The Art of Chess Analysis

Jan Timman

First published in 1997 by Gloucester Publishers plc, (formerly Everyman Publishers plc), Northburgh House, 10 Northburgh Street, London, EC1V 0AT

Reprinted 2003

British Library Cataloguing-in-Publication Data
A catalogue record for this book is available from the British Library.

ISBN 1 85744 179 6

Distributed in North America by The Globe Pequot Press, P.O Box 480, 246 Goose Lane, Guilford, CT 06437-0480.

All other sales enquiries should be directed to Gloucester Publishers plc, Northburgh House, 10 Northburgh Street, London, EC1V 0AT
tel: 020 7253 7887 fax: 020 7379 4060
email: info@everymanchess.com
website: www.everymanchess.com

Everyman is the registered trade mark of Random House Inc. and is used in this work under license from Random House Inc.

Proofreading: Tim Wall

Typeset and Edited by Petra Nunn

EVERYMAN CHESS SERIES (formerly Cadogan Chess)

Chief Advisor: Garry Kasparov
Commissioning Editor: Byron Jacobs

Printed by Lightning Source

Contents

Editor's Foreword

This renowned work by Jan Timman was first published in 1980 by RHM, but never reprinted in English due to the subsequent collapse of the publisher.

A second, updated edition was published in 1993, but this appeared only in Dutch. The current edition includes all the new analysis which appeared in the 1993 edition, together with some further minor corrections.

The Art of Chess Analysis remains one of the best examples of painstaking analytical work ever written. It is very unusual for a leading player such as Jan Timman to take on the difficult task of giving detailed annotations to the games of other players. He has succeeded magnificently. The book is particularly instructive in that Timman not only gives detailed analysis when required, but also covers the plans and counterplans available to both sides, illuminating many of the general principles governing chess strategy.

Petra Nunn
Chertsey, June 1997

Preface

In the winter of early 1971, at the Hoogoven tournament, I achieved my second master result and thus obtained the title of International Master. That summer my first Grandmaster tournament – the IBM – was on the program. The list of participants was an impressive one, and I decided to be as well prepared as possible. But how? During my high school years I had spent useful afternoons training with Bouwmeester, but that period was now definitely behind me; if I was to continue to grow and make progress, I would have to depend entirely on myself.

Not surprisingly, I turned to Botvinnik. The first chess book I had ever seen was Müller's biography of him, *Zo speelt Botwinnik,* and now I owned an English translation of Botvinnik's work, *One Hundred Selected Games.* In his Foreword, Botvinnik asks the rhetorical questions, 'How do I prepare?', and he immediately answers, 'That has never been any secret': fifteen to twenty days in the fresh country air, prescribes Dr Botvinnik.

So it was that Hans Böhm and I, among others, bid farewell to our carefree lifestyle and began a long retreat at a house in the Friesland countryside. For three months we lived like health fanatics. Our luggage contained little more than chess literature and track suits.

The tournament began ... and the first five games were lost. I remember exactly how I felt. During play my body was overflowing with so much energy that I could hardly stay seated in my chair. After each game I still had enough energy to run several times around the Vondel Park. But why bother?

This painful start drove me to a firm decision. I threw all my Spartan habits overboard and indulged myself in everything that had been declared unhealthy. In short, I went back to my old lifestyle. And lo and behold, immediately everything went wonderfully. Thanks to a good winning streak, a total catastrophe was averted and I managed a reasonable result.

So much for that part of the wisdom I had hoped to find in Botvinnik's work. The only lesson I really learned is that you must never change your normal rhythm just because you are faced with an important tournament. As Botvinnik says a little later in the same Foreword: 'Possibly some of my suggestions will not be of much benefit to some players; each must consider them critically and apply them with caution, taking his own individual capacities and habits into account.'

Far more useful was Botvinnik's advice to analyse games at home and then publish the analysis. As he put it: 'During play your analytical work is continually being tested against your critically-minded opponents, but in home-analysis it is very easy to be unobjective. To fight this tendency and to get away from poor analysis it is useful to publish your individual analytical work. Then you are subject to objective criticism.'

So I began to analyse games. Luckily, there was an independent magazine in Holland, *Schaakbulletin*, which was eager to publish this analytical work. In the framework of 'The Game of the Month,' a more-or-less thorough analysis was published in every issue. I limited myself to games between top players, hoping for as much critical comment as possible. In that respect the result was disappointing: only after the game Fischer-Petrosian, which I had worked on for about forty hours all told, did two reactions arrive (both of which have been gratefully worked into this book)

Even more disappointing was the reaction to my book about the Fischer-Spassky match, which appeared a year later. To put it plainly, the reactions were very enthusiastic and full of praise. But that was just the trouble! There had been a lot of competition to bring out the quickest books on the match. Commerce had run riot, and countless rushed works had appeared in a colourful variety of languages. In a way, my book stood out: despite its fairly quick appearance, it consisted of analysis over which some care had been taken. It was inevitable that a number of experts would declare it the best book on the match. But good heavens, imagine what would have happened if they had examined all the variations critically! A new book would have been necessary to accommodate all the mistakes and inadequacies in the analysis. I actually considered writing such a book, but it very quickly became apparent that not a single publisher had the slightest interest in it. There remained no other course for me but to completely revise the most interesting games from that match for this collection. The only real support in this respect was the Icelandic book on the match written by Fridrik Olafsson. It did not appear until a year after the match, and only in Icelandic, so it fell quite outside the commercial book category. Modestly, but with my heart at peace, I can say that there is no doubt which is the best book of that match.

The match in Reykjavik signalled the end of the Fischer era. His sudden indolence had a chaotic effect on the chess world. The number of chess enthusiasts the world over, particularly in the United States, had increased frighteningly, and although countless numbers of people were interested exclusively in Fischer's games, there was no fresh supply. My own state of mind was adversely affected. My analytical work was put aside a little. In the summer of 1979 I completely revised my analysis of Bronstein-Ljubojević (game 10 in this book), trying to show that interesting play was still taking place in the interval between the eras of Fischer and Karpov.

We must learn to live with Karpov as World Champion. His games are generally less absorbing than Fischer's, but on the other hand, the title has had a beneficial effect on Karpov. He has continued to play, and his games have even begun to show a little more colour. Games 17 and 18 are good examples.

My own play underwent a ripening process, and the analysis of games 14-18 (game 13 was done later) flowed from my pen with great ease. There is a definite difference between the analysis of games 1-6 and that of games 14-18.

During the last two years I have published little detailed analysis. But on those few occasions I received more response than ever before – a happy phenomenon. Four of the last five games in this book are brand new. I gave them a great deal of attention and tried for the greatest possible precision. Obviously, imagination takes its own course, like time and tide. Not only play itself but also analysis must be fed by inspiration. My hope is that you will feel free to make critical comments.

J. H. Timman
Amsterdam, August 19, 1979

Game One
Portisch – Smyslov
Candidates play-off Match (3), Portorož 1971
Dutch Defence

In chess it is customary to play off ties for reserve places in the candidates matches. Portisch and Smyslov, who had shared seventh place in the Interzonal tournament in Palma de Majorca 1970, played a six-game match which ended in a tie, 3-3. Since none of the eight candidates withdrew to make room for a reserve, the match stopped at that point instead of continuing to a decision.

Though it was in effect only a practice match, Portisch-Smyslov left us with some interesting games, particularly this one. Smyslov played the Leningrad Variation of the Dutch Defence very unconventionally. Portisch, who is known for his methodical opening play and rather dogmatic handling of the middlegame, was evidently thrown into confusion. Instead of striving for a small positional advantage, he entered complications which Smyslov seems to have evaluated better.

1 d4   f5
This in itself is already a surprise. As far as I know, Smyslov has never played this before.

2 g3   ♘f6
3 ♗g2   g6
4 ♘f3
Also somewhat surprising. One would have expected Portisch to fight the Leningrad in the manner popularised by Taimanov; namely, 4 c4 ♗g7 5 ♘c3 0-0 6 ♘h3, as was shown in the Championship of the Netherlands 1971, among other tournaments.

4 ...   ♗g7
5 b3 *(D)*
A fairly unknown move, first used in 1960 by Trifunović against Matulović.

5 ...   0-0

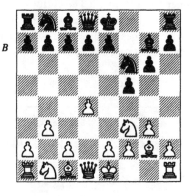

B

6 ♗b2   d5!?
A very unusual move in this position. Known is the continuation 6...d6 7 0-0 and now:

1) 7...a5 8 a3 c6 9 ♘bd2 ♘a6 10 e3 ♗d7 11 ♕e2 ♕c7 12 a4 with slightly better play for White (Bolbochan-Garcia, Mar del Plata 1966).

2) 7...♘e4 8 ♕c1 e6 9 c4 ♕e8 10 ♘c3 ♘xc3 11 ♗xc3 ♘d7 12 c5 ♕e7 13 cxd6 cxd6 14 ♕a3 ♘f6 15 ♖fe1 ♘d5 16 ♗d2 ♗f6 and the position is balanced (Garcia-Petersen, Lugano 1968).

3) 7...♘c6 8 d5 ♘a5 9 ♘fd2 c5 10 a4 ♗d7 11 c3 and now 11...♘e8 (instead of 11...♖c8) is good (Larsen-Reyes, Lugano 1968).

Perhaps Smyslov passed over 6...d6 because of 7 d5!?, an interesting field for further research.

7 c4   c6
8 0-0   ♗e6!?

If this was his intention, 8...♔h8 might have been considered, with the idea of being able to retreat the bishop later from e6 to g8. The curious textmove is somehow typical of Smyslov he sometimes has a definite preference for knights over bishops.

9 ♘g5   ♗f7
10 ♘c3   ♕e8 (D)

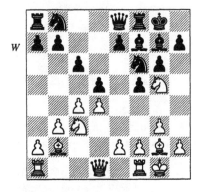

The last 'strange' move.
11 ♕d3

An unfortunate square for the queen in certain cases. 11 ♖c1 comes strongly into consideration, although the consequences of 11...dxc4 are not so easy to foresee. White gets the advantage after 12 ♘xf7 ♕xf7 13 bxc4 ♕xc4 14 ♘d5 ♕xa2 15 ♘c7 ♘a6 16 ♘xa8 ♕xb2 17 d5! due to the poor coordination of the black pieces. In other cases White can develop his queen elastically to e2 after 12 e3.

11 ...   h6
12 ♘xf7   ♕xf7
13 f3   ♘bd7

When you see the continuation of the game, you wonder why Black did not play 13...dxc4 first and then 14...♘bd7. After 15 e4 ♘b6 the same position as in the game would arise, but White would have the better 15 ♘a4, so as to meet 15...♖ad8 strongly with 16 ♕b3. With the text, Smyslov hopes for the move Portisch now plays, a move that looks good and was undoubtedly played without much thought; otherwise, Portisch would have realised the dangers involved.

14 e4?

Now the unusual position of the black queen on f7 becomes optimally justified. The correct move is 14 cxd5 and then:

1) 14...cxd5? 15 e4 e6 16 e5 ♘h7 (unfortunately, 16...♘e8 fails after 17 ♗a3) 17 ♘b5 and wins.

2) 14...♘xd5 15 e4 ♘xc3 (15...♘b4 16 ♕d2 ♖ad8 17 ♘a4! and Black loses time) 16 ♗xc3 ♖ad8 17 ♖ad1 with a slight advantage for White.

14	...	dxc4
15	bxc4	♘b6! *(D)*

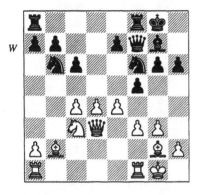

White is suddenly in great difficulties. The pawns on c4 and d4 are weak and the queen is uncomfortably situated on d3.

16 c5?

Portisch goes wrong again, but now this was very difficult to foresee. 16 exf5 is even worse on account of 16...♛xc4, but 16 d5 seems to be White's best practical chance. After 16...♘fd7 White can play:

1) 17 f4? fxe4! (not 17...♘c5 18 ♕e2 ♗xc3 19 ♗xc3 ♘xe4 20 ♗xe4 fxe4 21 dxc6) 18 ♗xe4 ♘c5, etc.

2) 17 ♕e2 ♗d4+ 18 ♔h1 ♘e5 19 ♖ad1 c5! and White loses a pawn without much compensation; e.g., 20 ♘b5 ♗xb2 21 ♕xb2 ♘exc4 22 ♕c3 ♕f6.

3) 17 ♘d1! ♘a4! 18 ♗xg7 ♔xg7 19 ♘e3 ♘ac5 20 ♕d2 fxe4 21 fxe4 ♖xf1+ 22 ♖xf1 ♖f8 and White can hold the game although Black has a positional advantage.

16	...	♘c4
17	♗c1	♖ad8
18	♖b1 *(D)*	

After 18 exf5 gxf5 19 ♕xf5 ♖xd4 Black has too many squares; e.g., 20 ♖b1 e6 21 ♕c2 ♘d5.

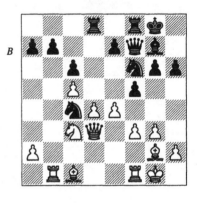

18	...	♘d7
19	d5	

White was probably relying on this move, but Smyslov's reply strikes at the core of the position with an iron fist.

| 19 | ... | b5! |

Actually very logical. The strong knight must be maintained on c4.

20 dxc6

After 20 cxb6 ♘dxb6 White has no more play at all; e.g. 21 f4 fxe4 22 ♗xe4 ♗xc3 23 ♕xc3 cxd5.

20	...	♘xc5
21	♕c2	a6 *(D)*

Everything is as strong as it is simple. White is at an impasse: after either 22 a4 or 22 f4 Black exchanges off his other bishop.

| 22 | f4 | ♗xc3 |

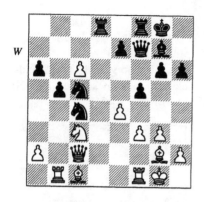

Smyslov plays the concluding moves in the most efficient manner.

26	axb5	axb5
27	♗b2	♖f6
28	♗a1	♕c5+
29	♔h1	♕xc6
30	♖bd1	e3+
31	♔g1	♖d2
32	♖xd2	exd2
33	♕d3	♖d6
34	♕c3	e5
35	♖d1	♕c5+
36	♔h1	♕e3
37	fxe5	♖d3

23	♕xc3	♘xe4
24	♗xe4	fxe4
25	a4	♕d5

0-1

Game Two
Polugaevsky – Mecking
Mar del Plata 1971
English Opening, Slav Formation

Polugaevsky has a very clear style: somewhat classical, enterprising, and not very dogmatic. In the following game we see him go to work turning a well-known type of positional advantage into victory. He was rather helped by Mecking's eighteenth move, after which he only once strayed from the best path. The bishop endgame contains study-like continuations. The game is a convincing whole, which, like the rest of the tournament, Polugaevsky played with great power. He allowed only four draws and finished first, three points ahead of his closest rival. Perhaps he was inspired by the manner in which Fischer was making himself at home in tournaments of the same calibre around that time.

1	c4	c6
2	♘f3	d5
3	e3	♘f6
4	♘c3	e6

More active is 4...♘bd7 to answer 5 b3 with 5...e5. After 4...♘bd7 5 d4 e6 the game follows Slav paths, but with 5 cxd5 cxd5 6 d4 White can try a sort of Exchange Variation where the black knight does not stand very well on d7.

5	b3	♘bd7
6	♗b2	♗d6
7	d4 *(D)*	

The point of the white set-up. In the normal Slav opening the fianchetto of the white queen's bishop is hardly possible because b2-b3 can always be answered by ...♗b4. Whether this set-up actually promises much is doubtful.

7	...	0-0
8	♗d3	♖e8

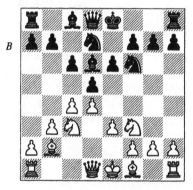

B

The correct way to equality. Black wants to answer 9 0-0 with 9...e5, when 10 cxd5 does not work because of 10...e4. Therefore White's following move.

9	♕c2	e5
10	cxd5	cxd5
11	dxe5	♘xe5
12	♘xe5	♗xe5
13	♘e2 *(D)*	

White wants to prevent Black from dissolving his isolated pawn with ...d5-d4 and practices Réti's dictum: castle only if there are no better moves.

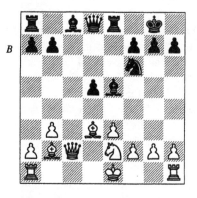

13 ...   ♛d6

Black should have tried to exploit the position of the white king in the centre. The most obvious continuation was 13...♛a5+, but after 14 ♗c3! ♗xc3+ 15 ♕xc3 ♕xc3+ 16 ♘xc3 the move 16...d4 is not good, due to 17 ♘b5 dxe3 18 ♘c7 exf2+ 19 ♔xf2. *(Precisely this line was later played in Makarychev-Chekhov, USSR Team Championship 1981. Black lost without having a chance after 19...♘g4+ 20 ♔g1 ♖d8 21 ♘xa8 ♖xd3 22 h3 ♘f6 23 ♔h2 ♗d7 24 ♖hd1 ♖xd1 25 ♖xd1 ♔f8 26 ♘c7 ♗c6 27 ♖e1 etc.)* Therefore 16...♗d7 is best, but after 17 0-0 ♖ac8 18 ♖ac1 White keeps a small positional advantage. However, there has to be something here, and that 'something' is 13...d4!, a move that is easily missed. My analysis:

1) 14 ♖d1 or 14 f4 then 14...♕a5+ etc. In general the possibility of this check ensures the correctness of Black's play.

2) 14 e4 and now:

2a) 14...♘xe4 15 ♗xe4 d3 16 ♗xd3 ♗xb2 17 ♗xh7+ ♔h8 18 ♕xb2 and Black has insufficient compensation for the pawn (this and subsequent annotations, also to other games in this book, stem from Dvoretsky, published in *New in Chess*, and also from a private letter).

2b) 14...♘g4. A good suggestion by Dvoretsky. After 15 h3 ♕h4 16 g3 ♕h6 17 ♘xd4 he gives 17...♕b6, but then Black does not have adequate compensation for the pawn after 18 ♘f3. Much stronger is 17...♖d8, after which White is in trouble. This means that he probably cannot capture the d-pawn.

3) 14 0-0-0 ♗d7! and the situation is critical for White; e.g.: 15 exd4 ♖c8 16 ♗c4 ♗b8 or 16 ♗c3 ♗d6.

4) 14 exd4(!) ♗xd4 15 ♗xd4 ♕xd4 16 0-0 ♕b6 with an equal position. The text-move, by the way, is also not so bad.

14 ♗xe5   ♕xe5
15 0-0   ♗d7

Here Mecking had perhaps intended 15...♘g4, which was probably stronger. Great complications may arise, such as:

1) 16 g3? ♕h5 17 h4 and now 17...g5! is strong, but not 17...♘e5 18 ♘f4 ♘f3+ 19 ♔g2 ♕g4 20 ♖h1 (Dvoretsky).

2) 16 ♘g3 h5! 17 ♖fe1 h4 18 ♘f1 and Black has an excellent position. He can perhaps even continue 18...h3 19 g3 ♕f6.

3) 16 ♘f4 and now *(D)*:

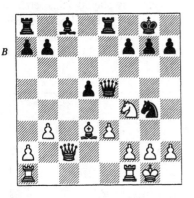

3a) 16...d4 17 ♗xh7+ ♔h8 18 h3 dxe3! (18...♘xf2 19 ♕xf2 dxe3 20 ♕h4 g5 21 ♕h6! ♕g7 22 ♕xg7+ ♔xg7 23 ♘h5+ ♔xh7 24 ♘f6+ and 18...♘f6 19 ♗g6!! dxe3 20 ♗xf7 ♕xf4 21 ♗xe8 ♘xe8 22 fxe3! ♕xe3+ 23 ♔h1 are winning for White) 19 hxg4 ♕xf4 with a roughly equal position. Black also has no problems after the continuation 17 ♖ae1 g5 18 h3 gxf4 19 hxg4 ♗xg4.

3b) 16...g5 17 h3 gxf4 18 exf4 ♕xf4 19 hxg4 ♗xg4 with excellent play for Black.

3c) 16...♘f6 and it is difficult for White to arm himself against the neutralising 17...d4, because after 17 ♘e2 Black can get a draw by repetition with 17...♘g4. Perhaps he can try 17 ♗b5 ♖d8 18 ♕c5, possibly followed by 19 ♕d4.

4) 16 ♗xh7+. Dvoretsky suggests that White has to seriously consider playing this way, since the alternatives are unsatisfactory. After 16...♔h8 17 ♘g3 g6 18 ♗xg6 fxg6 19 ♕xg6 ♖g8 20 ♕h5+ he finds the position difficult to evaluate. It seems to me that White's chances after 20...♕xh5 21 ♘xh5 ♗e6 22 h3 ♘e5 23 ♘f4 have to be assessed as somewhat better. Probably slightly more precise is 16...♔f8, in order after 17 ♘g3 to continue 17...g6 18 ♗xg6 fxg6 19 ♕xg6 ♕f6. If White then exchanges queens, Black can cover his d-pawn more securely, while his king is rather more central.

16 ♘d4

Now all complications are out of the way and a simple position with a slight plus for White has arisen.

16 ...	**♖ac8**
17 ♕e2	**♕d6**
18 ♕b2	**a6?** *(D)*

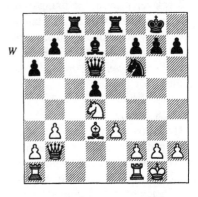

It was difficult to see at this moment that this move would be the root cause of Black's defeat. The fact is, however, that it violates the general positional rule against placing one's pawns on the same colour squares as one's bishop.

| 19 | ♖ac1 | ♘g4 |

Now this is only an innocuous demonstration.

20	♘f3	♕b6
21	♖xc8	♖xc8
22	♖c1	

White can ignore the 'threat' 22...♘xe3 because after 23 ♖xc8+ ♗xc8 either 24 ♕c1 or 24 ♕e5 wins.

22	...	♘f6
23	♖xc8+	♗xc8
24	♕c3	♗d7
25	♘d4	♘e8
26	a4!	

White is going to fix the black queenside pawns on squares the same colour as Black's bishop, the result of Black's eighteenth move.

| 26 | ... | ♕c7 |

Black can prevent the fixing of his queenside pawns with 26...a5, but the cure seems worse than the disease because after 27 ♗b5 ♗xb5 28 ♘xb5 both White pieces have optimal possibilities.

| 27 | ♕xc7 | ♘xc7 |
| 28 | a5 (D) | |

Black now has not only the weakness on d5 but also a more serious weakness on b7. If the knights were not on the board and White's king could reach d4 (which should be possible because White could keep the black king off the squares e5 and c5

with the moves b3-b4 and f2-f4), the position would be won because White could then play e3-e4 at the right moment.

Still, Black would have great drawing chances by playing 28...♘e6 here; e.g., 29 ♘xe6 (otherwise White cannot make progress: 29 ♘f5 is answered by 29...♘c5) 29...fxe6 30 f4 ♔f7 31 ♔f2 h6.

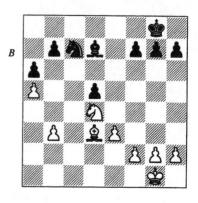

| 28 | ... | ♔f8? |
| 29 | ♔f1 | |

The immediate 29 e4 ♔e7! promised little.

| 29 | ... | ♔e7 |

Again, Black should try 29...h6 followed by 30...♘e6.

| 30 | ♔e2 | g6 |

Another pawn on the wrong colour, but this was difficult to avoid because if 30...♘e6 31 ♘f5+.

| 31 | ♔d2 | ♘e6 (D) |
| 32 | ♘xe6?! | |

I think a better idea is 32 ♔c3 ♘c5 33 ♗e2! (not 33 f3 ♘xd3 34 ♔xd3 ♔d6 35 b4 g5! and the winning chances are

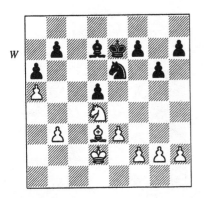

nil. White must keep his bishop on the board for the time being; it is unimportant that Black can win the f2-pawn, because then the white king can penetrate.) 33...♘e4+ (33...♔d6 is safer, but then White can strengthen his position with 34 f3 possibly followed by 35 g4, 36 h4, 37 g5, and bringing his bishop to c2) 34 ♔b4 ♘xf2 (again, 34...♔d6 is safer) 35 ♔c5 and now:

1) 35...♘e4+ 36 ♔b6 ♘d6 37 ♔c7 g5 38 ♗f3 ♗e6 39 g4 and 40 ♘f5+, or 37...f5 38 ♗f3 ♗e6 39 ♘e2, and in either case both d5 and thus also b7 fall.

2) 35...♔d8 36 ♔xd5! ♔c7 37 ♔e5 with a great spatial advantage for White.

32	...	fxe6
33	f4	e5
34	g3	♔d6?

Strange as it seems, this may be the losing mistake. 34...♗b5! is imperative because the pawn endgame after 35 ♗xb5 axb5 is drawn; e.g., 36 ♔c3 ♔e6 37 ♔b4 d4!. White must therefore

play 35 ♗c2 whereupon there can follow 35...♔d6 36 ♔c3 ♗e2 37 ♗b1! (White first tempts the black bishop to f1 where it stands less well) 37...♗f1 (Black has nothing better) 38 ♔b4 d4! 39 exd4 exd4 40 ♗e4 ♔c7 41 ♔c5 d3 42 ♔d4 d2 43 ♗f3 b6! *(D)* and White has these choices:

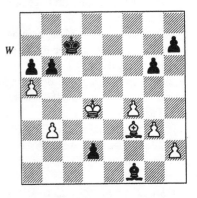

1) 44 b4 bxa5 45 bxa5 ♔d6 46 ♔c3 ♔c5 and Black wins the a5-pawn with an easy win.

2) 44 axb6+ ♔xb6 45 ♔c3 ♔c5! 46 ♔xd2 ♔d4 and Black can hold the draw thanks to the strong position of his king.

3) 44 ♔c3! bxa5 45 ♔xd2 ♗b5! 46 ♗d1! (White must prevent 46...a4 dissolving the doubled pawn) 46...♔d6 47 ♔c3 ♔d5! 48 ♗c2 ♗d7 with the threat 49...♗f5, and White has no real winning chances.

35 ♔c3 ♗e6

Now the pawn endgame after 35...♗b5 is lost: 36 ♗xb5 axb5 37 ♔b4 d4 38 fxe5+ (this is the difference: if the black king were on e6 this capture would not be with check) 38...♚xe5 39 exd4+ etc.

36 ♚b4 *(D)*

When a top player makes a mistake in a purely technical position, it often results from being too hasty. This is the case here. White wishes to capture on e5 and then invade with his king via c5. However, he should have prepared the execution of this plan.

The right move was 36 ♗e2, in order firstly to play the bishop to f3 and only then move the king to b4.

Black then has no good defensive set-up, as can be seen from the following variations:

1) 36...d4+ 37 exd4 exd4+ 38 ♚xd4 ♗xb3 39 ♗f3 ♚c7 40 ♚c5 ♗e6 41 g4 and White's majority on the kingside is decisive.

2) 36...♗d7 37 ♗f3 ♗c6. Black has defended as well as possible against the threatened incursion of the white king. After 38 ♚b4 d4, however, White wins the pawn ending: 39 ♗xc6 bxc6 40 exd4 exd4 41 ♚c4 c5 42 b4 cxb4 43 ♚xd4 ♚c6 44 ♚c4 and now White remains one tempo ahead in the race after 44...h5 45 ♚xb4 ♚d5 46 ♚c3 ♚e4 47 ♚c4 ♚f3 48 ♚c5 ♚g2 49 ♚b6 ♚xh2 50 ♚xa6 ♚xg3 51 ♚b6 h4 52 a6 and Black has the misfortune to have his pawn stopped by White's promotion on a8.

36 ...   exf4

Black fails to take advantage of White's slip. By the exchange of pawns he is able to keep White's king away from c5, but in another respect it

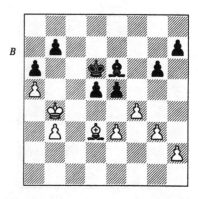

is a serious concession in that White gets the d4-square for his king. Black should have played the move given by Dvoretsky: 36...d4!. This thrust is fully in accordance with the demands of the position: Black holds on to the centre for as long as possible.

'I don't think it would have saved the game', Dvoretsky remarked with regard to 36...d4. But in my opinion he is too pessimistic about the consequences of his own recommendation. First of all it should be established that 37 e4 achieves nothing after 37...♗d7, followed by 38...♗c6. By virtue of his (for the time being) protected passed pawn on d4 Black runs no risk of losing.

White's best attempt to win here begins with 37 exd4 exd4 38 h4. The threat of 39 h5 compels Black to be very alert in defence. My analysis:

1) 38...♗f5 39 ♗xf5 gxf5 40 ♚c4 d3 41 ♚xd3 ♚c5 (or 41...♚d5) 42 h5! and the pawn ending is won for White.

2) 38...♚c6! The only defence. The point of the move with the king

becomes evident after 39 h5 gxh5 40 ♗e4+ (on 40 ♗xh7 at once Black has the strong centralisation 40...♔d5) 40...♗d5 41 ♗xh7 b5!. In this way Black sets about isolating the enemy king so that his bishop has a free game. He is just in time with this; on 42 ♗g6 he now has 42...♗f3, while White makes just as little progress with 42 axb6 ♔b6 43 ♗g6 a5+ 44 ♔a3 ♗f3.

37	gxf4	♗g4
38	♔c3	♗f3
39	♔d4	♗g2
40	h4	♗f3
41	b4	♗h1

If 41...♗g4 42 ♗f1 ♗e6 43 ♗g2 followed by 44 e4 would win even more quickly.

42	♗e2	♗g2
43	♗g4	♗e4
44	♗c8	♔c7
45	♗e6	♔d6
46	♗g8	h6

47	♗f7	h5
48	♗e8	♗c2
49	♗f7	

49 b5 also wins, but less convincingly; for example, 49...axb5 50 ♗xb5 ♗e4 51 ♗a4 ♗f5 52 ♗b3 ♗e4 53 ♗a2 ♔c6 54 ♔e5 ♔c5.

49	...	♗e4
50	f5!	♗xf5

Or 50...gxf5 51 ♗xh5 ♔e6 52 ♗e2 followed by h5-h6 and possibly ♗xa6 and b4-b5.

51	♗xd5	♗c8
52	e4	

The crowning of White's refined manoeuvres: Black is in zugzwang.

52	...	♔e7
53	♔e5	g5
54	hxg5	h4
55	g6	h3
56	g7	h2
57	g8♕	h1♕
58	♕f7+	♔d8
59	♕f8+	1-0

Game Three
Gligorić – Portisch
IBM Tournament, Amsterdam 1971
Grünfeld Defence

Neither Gligorić nor Portisch had a good start in this IBM tournament. A tense duel was therefore expected in their fifth-round encounter, as indeed occurred. The Yugoslav showed his most inventive side; his three pawn sacrifices were reminiscent of the two occasions when he showered Hort with a total of four exchange sacrifices. There were relatively many mistakes for grandmasters of this class, but no one can take this amiss. Such complicated problems can hardly be solved in the limited two and a half hours available for thinking. Indeed, the players are to be complimented for not fearing to enter such dense thickets, even against each other. This was certainly the most interesting game of the tournament.

1	d4	♘f6
2	c4	g6
3	♘c3	d5
4	♗g5	♘e4
5	♗h4 *(D)*	

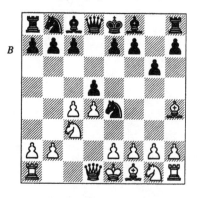

5 ...   ♘xc3

Fischer also preferred this to the more usual 5...c5. White has two possibilities in that case:

1) 6 cxd5 ♘xc3 7 bxc3 ♕xd5 8 e3 cxd4! 9 ♕xd4 ♕xd4 10 cxd4 e6! and practice has shown that Black has at least equal chances. On 11 ♗f6 there comes 11...♗b4+ followed by 12...0-0.

2) 6 e3! and now:

2a) 6...♗g7 7 cxd5 ♘xc3 8 bxc3 ♕xd5 9 ♕f3 ♕d8 (bad is 9...♕xf3 10 ♘xf3 cxd4 11 cxd4 ♘c6 12 ♗b5 ♗d7 13 0-0 e6 14 ♖ab1, Taimanov-Uhlmann, USSR-'World' 1970) 10 ♗b5+ ♘d7 11 ♘e2 and Black has a choice:

2a1) 11...cxd4 12 exd4 0-0 13 0-0 a6 14 ♗d3 ♕c7 15 ♕e3 e5 16 f4 exd4 17 cxd4 ♘f6 18 ♖ae1 ♕b6 19 h3 drawn (Forintos-Witkovsky, Wijk aan Zee 1971). 15 ♗g3 comes into consideration as an improvement for White.

2a2) 11...a6!? 12 ♗d3? (better seems the continuation 12 ♗xd7+ ♕xd7 13 0-0) 12...♘e5! 13 dxe5 ♕xd3

14 ♖d1 ♕c4 15 ♕d5 ♕xd5 16 ♖xd5 b6 with advantage to Black (Mititelu-Hort, Luhačovice 1971).

2b) 6...♘c6!? 7 cxd5 ♘xc3 8 bxc3 ♕xd5 9 ♕f3 ♕xf3 10 ♘xf3 cxd4 11 cxd4 e6 and Black gets the same sort of play as in variation 1. In this case 7 ♘f3 seems the correct method.

2c) 6...♕a5 7 ♕b3 cxd4 (stronger than 7...♘c6 8 ♘f3 cxd4 9 exd4 ♘xc3 10 bxc3 ♗e6 11 ♗e2 ♗g7 12 0-0 0-0 13 c5 with the better chances for White, Taimanov-Filip, Wijk aan Zee 1970) 8 exd4 ♗h6! 9 ♖d1 (9 ♘f3? g5! 10 ♗g3 g4) 9...0-0 10 cxd5. So far Donner-G. Garcia, Cienfuegos 1973, and now, according to Donner, 10...♘d7 11 ♗d3 ♘xc3 12 bxc3 ♘b6 13 ♘e2 ♕xd5 leads to an equal game. This approach by Black is probably the main reason many players with White now play 4 ♘f3 ♗g7 before continuing with 5 ♗g5.

6	bxc3	dxc4
7	e3	♗e6
8	♗e2	

Two games with Fischer as Black continued with 8 ♖b1 b6:

1) 9 ♘f3 ♗g7 10 ♘d2 0-0 11 ♘xc4 ♗d5 12 ♕d2 ♕d7 13 ♘a3 c5 14 f3 ♕a4 15 ♘b5 with equal chances (Mecking-Fischer, Buenos Aires 1970).

2) 9 ♗e2 ♗h6 (seems strange at first, but it is directed against both 10 ♗f3 c6 11 ♘e2 and 10 ♘f3 followed by a later ♘g5) 10 ♘f3 c6 11 ♘e5 ♗g7 12 f4 ♗d5 13 0-0 ♘d7 14 ♘xc4 0-0 15 a4 c5 16 ♘e5 ♘xe5 17 dxe5 f6

18 ♖b2! with some advantage for White (Taimanov-Fischer, Vancouver 1971).

| 8 | ... | ♗g7 |
| 9 | ♘f3 | |

Very interesting positions can arise after 9 ♖b1 ♗d5 and now:

1) 10 f3 f5 11 ♘h3 h6 12 ♘f4 g5 13 ♘xd5 ♕xd5 14 ♗f2 or 14 ♕a4+ ♕d7 15 ♕xd7+ ♘xd7 16 ♗g3 0-0-0 17 ♗xc4 e5 (18 ♗e6 ♖he8!) and Black does not stand badly in either case.

2) 10 ♗f3 c5!? (10...0-0 11 e4 ♗c6 12 ♘e2 is good for White) 11 ♕a4+ ♗c6 12 ♗xc6+ ♘xc6 13 ♖xb7 ♕c8 and now 14 ♖xe7 ♔f8 15 ♖e4 leads to intricate complications which are probably not unfavourable for Black.

| 9 | ... | 0-0 |
| 10 | 0-0 | c5 |

Perhaps too sharp. If Black wants to keep the pawn he can also try 10...c6 11 ♘g5 b5. White would then have to decide whether to capture on e6 or to bring his knight later to c5 via e4.

11 ♘g5! *(D)*

This leads forcibly to advantageous play for White.

| 11 | ... | ♗d5 |
| 12 | e4 | ♗c6 |

The alternative is 12...h6. In the tournament bulletin Gligorić then gives the variation 13 exd5 hxg5 14 ♗xg5 cxd4 15 ♗xc4 dxc3 16 h4 with a strong attack for White. I find this unclear because Black can build a sturdy position with 16...♘d7 17 h5

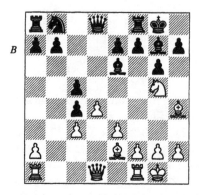

B

♘e5 18 ♗b3 ♕d6 (19 f4 ♘c4!). However, White has the much better 16 ♖e1!, as 16...♖e8 17 d6 ♘c6 18 ♕f3 wins easily. Black must play 16...♕c7, but even then his position is hardly playable after 17 ♕b3 ♘d7 18 ♖xe7.

13 d5   ♗b5
14 a4   ♗a6 (D)

Black has taken the necessary trouble to hold the c4-pawn, but the price has been high. White has a great preponderance in the centre and the black bishop on a6 cannot help in the defence.

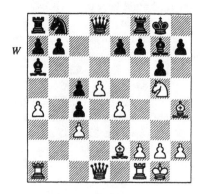

W

White's plan is the natural f2-f4 followed by e4-e5 or f4-f5, but first he must defend c3. Both 15 ♖c1 and 15 ♕c2 (perhaps followed by ♖ad1) are possible. The move Gligorić chooses is weak as the unprotected queen on d2 gives Black a chance for counterplay.

15 ♕d2   e6

Another manner of profiting from the unprotected position of the queen is 15...e5, intending an immediate blockade. In that case White opens the position at once with 16 f4; e.g., 16...♘d7 17 f5 h6 18 ♘f3 g5 19 ♗f2 and White's prospects are more favourable.

16 ♘f3   ♕d6

If Black knew what awaited him, maybe he would have played 16...♕e8, where the queen covers many vital squares. White would then have three possibilities:

1) 17 d6 ♘c6 18 d7 ♕b8 and White has achieved nothing. After 19 ♗g3 ♕d8 20 ♗d6 Black sacrifices the exchange with 20...♕xd7.

2) 17 e5 exd5 18 ♕xd5 ♘c6 and it is Black who stands better.

3) 17 ♖e1! ♘d7 18 ♗f1 and Black has a problem with his queen vis-à-vis the rook on the e-file. He would do best to close the file with 18...e5.

17 e5! (D)

White correctly feels nothing for 17 ♗g3 e5 but offers a pawn which can be accepted in two ways. One of them, 17...♗xe5 18 ♘xe5 ♕xe5 19 ♗f3, leads to an uncomfortable position, so Black actually has no choice.

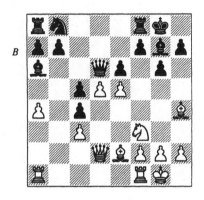

B

17 ...   ♕xd5
18 ♕e3

White had the difficult choice between 18 ♕e3 and 18 ♕f4. Gligorić wrote that he did not play 18 ♕f4 because of 18...♘d7 19 ♖fd1 ♗xe5. This is astonishing: either 20 ♕e3 (which Gligorić gives) or 20 ♖xd5 ♗xf4 21 ♖xd7 wins a piece.

Such notes for the bulletin are sometimes written in great haste. The question remains whether 18 ♕f4 is better than the text-move. In my original notes I gave the variation 18...♘d7 19 ♖fd1 ♕c6 20 ♗f6 ♘xf6 21 exf6 e5 22 ♘xe5 ♕xf6 23 ♕xf6 ♗xf6 24 ♘d7 ♗xc3 25 ♖ac1 ♗d4 and evaluated the ending as tenable for Black. This is certainly true; if anything, he stands slightly better. An attempt to strengthen this line with 19 ♖ad1 ♕c6 20 ♖xd7 ♕xd7 21 ♗f6 would fail, because Black has the reply 21...♖fd8. These two variations demonstrate how little I understood such positions at that time. Twenty years later I analysed it as follows: 19 ♖fd1 ♕c6 20

♖d6 ♕c7 21 ♖ad1 ♘b6 22 a5 ♘d5 23 ♖1xd5! exd5 24 ♗f6.

White certainly has a dangerous attack here, but I am not sure whether it breaks through after the strong defensive move 24...♖fe8!. Perhaps it is still better for White to continue, as in the game, with 20 ♗e7 (instead of 20 ♖d6) in order to bring the bishop to d6. In that case, however, I think the queen is better placed on e3.

18 ...   ♘d7
19 ♖fd1   ♕c6
20 ♗e7 (D)

White is going to overprotect his e5 outpost. 20 ♖d6 ♕c7 21 ♖ad1 is not good because of 21...♘b6 followed by 22...♘d5. If White first tries 20 a5 then Black replies 20...♕c7, and the e5-square is difficult to defend; on 21 ♗e7 Black again offers the exchange with 21...♘xe5, and after 22 ♗d6! ♘xf3+ 23 ♗xf3 ♕c8 24 ♗xf8 ♗xf8 the position is roughly in balance.

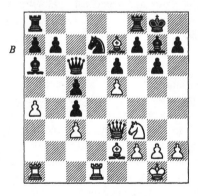

B

20 ...   ♖fe8
21 ♗d6   f6

22 h4   ♖ad8

The players strengthen their positions in the prescribed manner.

23 h5

Probably an inaccuracy, which, however, is not taken advantage of. With 23 a5! White can prevent Black's possible knight manoeuvre and thus also his counterplay.

23 ...   gxh5

The tendency to take such pawns has been seen in Portisch's games before. This time he misses the chance, prepared by his last two moves, to further undermine the configuration e5-d6 with the strong 23...♘b6! 24 hxg6 ♘d5! (not 24...hxg6 25 ♘h4 ♘d5 26 ♕g3 g5 27 ♘g6!) 25 gxh7+ ♔h8 26 ♕c1 (White must keep c3 defended) 26...♖xd6! 27 exd6 f5 and Black has good play in the centre for the exchange.

24 ♖d2

Now White has some control over the game again because 24...♘b6 is bad on account of 25 exf6 ♘d5 26 ♕g5.

24 ...   b6
25 ♖ad1   ♗b7

One can understand that Black is losing patience. Whatever he does, his position will worsen. The pressure on e5 must not be eased, so his knight must remain on d7. As a result, the squares e7 and c7 must remain protected. I cannot give a reasonable alternative to the text-move.

26 ♗xc4   ♕xa4 (D)
27 exf6

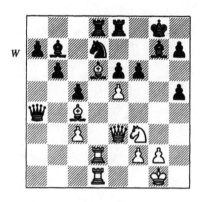

White can win here in an intricate manner with 27 ♗c7!. Here is the analysis:

1) 27...♗xf3 28 exf6 ♕xc4 (or 28...♗xd1 29 ♗xe6+) 29 ♕xf3 and then continuing as in the game.

2) 27...♘xe5 28 ♖xd8 ♘xc4 29 ♕xe6+, etc.

3) 27...♕xc4 28 ♖xd7 'with a decisive attack', I wrote in the first edition of this book. Some further explanation is called for. After the continuation 28...♖xd7 29 ♖xd7 ♕e4 White has the crushing 30 ♖xg7+! ♔xg7 31 exf6+ and the black king has no good escape.

27 ...   ♕xc4
28 ♗e7   ♗xf3?

Black will finally come out of the complications an exchange behind and without compensation. 28...♕g4! keeps the struggle alive; e.g., 29 ♗xd8 and now:

1) 29...♘xf6 30 ♘e1 ♕g6 31 ♗xf6 ♕xf6 with rough equality.

2) 29...♗xf3. This move, which I gave in my original notes, loses on the

spot, on account of 30 f7+! ♔xf7 31 ♖xd7+, followed by 32 ♕xf3.

29	♕xf3	♗xf6
30	♗xd8	♖xd8
31	♖xd7	♖f8
32	♖xa7	♗h4 *(D)*

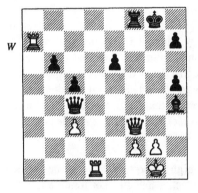

Gligorić indicates that 32...♗xc3 does not work because of 33 ♕g3+

and 34 ♖c1. Even better is 33 ♕xf8+ and mate. Relatively best, according to Gligorić, is 32...♕g4, even though White must win eventually after 33 ♕d3. After the text-move it ends quickly.

33 ♖a8

The Dutch Master, Pliester, found an immediate win here with 33 ♖d8!! ♗xd8 34 ♕b7, followed by mate. An attractive combination.

33	...	♖xa8
34	♕xa8+	♔f7
35	♖d7+	♗e7
36	♕f3+	♔e8
37	♖b7	♕d5
38	♕xd5	exd5
39	♖xb6	♔f7
40	♔f1	c4
41	♔e2	h4

1-0

Game Four
Fischer – Larsen
Semi-final Candidates Match (1), Denver 1971
French Defence, Winawer Variation

Despite the overwhelming manner in which Fischer accounted for Taimanov in the first of the series of candidates matches, various experts thought that the ensuing match against Larsen could go either way. After all, Larsen had beaten Fischer in the Interzonal. Larsen himself was, as usual, optimistic. Even before the candidates matches had begun, he was declaring that the next World Champion would be named Bent Larsen. Fischer thoroughly awakened him from that dream.

The first game of the match was undoubtedly the most interesting one. Larsen played uninhibitedly yet without being too reckless, but in the end he could not match Fischer's precise, direct play.

1 e4   e6

An unusual choice for Larsen, and the last time in the match that he deviates from his usual Sicilian.

2 d4   d5
3 ♘c3

Larsen had undoubtedly reckoned on this. Fischer is the sort of fighting player that never plays the Tarrasch Variation.

3 ...   ♗b4
4 e5

This may have been a slight surprise for Larsen. Fischer always used to be willing to enter the Winawer Variation, but when he returned to the chess world in the tournament at Rovinj-Zagreb 1970 he changed to the treatment with 4 a3 ♗xc3+ 5 bxc3 dxe4 6 ♕g4, at first with success against Uhlmann, then with catastrophic consequences against Kovačević. Larsen

might therefore have assumed that Fischer had still not found a reliable weapon against the Winawer.

4 ...   ♘e7
5 a3   ♗xc3+
6 bxc3   c5
7 a4

Like Smyslov, Fischer had always much preferred the positional method to the pawn snatch with 7 ♕g4.

7 ...   ♘bc6
8 ♘f3   ♗d7

Larsen does not enter the system with 8...♕a5 which the chief exponents of this variation, Uhlmann and Korchnoi, always use (see Game 19, Spassky-Korchnoi).

9 ♗d3   ♕c7

Now 9...♕a5 has less point because White does not have to defend the pawn: 10 0-0 c4 11 ♗e2 ♕xc3 12 ♗d2 ♕b2 13 ♖b1 followed by 14

🜚xb7 and White has a dangerous initiative.

10 0-0 c4

In combination with the next move, this plan carries great danger. The alternative is 10...h6 followed by castling short and only then, perhaps, to aim for ...f7-f6, recapturing on f6 with the rook.

11 ♗e2 f6 (D)

Obviously, Larsen had studied his opponent's rare losses well. Fischer lost a long game against Mednis in the 1960/61 U.S. Championship after 12 ♗a3 0-0! 13 ♖e1 ♖f7 14 exf6 gxf6 15 ♗f1 ♖e8 16 ♘h4 ♘g6 17 ♕h5 ♖g7 18 g3 ♕a5 19 ♗b2 ♘d8 20 ♖e3 ♘f7 21 ♔h1 ♘d6 and Black already had the initiative.

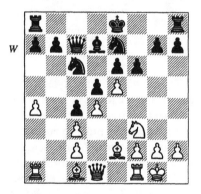

W

12 ♖e1!

An important improvement. If Black now castles short, White can capture on f6 and answer the pawn recapture with ♗h6. Black must therefore play to win the e5-pawn.

12 ... ♘g6

Again Fischer has the chance to capture on f6, but he does not concern himself with this possibility.

13 ♗a3

According to Byrne, 13 g3 would also give White a small advantage. But in that case Black could accept the pawn offer without too many problems: 13...fxe5 14 dxe5 ♘cxe5 15 ♘xe5 ♕xe5 16 ♗g4 ♕xc3 17 ♗xe6 0-0-0 and the position is far from clear.

13 ... fxe5
14 dxe5 ♘cxe5
15 ♘xe5 ♘xe5

Capturing with the queen is hardly to be considered: 15...♕xe5 16 ♗xc4 ♕xc3 17 ♗xd5 0-0-0 18 ♗b3 and Black has no compensation at all for the pair of bishops.

16 ♕d4 (D)

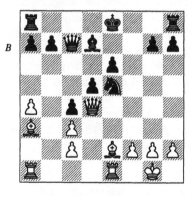

B

The queen keeps an eye on both flanks from here. Larsen, in his notes to this game, points out an interesting opening finesse. If this position had come about in a slightly different way (the way that has repeatedly occurred in practice up to Black's eleventh move) – namely, 7...♕c7 (instead of 7...♘bc6) 8 ♘f3 b6 9 ♗b5+ ♗d7 10 ♗d3 ♘bc6 11 0-0 c4 12 ♗e2 f6 13 ♖e1 ♘g6 14 ♗a3 fxe5 15 dxe5 ♘cxe5 16 ♘xe5 ♘xe5 – then, because of the extra move ...b7-b6, Black could have taken the sting out of the text-move, 17 ♕d4, with 17...0-0-0. However, in that case White would gain the advantage in another way: 17 f4 ♘c6 18 ♗g4 0-0-0 19 ♗xe6 ♗xe6 20 ♖xe6. Now we see the drawback of Black's extra move: his knight on c6 hangs if Black takes on f4, and this ensures that White can maintain the initiative.

16 ...   ♘g6

Actually, this is already the decision to keep the king in the middle. After 16...0-0-0 17 ♕xa7 ♘c6 18 ♕e3 White has a clear advantage because of Black's damaged king's position, and 16...♘c6 17 ♗h5+ loses directly. An alternative worth considering is the curious 16...h5 to prevent the bishop check on h5, and then 17...♘c6 or 17...♘g4 to aim at castling long. White, however, answers with the very powerful 17 ♕h4! with dangerous threats.

17 ♗h5   ♔f7

Black can force the exchange of queens by returning the pawn with 17...0-0-0, but his king would not be much safer than in the game: 18 ♕xa7 b6 19 ♕a8+ ♕b8 20 ♕xb8+ ♔xb8 21 a5! and now:

1) 21...bxa5 22 ♗d6+ ♔b7 23 ♖xa5 ♖a8 24 ♖c5 ♖hc8 (24...♖a7 is

tougher) 25 ♖b1+ ♔a6 26 ♗c7 ♗b5 27 ♖5xb5 ♖xc7 28 ♖5b2 ♖c5 29 ♖a2+ ♖a5 30 ♖xa5+ ♔xa5 31 ♖a1+ and wins a rook.

2) 21...♔c7 was suggested in English circles to make the black position defensible. However, after 22 axb6+ ♔xb6 23 ♗g4! Black has no satisfactory answer (23...♖he8 24 ♗b4 or 23...♖a8 24 ♗xe6 ♖he8 25 ♖eb1+).

18 f4 (D)

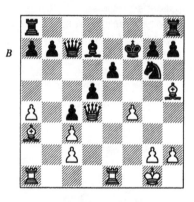

'Typical of Fischer's style,' is the accurate remark found in *The Games of Robert J. Fischer*. White seeks to clear the centre in order to attack the black king on an open board. I assume that a player like Karpov or Romanishin would continue less energetically with 18 ♖e3 or even 18 ♖e5 to continue the attack in a half-open position purely on the dark squares after a possible exchange on g6.

18 ...   ♖he8

The only answer. Black is forced to put his king on f6 where it will be exposed to some draughts.

19	f5	exf5
20	₩d5+	♔f6

20...♗e6 loses directly because of 21 ♖xe6 ♖xe6 22 ₩xf5+ ♖f6 23 ₩d5+ ♖e6 24 ♖f1+ and White is a piece up.

21 ♗f3!

Once again correctly called typical of Fischer's style in the above-mentioned book. Having converted a half-open position directly into an open one, he continues his attack slowly but clearly. The sharp 21 g4, to immediately demonstrate the compromised position of the black king, was recommended in the Russian press. The variations given after 21...♖ad8 22 ₩d4+ *(D)* are attractive:

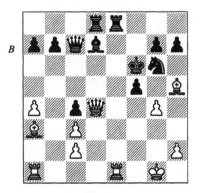

1) 22...♔f7 23 ♗e7! ♖xe7 24 ♖xe7+ ♔xe7 25 ₩xg7+ ♔d6 26 ₩f6+ and wins.

2) 22...♔g5 23 ♖e7! (a nice dual with move 23 in variation 1) 23...♘xe7 24 ₩e3+ f4 25 ♗xe7+ ♖xe7 (not 25...♔h6 26 ♗xe8 and the queen is immune due to 27 g5 mate) 26 ₩xe7+

♔h6 27 ♗f7! g6 (27...₩b6+ 28 ♔f1 ₩f6 offers no salvation because of the deadly pin after 29 ₩xf6+ gxf6 30 ♖d1) 28 ♖d1 ₩b6+ 29 ♔f1 ₩e3 (the only chance) 30 ₩xe3 fxe3 31 ♔e1 and Black must give up the exchange with 31...♔g7 32 ♗e6 ♗xe6. The endgame is then only a matter of technique for White.

These results are hardly satisfying for Black. But he has a far better defence than 21...♖ad8; namely, 21...₩b6+! 22 ♗c5 ₩c6. At first sight it appears that White's extra bishop move only makes things more difficult for Black, but the point is that after 23 ₩d4+ the black king can go to g5 without the white queen's decisive capture on g7 (but not 23...♔f7 24 gxf5 ♗xf5 25 ♖f1 and wins). Partly because of the centralised position of Black's pieces, White cannot take direct advantage of the position of Black's king; e.g., 23 ₩d4+ ♔g5 24 h4+ ♔xh4! 25 gxf5+ ♔xh5. The white king has become as exposed as the black one due to the reckless push 21 g4.

Fischer's intuition – I assume he chose the text-move mainly on intuitive grounds – was thus (again) faultless. The text-move, after a forest of complications, ultimately gives him the better chances in every variation.

21 ...   ♘e5! *(D)*

Byrne gives this a question mark without any reason at all; as he points out, there are no decent alternatives. Indeed, the endgame after 21...♗e6 22 ₩xb7 ₩xb7 23 ♗xb7 ♖ab8 24 ♖ab1

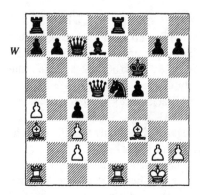

would be discouraging to play, especially against Fischer. The text-move shows a sharp appraisal of the coming complications and demonstrates how lively and fresh Larsen's play still was at the beginning of the match.

22 ♕d4

This looks like an unpleasant pin, but Larsen shows that the consequences are bearable.

22 ...   ♔g6

23 ♖xe5

There is no more to be squeezed out of the position; e.g., 23 ♗xb7 ♕xb7 24 ♖xe5 ♖xe5 25 ♕xe5 ♖e8 and White has achieved nothing. An interesting attempt is 23 ♔h1 to clear g1 in advance for the rook should the g-file be opened by an exchange on f3. However, Black can see to it that if there is an exchange, the kingside will remain closed: 23...♘g4! and White has nothing better than repetition of moves with 24 ♗d6 ♕b6 25 ♗c5 ♕c7 26 ♗d6.

23 ...   ♕xe5

Naturally not 23...♖xe5 24 ♗d6.

24 ♕xd7   ♖ad8

Centralising the heavy artillery to the utmost.

25 ♕xb7 *(D)*

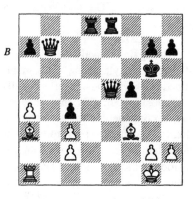

25 ...   ♕e3+

A difficult choice, but the consequences are slightly more favourable than those following the alternative 25...♕xc3. That move looks overwhelming at first; the white pieces do not seem to be working together while the black ones are all itching to give mate. However, it seems the attack against Black's king still continues: 26 ♕c6+! ♔g5 27 ♗c1+ f4 (or 27...♔h4 28 g3+ ♔h3 29 ♗g2+ ♔g4 30 h3+ ♔xg3 31 ♕c7+ ♕e5 32 ♕xe5+ ♖xe5 33 ♗g5! and Black must lose material to avoid mate) 28 h4+ ♔f5 (but not 28...♔xh4 29 ♔h2 and the black king is ensnared in a mating net) 29 g4+! (this energetic continuation of the attack was found by Zaitsev) 29...fxg3 30 ♔g2 *(D)*.

The black attack has been beaten off and, although there are no direct

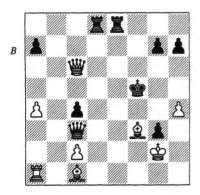

threats, he is in difficulties. Taking the rook is too dangerous: 30...♕xa1 31 ♗g4+ ♔e5 (31...♔xg4 32 ♕f3+ and mates) and now not 32 ♕b5+ ♔d6 33 ♕b4+ ♔d5 34 ♗a3 (as given by Zaitsev), because of the saving 34...♕e5!, but 32 ♕c5+ ♖d5 33 ♕e3+ ♔d6 (or 33...♔f6 34 ♕xe8 with mating threats on e6) 34 ♗a3+ ♔c7 35 ♕xa7+ ♔c6 36 ♕a6+ ♔c7 37 ♕xc4+ ♔b8 (or 37...♔b6) 38 ♕xd5 ♕xa3 39 ♕b5+. Brilliant teamwork by queen and bishops on an open board.

Still, the best for Black is 30...♕d4 (instead of 30...♕xa1), but after the calm 31 ♔xg3 White has the better prospects because his king is in just a little less danger.

26 ♔f1   ♖d2

This looks threatening, but Fischer must have seen it all long before and now comes up with the precise defence.

27 ♕c6+   ♖e6
28 ♗c5!

Improbable but true. The black attack is refuted in the nick of time. The following series of moves is forced.

28	...	♖f2+
29	♔g1	♖xg2+

Making the best of it.

30	♔xg2	♕d2+
31	♔h1	♖xc6
32	♗xc6 *(D)*	

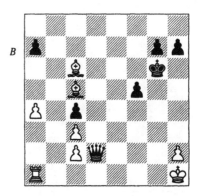

32 ...   ♕xc3?

Optimism or desperation? Knowing Larsen, I choose the first. Having conducted an enervating defence with extraordinary strength, Black suddenly loses his way. A pity, really, because one could expect a very interesting fight after 32...a5. At first sight the white bishops seem supreme, particularly with the possession of d4, but the black king can still find shelter behind the kingside pawns; e.g., 33 ♗d4 ♔h6 34 ♖g1 g5 or 33 ♖g1+ ♔f7 (33...♔h6 34 ♗f8) 34 ♗d4 g5. It is difficult to judge the position. A comparison with 'La Grande Variante' of the Open Ruy Lopez is not out of place. The theoreticians are still not agreed on who stands better after 1 e4 e5 2 ♘f3 ♘c6 3 ♗b5 a6 4 ♗a4 ♘f6 5

0-0 ♘xe4 6 d4 b5 7 ♗b3 d5 8 dxe5 ♗e6 9 c3 ♗c5 10 ♘bd2 0-0 11 ♗c2 f5 12 ♘b3 ♗b6 13 ♘fd4 ♘xd4 14 ♘xd4 ♗xd4 15 cxd4 f4 16 f3 ♘g3 17 hxg3 fxg3 18 ♕d3 ♗f5 19 ♕xf5 ♖xf5 20 ♗xf5 ♕h4 21 ♗h3 ♕xd4+ 22 ♔h1 ♕xe5 (D).

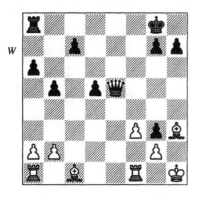

In the *Encyclopedia of Chess Openings* Korchnoi judges the chances to be equal, but he gives a few examples to show that every seemingly trivial inaccuracy can swing the balance strongly. The position after 32...a5 in the Fischer-Larsen game is perhaps a little better for White than in 'La Grande Variante,' but only if White can prevent the formation of the pawn duo f5-g5. Therefore, the best appears to be 33 ♗d4 ♔h6 34 ♖f1!, which forces 34...f4. White must still remain on his guard; e.g., 35 ♗e5 g5 36 h4? ♕e2! 37 hxg5+ ♔g6 38 ♗e8+ ♔f5 with win of material. A good move

seems to be 35 h4 and only after 35...♕xc2 36 ♗e5. After 36...♔h5 37 ♗xg7 (not 37 ♖xf4 ♕d1+ 38 ♔g2 ♕e2+) the black pawns have been split, which ensures White's advantage.

| 33 | ♖g1+ | ♔f6 |
| 34 | ♗xa7 (D) | |

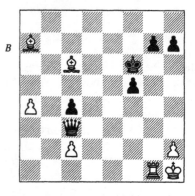

The white bishops come into their own even more with a passed a- pawn. Black is helpless against its advance.

34	...	g5
35	♗b6	♕xc2
36	a5	♕b2
37	♗d8+	♔e6
38	a6	♕a3
39	♗b7	

Little by little, White's passed pawn progresses toward promotion.

39	...	♕c5
40	♖b1	c3
41	♗b6	1-0

If 41...c2 42 ♖e1+.

Game Five
Taimanov – Stein
39th USSR Championship, Leningrad 1971
Modern Benoni Defence

Stein's sudden death in 1973, just before he was due to travel to the European Team Championship in Bath, England, shocked all genuine chess lovers. His enterprising style had a very personal tint. Keene analysed sixty of the Ukrainian grandmaster's games in his book, *Master of Attack*. The book includes only games he won, all the more clearly to emphasise Stein's impressive attacking skill.

The following game does not appear in the book. Though it is not really an attacking game, it does show his individual, enterprising style. Taimanov, who had just recently lost disastrously to Fischer, is defeated in a difficult positional game.

1	d4	♘f6
2	c4	c5
3	d5	g6
4	♘c3	d6
5	e4	♗g7
6	♘f3	0-0
7	♗e2	e6
8	0-0	exd5
9	cxd5	a6

The alternative 9...♖e8 is more current. After 10 ♘d2 extensive complexes of variations begin after both 10...♘bd7 and 10...♘a6.

10	a4	♗g4
11	♗f4 (D)	

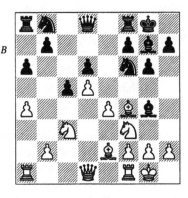

B

This position can also be reached via a different move order (1 d4 ♘f6 2 c4 c5 3 d5 e6 4 ♘c3 exd5 5 cxd5 d6 6 ♘f3 g6 7 ♗f4 a6 8 a4 ♗g7 9 e4 0-0 10 ♗e2 ♗g4 11 0-0). The text-move is not the sharpest. Alternatives are:

1) 11 ♗g5 ♘bd7 (11...h6!? 12 ♗h4 ♗xf3! with equal chances;

11...h6!? 12 ♗f4! ♖e8 13 ♘d2 ♗xe2 14 ♕xe2 ♘h5 15 ♗e3 ♘bd7 16 ♔h1 and White stands a little better. However, not 16 f4 f5! 17 exf5? ♖xe3.) 12 ♘d2 ♗xe2 13 ♕xe2 ♖e8 14 f4! ♕c7 15 ♕f3 c4 16 ♔h1 b6?! 17 ♖ae1 h6 18 ♗xf6 ♘xf6 19 e5 with advantage to White (Gligorić-Hartoch, Amsterdam 1971). In the game Timman-Nunn, London 1975, Black tried 16...♖b8 (instead of 16...b6), a slightly more purposeful move but nevertheless not satisfactory. After 17 ♖ae1 b5 18 axb5 axb5 19 e5 dxe5 20 f5 ♖f8 21 ♘de4 White had a known type of pressure on the black position.

2) 11 ♘d2 ♗xe2 12 ♕xe2 ♘bd7 (not 12...♖e8? 13 ♘c4, Donner-Hug, Berlin 1971) 13 ♘c4.

11 ...   ♖e8
12 ♕c2

12 ♘d2 also comes into consideration here: 12...♗xe2 13 ♕xe2 ♘h5 14 ♗e3 ♘d7 with chances for equal play. Black has the same position as in variation 1 after White's 11th move, but without the slight weakness at h6.

A well-known mistake is 12 h3? due to 12...♘xe4 (Uhlmann-Fischer, Palma de Mallorca 1970).

12 ...   ♕c7
13 h3   ♗xf3
14 ♗xf3   ♘bd7
15 a5

Many games have taken an almost identical course. For example, after 15...♖ab8 16 ♖fe1 we have the game Tal-Stein, Rostov 1971, by transposition of moves. Black continued with 16...b5?! 17 axb6 ♖xb6 18 ♖a2 ♖eb8 19 ♗e2 a5 20 ♖ea1 and White stood a little better.

I played Black against Portisch in Hastings 1969/70 and tried 15...c4, which led to the interesting continuation 16 ♘b1 (16 ♘e2 ♖ac8) 16...♘c5 (16...♖ac8!?) 17 ♕xc4 (17 ♘d2 ♘d3 18 ♗e3 ♘e5 with chances for both sides) 17...♘fxe4 18 ♖a2 f5 19 ♘d2?! (if 19 b4 ♘e6!, but 19 ♖c1! should be

considered) 19...♘xd2 20 ♗xd2 ♖ac8 and Black had the advantage. Stein's move is solid, but probably not better.

15 ...   ♖e7 (D)

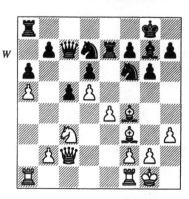

16 g4

An interesting idea. White wants to increase his influence on the centre with his bishops on g2 and g3 and then to follow with f2-f4. The other side of the coin is that the squares f4 and thereby e5 are weakened. In any case, 16 ♖fe1 is a good alternative.

16 ...   h6
17 ♗g2   ♖ae8
18 ♗g3   ♘h7
19 ♘b1

Why not 19 f4? If 19...g5 then 20 e5 is strong: 20...dxe5 21 fxg5 hxg5 22 d6 or 20...gxf4 21 exd6 ♕xd6 22 ♗xf4 ♗e5. Black, however, has the stronger 19...c4 with good play.

19 ...   g5
20 ♘d2   ♘e5
21 ♖a4

A rather strange move but not a bad one. White wants to prevent 21...c4. If he does this with 21 ♖fc1, to simultaneously free f1 for his knight, there follows, for instance, 21...♘f8 22 ♘f1 ♘fg6 23 ♘e3 ♘f4 24 ♘f5 ♖d7 and Black stands satisfactorily. The immediate f2-f4 may also be considered, however.

21 ...　　　　♘f8 (D)

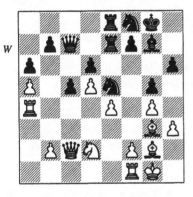

22 f4!
Now or never.

22 ...　　　　gxf4
23 ♖xf4　　　　♘fg6
24 ♖f1

The alternative idea 24 ♖f5, so as possibly to play the rook to h5 later, springs to mind. A double-edged business.

24 ...　　　　♕d8!
A strong move, the prelude to a regrouping.

25 ♖a3　　　　♖c7?!
More accurate is 25...♖d7 to overprotect d6, followed by 26...♕e7 and 27...♖c8. The reason becomes clear in the next moves.

26 ♖b3　　　　♘h4

Also dubious: the queen becomes tied to the protection of the knight. One gets the impression that Stein was in time trouble. Still good is 26...♕e7 27 ♖b6 ♖d8, after which there is little wrong with the black position.

27 ♖b6　　　　c4?!
28 ♕a4!
Threatens to take on d6. The black pieces are in one another's way.

28 ...　　　　♖f8
29 ♕a3　　　　♖c5
30 ♗f2

30 ♖xb7 ♘xg2 (30...♖xa5 31 ♗xh4) 31 ♔xg2 ♖xa5 gives Black counterplay.

30 ...　　　　♖b5
31 ♖xd6　　　　♕e7

31...♕g5 is no better, because of 32 ♗e3 ♕e7 33 ♗xh6. Now, however, the knight on h4 still hangs.

32 ♖b6　　　　♕xa3
33 bxa3　　　　♘xg2 (D)

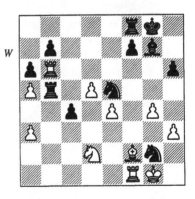

34 ♖xb5?
A mistake which hands the initiative over to Black. After 34 ♔xg2

Black can hardly play the 34...♖xa5 that Taimanov feared: 35 ♗d4! ♖xa3 (35...♘xg4 36 ♗xg7 ♘e3+ 37 ♔f2 ♘xf1 38 ♗xf8) 36 ♗xe5 ♗xe5 37 ♘xc4 ♖a2+ 38 ♔f3 f6 (the best) 39 ♖d1! ♖c8 40 ♘xe5 fxe5 41 ♖d3 and the white king can reach h4 safely.

Black must therefore try 34...c3 35 ♘b3 ♘c4 36 ♖xb5 axb5, but then 37 ♗c5 is very good (37...♖e8 38 d6).

| 34 | ... | axb5 |
| 35 | ♔xg2 | ♖a8! |

Here lies the difference. Black immediately becomes active.

36	♗b6	♘d7
37	♗c7	♗c3
38	♘f3	♗xa5

Perhaps the prophylactic 38...f6 is preferable to the text-move. The weakening is a lesser evil than the advance of the white centre pawns. The a5-pawn, as the saying goes, will not run away.

39 ♗d6?!

White should lose no time in playing 39 ♗xa5 ♖xa5 40 e5!; for example, 40...b4? 41 e6 fxe6 (41...♘f6 42 ♘e5 ♔g7 43 ♘d7!) 42 dxe6 ♘f6 43 axb4 and White stands better. Black must therefore defend with 40...♘f8, whereupon 41 g5 comes into consideration.

39	...	♘f6
40	♗e7	♘xe4
41	♘d4	

The best chance.

41 ... b4 (D)

It is clear that the time-trouble is over. Black's last move is very strong

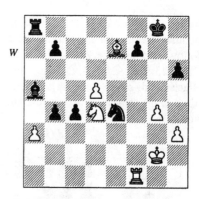

and well founded because the a-file is opened for the rook.

42	axb4	♗b6
43	♖f4	♖a2+
44	♔f3	♘d2+

44...♘g5+ 45 ♗xg5 hxg5 46 ♖e4 gives White counterplay.

45 ♔e3?

This loses in a prosaic fashion. With 45 ♔g3 he would pose a more troublesome problem:

1) 45...c3 46 d6 c2 47 ♘e2 (not 47 ♘xc2 ♖xc2 48 d7 ♖c3+ and ...♖d3) is holdable.

2) 45...♘b3!? 46 ♘xb3 cxb3 47 ♖f1 (the only move) 47...b2 48 ♗f6 or 47...♗d4 48 d6.

3) 45...♖a3+ 46 ♔g2 ♖d3 47 ♗c5.

4) 45...♗xd4! 46 ♖xd4 c3. This solution to the problem was given by Stam. At first sight it seems improbable that it can be good, because White queens with check. However, the black attack arrives first after 47 d6 c2 48 d7 c1♕ 49 d8♕+ ♔h7; the question is whether it is a mating attack. Assume that White plays 50 ♗f6

(D), the only possibility to create counterthreats.

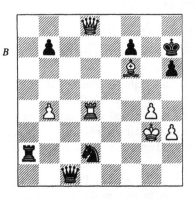

Black now has various checks at his disposal, but, since all the white pieces are protected, he must be all the more careful that the white king does not escape to safety on the queenside; e.g., 50...♖a3+ 51 ♔f4 ♘c4+ 52 ♔e4 ♕e3+ 53 ♔d5 ♕e6+ 54 ♔c5 b6+ 55 ♔b5 and Black has no continuation. He need not let it get that far, of course. On the 51st move, 51...♘f3+ is far stronger; but even that is not the nicest or most forcing win. From the diagram position, that distinction is held by 50...♘f1+ 51 ♔h4 ♕e1+ 52 ♔h5 and now the well-known smothered mate follows, in a very unusual part of the board: 52...♘g3+ 53 ♔h4 ♘f5+ 54 ♔h5 ♕h4+ 55 ♗xh4 ♘g7 mate.

45	...	♘b3
46	♗c5	

Or 46 ♗f6 c3 47 ♔d3 ♗xd4 48 ♗xd4 c2.

46	...	♘xc5
47	bxc5	♗xc5
48	♔f3	♖b2 *(D)*

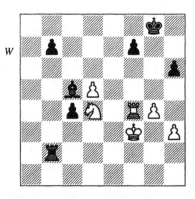

Thus the queenside pawns become mobile while the bishop restrains the white d-pawn. The rest of the game is simple.

49	♖e4	b5
50	♘f5	♖f2+
51	♔g3	♖d2
52	♖e8+	♔h7
53	♖c8	♖xd5
54	♔f4	♗a3!
55	♖c6	♖c5
56	♖xh6+	♔g8
57	♖a6	c3
58	♘d4	c2!
59	♘xc2	♗c1+
60	♘e3	♖c3
61	♖a8+	♔g7

0-1

After 62 ♖e8 b4 and 63...b3 followed by the exchange of pieces on e3, the black b-pawn queens.

Game Six
Fischer – Petrosian
Final Candidates Match (1), Buenos Aires 1971
Sicilian Defence, Taimanov Variation

The first game of the Fischer-Petrosian candidates match is, like the first Fischer-Larsen match game, the most interesting one – in any case, it is the richest in content. Fischer played a variation that he had earlier used with success against Taimanov, among others. Petrosian obviously entered it willingly, and it appeared that he and his seconds, Averbakh and Suetin, had prepared very well. Fischer had no ready answer to their new approach.

I was in Moscow during the first games of this match. The experts there thought Petrosian had let winning positions slip in each of the first five games (except the second, of course, which he had won). In this first game, in fact, I have been able to prove, more or less, that Petrosian had obtained a virtually won position after only fifteen moves. He missed his chance, and the struggle was wide open again. In the continuation, it was Fischer who found his way best in a difficult struggle, and just before the time control he achieved a decisive advantage.

This game was Fischer's twentieth successive victory over (strong) grandmasters, a record that has even found its way into the *Guinness Book of World Records*.

1	e4	c5
2	♘f3	e6
3	d4	cxd4
4	♘xd4	♘c6
5	♘b5	d6
6	♗f4	e5
7	♗e3	♘f6
8	♗g5	♗e6

The justification of this move is to be found in Black's eleventh, and so it must be regarded as the best reaction to the system chosen by White. Two alternatives are, in brief:

1) 8...a6 9 ♗xf6 gxf6 10 ♘5c3 f5 11 ♕h5 ♘d4 12 ♗c4! ♕c7 (also 12...♘xc2+ 13 ♔e2 ♗e6, as suggested in *Schaakbulletin 46*, gives White the advantage after 14 ♗xe6 ♘d4+ 15 ♔f1 ♘xe6 16 exf5 ♘f4 17 ♕f3 or 16...♘d4 17 ♘d2) 13 ♘d2 ♘xc2+ 14 ♔e2 ♘xa1 (Bronstein-Polugaevsky, 1964), and now after 15 ♖xa1 White stands better (Fischer).

2) 8...♕a5+ 9 ♕d2 ♘xe4 10 ♕xa5 ♘xa5 11 ♗e3 ♔d7 12 ♘1c3! ♘xc3 13 ♘xc3 and now:

2a) 13...♔d8 14 ♘b5 ♗e6 15 0-0-0 b6 16 f4 and White held the advantage (Fischer-Taimanov, 2nd match game 1971).

2b) 13...♗e7 14 0-0-0 ♖d8 15 ♘d5
♘c6 16 ♗b5, again with advantage to
White (Adorjan-Bobotsov, Amster-
dam-IBM 1971).
2c) 13...b6! 14 ♗b5+ ♘c6 15 0-0-0
♗b7 16 f4 ♖e8! and White's advantage is small.

9	♘1c3	a6
10	♗xf6	gxf6
11	♘a3	d5! *(D)*

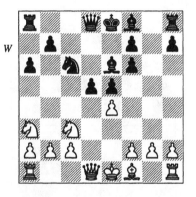

The idea of this move is not new; it
is also found in the Pelican Variation.
There it is insufficient for equality, but
here it is at least sufficient.

12 exd5

On 12 ♘xd5 ♗xa3 13 bxa3 Black
has two good continuations: 13...♕a5+
14 ♕d2 ♕xd2+ 15 ♔xd2 0-0-0 16 c4
f5, or directly 13...f5.

12	...	♗xa3
13	bxa3	♕a5
14	♕d2	0-0-0
15	♗c4	

Unremarked upon everywhere, but
in my opinion this is the mistake
which gets White into trouble. In most

cases the bishop should stand on d3,
and it is therefore logical to postpone
making the choice between ♗c4 and
♗d3 by playing 15 ♖d1!:
1) 15...♘d4? 16 dxe6 ♘f3+ 17
gxf3 ♖xd2 18 ♔xd2 and wins.
2) 15...♖hg8 16 ♗d3!.
3) 15...♗xd5 16 ♘xd5 ♖xd5 17
♕xa5 ♖xd1+ 18 ♔xd1 ♘xa5 19 ♗d3
or 17...♖xa5 18 ♗c4; in either case
both sides' pawn structures have been
weakened, but White has the better
prospects as his light-squared bishop
is stronger than the knight in this position.
4) 15...♔b8!? 16 ♘e4! ♕xd2+ 17
♖xd2 ♗xd5! 18 ♘xf6 ♗xa2 19 ♖xd8+
♖xd8 20 ♗d3 with a slight advantage
to White (20 ♘xh7? ♘d4 21 ♗d3 f5).
5) 15...♘e7! 16 d6! ♘c6 17 ♘e4
with a small advantage to White; for
example, 17...♕xd2+ 18 ♖xd2 f5 19
♘c5 ♖hg8.

15 ... ♖hg8

In *Schaakbulletin 47* the alternative 15...♗f5 is given, with the intention 16 0-0 ♘d4 17 ♗d3 ♔b8 18
♗xf5 ♕xc3. After 19 ♕xc3 ♘e2+ 20
♔h1 ♘xc3 21 f4! White does not
stand badly in the ending; e.g., 21...e4
22 ♖ae1 or 21...♖xd5 22 ♖f3 e4 23
♖xc3 ♖xf5 24 g3.
The move Petrosian chooses holds
the white position in a vice; White
cannot play 16 0-0 due to 16...♗h3.

16 ♖d1 *(D)*

A very critical point indeed. Before
investigating the consequences of
the much-discussed 16...♖xg2, I first

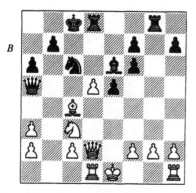

want to examine the following possibilities, most of which are also good for Black:

1) 16...♖g4? 17 ♗d3! (17 ♗b3 ♖d4) and Black has had his say.

2) 16...♘e7. Given by O'Kelly in *Europe Echecs*. The threat is the manoeuvre ...♖g8-g4-d4. He gives the following variation: 17 ♘e4 ♕c7 18 ♕c3 ♘xd5 19 ♗xd5 ♗xd5 20 ♕xc7+ ♔xc7 21 ♘xf6 ♗xg2 22 ♘xg8 ♗xh1 with advantage to Black. Indeed in this case Black is even winning. Therefore White should play the better 17 ♗b3 profiting from the fact that the black knight can no longer go to the strong square d4. White has counterplay with 18 ♘a4 in answer to either 17...♖xg2 or 17...♖g4.

3) 16...♗g4. A good suggestion by Korchnoi and Furman in *64*, with the idea of playing 17...♗f5 only after 17 f3. They give the variation 17 f3 ♗f5 18 ♘e4 ♖xg2 19 ♕xa5 ♘xa5 20 ♗d3 ♖xd5 21 ♘xf6 and now the exchange sacrifice 21...♖xd3 22 cxd3 ♖xa2 is forced and strong.

At that time I even suggested 18 ♗b3 to answer 18...♘d4 with 19 ♘e4. M.Spanjaard, in his column in the *Utrechts Nieuwsblad*, pointed out that Black can then give mate immediately with 19...♖xg2 20 ♕xa5 ♖e2+ 21 ♔f1 ♗h3+ 22 ♔g1 ♘xf3 mate.

4) But why didn't Petrosian play 16...♖xg2? *(D)* it is more difficult to answer this question than to give variations.

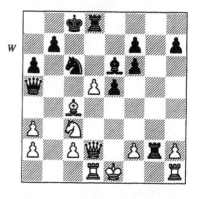

4a) First, let us look at 17 ♕e3, which in some columns was even given as a refutation. After 17...♘d4 18 ♔f1 there can follow:

4a1) 18...♘f5, here and there given as the best. After 19 ♕e1, ♖xf2+! is sufficient for a decisive attack. However, O'Kelly showed that White can force a draw as follows: 19 ♕a7! ♕xc3 20 ♗xa6! bxa6 21 ♕a8+ ♔c7 22 ♕a7+, etc.

4a2) 18...♘xc2 19 ♕d3! (not 19 ♕d2 ♗h3 or 19 ♕f3 ♖xf2+! with a decisive attack) 19...♖g4 (now 19...♖xf2+ 20 ♔xf2 ♕c5+ 21 ♔e2 ♗g4+ 22 ♔d2 is not sufficient) and now, besides 20 ♕xc2 ♖xc4 21 dxe6, which leads to better play for Black after 21...♕xc3! 22 ♕xc3 ♖xc3! 23 exf7 ♖f8, White can offer the queen with 20 dxe6. Langeweg judges that Black runs no risk with 20...♖xd3 21 ♖xd3 ♕xa3, but I cannot agree, because after 22 exf7, 22...♖xc4 fails to 23 ♖g1, and otherwise a white rook gains control of the g-file; for example, 22...♘d4 23 ♖g1 ♖xg1+ 24 ♔xg1 ♘f5 (to stop ♖g3) 25 ♗e6+.

4a3) 18...♗g4!. Although not mentioned by anybody, this move is very strong. The main variation runs: 19 ♔xg2 ♗f3+ 20 ♔h3 (otherwise he loses the rook with a lost position) 20...♕c7! 21 ♖xd4 (mate in two was threatened) 21...♕d7+ and now:

4a31) 22 ♔h4 ♕f5!!, threatening 23...♕h5+ and 24...♖g8 and mate. Barendregt drew my attention to 23 ♕h6 which, it is true, does avert the mate, but after 23...exd4 24 ♖g1 dxc3 the black attack continues despite the restored material equality.

4a32) 22 ♔g3 ♗xh1 23 ♖g4 f5 24 ♕c5+ ♔b8 25 ♖g7 (25 ♖g5 f6) 25...♖c8 and White cannot hold on to his extra material; e.g., 26 ♕b4 f4+ 27 ♔h4 ♕d8+ 28 ♔h3 ♕f6 29 ♖g4 ♕h6+ 30 ♖h4 ♕g6 31 ♖g4 ♕h5+ 32 ♖h4 ♕f3 mate.

White must therefore play 19 ♗e2 or ♘e2, but in either case 19...♘f5 is strong, perhaps too strong.

My conclusion is that 17 ♕e3 must be rejected and that White must play:

4b) 17 ♘e4 *(D)*. Black then has three possibilities:

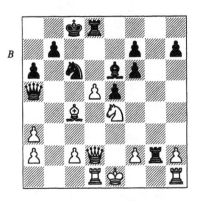

4b1) 17...♖g6 18 ♕xa5 ♘xa5 19 dxe6 ♘xc4 20 exf7 ♖f8 21 ♖d5 b6 and White stands a little better (Korchnoi and Furman).

4b2) 17...♗g4 18 ♕xa5 (if 18 ♗f1 ♗f3!) 18...♘xa5 19 ♗e2 ♗xe2 20 ♔xe2 ♖g6 21 ♘g3 e4 22 h4 with chances for both sides.

4b3) 17...♕b6! 18 ♕e3 (18 ♕c3 ♗f5 19 ♗f1 ♗xe4 20 ♕h3+ ♔b8 21 ♗xg2 ♗xc2 and Black wins) and now Black can get a decisive endgame advantage with 18...♕xe3+ 19 fxe3 ♗g4 followed by 20...♗f3. Also 18...♘d4 19 ♔f1 ♗g4 20 ♔xg2 ♗f3+ 21 ♕xf3 ♘xf3 22 ♔xf3 f5 is good because Korchnoi and Furman's suggested 23 ♘d2 is met by 23...♕d4, while the more natural 23 ♘g3 is strongly answered by 23...♕g6.

I hope I have shown with these lines that Black could have obtained a winning position by 16...♖xg2, which was indeed quietly assumed by others.

The move played by Petrosian is not bad either.

16 ...   ♝f5
17 ♝d3   ♝xd3

17...♞d4 leads to the same position after 18 ♝xf5 ♞xf5 19 ♛d3 (19 0-0 ♞h4) 19...♞d4, but Black can also try 19...♞d6. It is strange that Petrosian limits his choices like this.

17...e4 is a whole chapter in itself. White can react as follows:

1) 18 ♝xe4? ♝xe4 19 ♞xe4 ♜ge8 20 0-0 ♜xe4 21 ♛d3 f5 and Black wins.

2) 18 ♞xe4 ♝xe4 19 dxc6 ♛e5!.

3) 18 ♝e2! ♜xg2 19 ♛e3 ♞e5 20 ☫f1. White stands better, according to the *Deutsche Schachzeitung,* because 21 ♞xe4 is possible when the black rook withdraws. However, Black can play 20...♞g4 21 ♝xg4 ♜xg4 22 h3 ♜h4 with a difficult position for White (23 ♛g3 ♜h5 or 23 ♜d4 ♛c5!).

18 ♛xd3   ♞d4
19 0-0   ☫b8
20 ☫h1 *(D)*

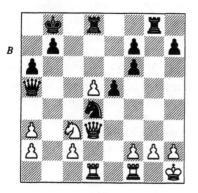

20 ...   ♛xa3

20...♜c8 is an important alternative. White gets the advantage after 21 ♞e4 ♛xd5 22 c3 f5 23 ♞g3 f4 24 cxd4 fxg3 25 fxg3. O'Kelly, however, points out the exchange sacrifice 22...♜xc3 23 ♛xc3 when Black has just enough compensation.

21 f4

In *Schaakbulletin 47,* 21 ♞e4 is correctly given as better. However, the possibility 21...♛xa2 is not mentioned: 22 ♞xf6 ♜g6 23 ♛e4.

21 ...   ♜c8
22 ♞e4   ♛xd3

22...♛xa2 leads to nice continuations such as 23 ♞xf6 ♜xg2! Then 24 ♞d7+ ☫a7 25 fxe5 ♜cxc2 26 ♛xd4+ leads to the beautiful king manoeuvre 26...☫a8 27 ♞b6+ ☫b8 28 ♞d7+ ☫c8 29 ♞b6+ ☫d8 30 ♛h4+ ☫e8 and Black wins. White must therefore play 23 ♜d2! (Korchnoi and Furman), after which Black has a draw with 23...♜xc2 24 ♜xc2 ♛xc2 (24...♞xc2 25 ♛e2) 25 ♛xc2 ♞xc2 26 ♞xf6 ♞e3! 27 ♜e1 (27 ♜f3 ♜c8!) 27...♞xg2 28 ♜g1 ♜g6 29 ♞d7+ ☫c7 30 ♞xe5 ♞xf4 31 ♞xg6 fxg6, as shown by Kholmov. Perhaps 26 fxe5 is worth trying as a winning attempt.

23 cxd3 *(D)*

This has not been commented on anywhere. Yet 23 ♜xd3, with the idea of attacking the knight's position, is interesting. A drawn position arises after the long, practically forced continuation 23...♜xc2 24 g3 ♜xa2! 25 ♞xf6 ♜c8 26 fxe5 ♜cc2 27 ♞g4 h5 28

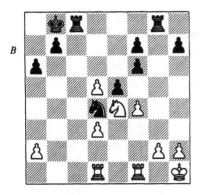

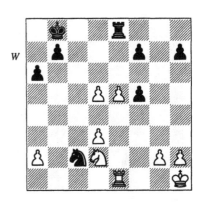

$\textcircled{2}$f2! (28 $\textcircled{2}$e3 Ξxh2+ 29 $\mathbf{\dot{g}}$g1 Ξh3)
28...Ξxf2 29 Ξxf2 Ξxf2 30 Ξxd4 Ξf5!
(31 d6 $\mathbf{\dot{g}}$c8 32 Ξc4+ $\mathbf{\dot{g}}$d8).

23 ...	Ξc2
24 Ξd2	

Now 24 g3 is bad due to 24...Ξxa2
25 $\textcircled{2}$xf6 Ξc8, etc.

24 ...	Ξxd2
25 $\textcircled{2}$xd2	f5

Sharply seen. Examine also these
lines:

1) 25...Ξe8? 26 f5, etc.

2) 25...Ξd8 26 fxe5 fxe5 27 Ξxf7.

3) 25...Ξc8!? 26 fxe5 Ξc2 (or
26...fxe5 27 Ξxf7 Ξc2 28 $\textcircled{2}$f1 Ξxa2
29 g4!) 27 $\textcircled{2}$e4 fxe5 28 g4! with
slightly better play for White.

4) 25...exf4 26 Ξxf4 Ξe8 27 Ξxf6
with advantage to White.

26 fxe5	Ξe8
27 Ξe1	$\textcircled{2}$c2 (D)
28 Ξe2	

28 Ξc1 is recommended by Panov.
The luminous point is 28...Ξxe5? 29
$\textcircled{2}$f3 Ξe2 30 d6! $\mathbf{\dot{g}}$c8 31 $\mathbf{\dot{g}}$g1! $\mathbf{\dot{g}}$d7 32
$\mathbf{\dot{g}}$f1 winning a piece. After 28...$\textcircled{2}$b4
(28...$\textcircled{2}$d4? 29 $\textcircled{2}$c4 b5 30 $\textcircled{2}$b6) little

is happening: 29 d4 $\textcircled{2}$xd5 and though
the black kingside pawns are indeed
weak, if White attacks them Black will
get the c-file. Furthermore, Black has
the advantage on the queenside. White
should occupy d6 with his knight by
playing 30 Ξc5 Ξd8 31 $\textcircled{2}$c4.

28 ...	$\textcircled{2}$d4

28...$\textcircled{2}$b4 was suggested here, with
the idea 29 $\textcircled{2}$c4 $\textcircled{2}$xd3 30 e6 fxe6 31
$\textcircled{2}$d6 Ξe7 32 $\textcircled{2}$xf5? Ξf7. Better seems
30 g3 and White stands a little better
(30...b5 31 $\textcircled{2}$a5).

29 Ξe3	$\textcircled{2}$c2
30 Ξh3	

Naturally.

30 ...	Ξxe5
31 $\textcircled{2}$f3	Ξxd5

Disapproved of by Kholmov. He
gives 31...Ξe2 as correct, with the
variation 32 Ξxh7 $\textcircled{2}$d4 33 Ξxf7 Ξxa2
34 h4 $\textcircled{2}$xf3 35 gxf3 Ξa4!, drawing.
But 33 Ξxf7 is ridiculous and must be
replaced with the immediate 33 h4.
Then the black f-pawns only make it
more difficult to stop the h-pawn.

32 Ξxh7 (D)

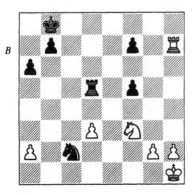

32 ...   ♖xd3

It is possible to say that this is the decisive mistake. It is much more logical to mobilise the majority on the queenside immediately with 32...b5. In *Schaakbulletin 47,* a variation ending in a draw is given: 32...b5 33 h4 a5 34 h5 b4 35 ♖xf7 a4 36 h6 ♖d6 37 h7 ♖h6+ 38 ♔g1 b3 39 axb3 a3 and White has nothing better than repetition of moves with 40 ♖f8+ and 41 ♖f7+. Foreign magazines again fail to comment here.

33 h4   ♘e3

This is the move generally considered to be the decisive mistake, and it is also mentioned that 33...♘d4 holds the draw. This is correct as far as the rook-endgame is concerned. Korchnoi and Furman analyse: 34 ♘xd4 ♖xd4 35 ♔h2 f6 36 ♔g3 ♖g4+ 37 ♔h3 ♖g6, or 36 ♔h3 ♖d3+ 37 g3 f4; also, 34 ♘e5 ♖e3 35 ♘xf7 f4 36 h5 f3 37 gxf3 ♘xf3 38 ♔g2 ♘h4+ 39 ♔f2 ♖f3+ 40 ♔e2 ♖f6 41 h6 ♘f5 leads to a draw, according to them. The variation is rather long and thus not quite

convincing. On the 35th move, worthy of consideration is 35 ♘d7+ followed by 36 ♖xf7. Kholmov however, shows an even more convincing way to keep White's advantage: 34 ♘g5! f6 35 ♘h3 and Black's f-pawns again get in the way of his pieces.

34 ♖xf7

If 34 h5, 34...♘g4 follows. Then 35 ♖xf7 is too late: 35...♖d1+ 36 ♘g1 ♘f2+ 37 ♔h2 ♘g4+, drawing.

34 ...   ♖d1+

A little better is 34...♔c8 to offer the exchange of rooks after 35 h5 ♖d1+ 36 ♔h2 ♖d7. But after 37 ♖f8+ ♔c7 38 ♔g3 or 37...♖d8 38 ♖xd8+ ♔xd8 39 ♔g3 White keeps matters firmly under control.

35 ♔h2   ♖a1

Perhaps still 35...♔c8, though now 36 h5 can be replaced by 36 ♔g3.

36 h5 (D)

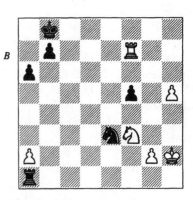

36 ...   f4

A critical moment. Petrosian is seized by panic and plays a move that loses quickly. In *Both Sides of the*

Chessboard Byrne states that Petrosian should have played 36...♖xa2. It is then unclear whether White has real winning chances. Originally I gave 37 ♘h4 in reply, but then Black gets an immediate draw with 37...f4! 38 ♖xf4 ♖a5 39 g4 ♘xg4+ and White has no pawns left. A better try is 37 ♖g7 (D). Black then has the following possibilities:

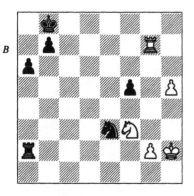

1) 37...♘g4+. This move is given by Kasparov in the *Encyclopaedia of Chess Endings*. He concludes that Black should be able to get a draw after the long variation 38 ♔g3 a5 39 ♘d4 a4 40 ♘xf5 ♘f6 41 h6 a3 42 h7 ♘xh7 43 ♖xh7 ♖b2 44 ♖h1 a2 45 ♖a1 b5 46 ♘d4 b4 47 ♘c6+ ♔c7 48 ♘xb4 ♖xb4 49 ♖xa2 ♔d6 50 ♖e2 ♖b8 when a theoretically known endgame has arisen. However, White can strengthen this variation considerably with 39 ♔f4! (instead of 39 ♘d4). The point is that 39...♖xg2 is not playable, because of 40 h6 and the h-pawn runs on to queen without being troubled.

Also winning for White is 39...a4 40 ♔xf5 ♘e3+ 41 ♔e4; for example: 41...♖e2 42 ♔d3 a3 43 ♔xe2 a2 44 h6 a1♕ 45 ♖g8+ ♔a7 46 h7 and promotion cannot be prevented.

2) 37...a5. Another suggestion by Kasparov, and one which contains a beautiful idea. After 38 h6 ♘g4+ 39 ♖xg4 fxg4 40 h7 gxf3 41 h8♕+ ♔a7 42 ♕d4+ ♔a8 43 ♕d5 ♖xg2+ 44 ♔h3 ♖g6 Black is going to build an impenetrable fortress. However, White can also strengthen this variation, namely with 38 ♘e5. Then it is not easy to see how Black is going to stop the h-pawn.

3) 37...f4. This move, given by Byrne, is easily the best. Black gets ready to stop the h-pawn via a5. Moreover, the white king is deprived of the g3-square. After 38 h6 ♖a5 39 h7 ♖h5+ 40 ♔g1 ♔a7 there is no win for White. If the worst comes to the worst, Black can give up his rook for the h-pawn, for his queenside pawns are then far enough advanced. Byrne elaborates on this as follows: 41 ♘g5 a5 42 ♖g8 a4 43 h8♕ ♖xh8 44 ♖xh8 a3 45 ♖c8 a2 46 ♖c1 ♘c2 with a draw. A more subtle attempt to win for White is 38 ♖g5, in order to keep the black rook at bay. Here Byrne gives the following variation: 38...♖c2 39 ♘e5 ♖c7 40 h6 ♖h7 41 ♘c6+ bxc6 42 ♖g8+ ♔c7 43 ♖g7+ ♖xg7 44 hxg7 ♘g4+ 45 ♔h3 ♘f6 and Black even wins. The move 41 ♘c6+ is a nice study idea, but there is little sense in playing it, since Black has a more than

adequate defence. Much stronger is 40 ♔h3 (instead of 40 h6), after which White does indeed threaten to win in this study-like manner and, besides, he throws his king forward in support of the h-pawn. Black then has difficulty in reaching the safe haven of a draw.

	37	♖xf4	♖xa2

38 ♖e4!

Fischer has played the whole second half of the game very accurately. The text-move prevents ...♖xg2+ because the black knight is hanging.

38	...	♘xg2
39	♔g3	♖a5
40	♘e5	1-0

Game Seven
Fischer – Spassky
World Championship Match (4), Reykjavik 1972
Sicilian Defence, Sozin Variation

Fischer had unnecessarily lost a drawn position in the first game of this world championship match and had failed to show up for the second, while Spassky had not put up much resistance in the third game, although he was playing the white pieces. It was not until the fourth game that we saw both players in their element.

Just as Petrosian in the first game of his match with Fischer had found an important improvement on Taimanov's handling of the Sicilian, so Spassky improved on Larsen's play in another Sicilian variation. He clearly took matters under control and even increased his advantage when Fischer evidently underestimated the seriousness of his situation. However, in the fifth hour Spassky failed to crown his work and Fischer succeeded in reaching a draw with precise defensive manoeuvres.

1 e4	c5
2 ♘f3	d6
3 d4	cxd4
4 ♘xd4	♘f6
5 ♘c3	♘c6
6 ♗c4	

The system Fischer had always used. This would be the main reason for Spassky's choosing to enter an unusual (for him) Sicilian.

6 ...	e6
7 ♗b3	♗e7
8 ♗e3	0-0

Larsen, who also castled at this point in his game against Fischer in the 1970 Interzonal tournament, remarks in his book, *Ich spiele auf Sieg,* that he did not want to play 8...a6 because he feared that White would then

castle short and the move a7-a6 would just be a lost tempo. We will see that Spassky has a different opinion about this.

9 0-0

The first significant decision. About five years before this game, Fischer had begun to prefer 9 ♕e2, intending to castle long. Then he lost to Larsen in the above-mentioned game, which went 9 ♕e2 a6 10 0-0-0 ♕c7 11 g4 ♘d7 12 h4 ♘c5 13 g5 b5 14 f3 ♗d7 15 ♕g2 b4 16 ♘ce2 ♘xb3+ 17 axb3 a5 and the black attack came first. The cause was mainly White's twelfth move, which, as indicated by Velimirović, should have been 12 g5. Nevertheless, a year later Fischer returned to the old system with kingside castling in two games of his match with Larsen, and he won both of them.

9 ...　　a6

Spassky sees ...a7-a6 as a waiting move rather than a tempo-loss. Other possibilities in this much-played position are:

1) 9...♘a5 (Botvinnik's move) 10 f4 b6 11 e5 (White must play sharply because after 11 ♕f3 ♗b7 the threat of the exchange sacrifice ...♖a8-c8xc3 is strong) 11...♘e8 12 f5 dxe5 13 fxe6 ♘xb3 14 ♘c6! ♕d6 15 ♕xd6 ♗xd6 16 axb3 ♗xe6 17 ♘xa7 and the endgame is a little better for White (Kostro-Doda, 1957).

2) 9...♗d7 10 f4 and now:

2a) 10...♘xd4 11 ♗xd4 ♗c6 12 ♕d3 b5 13 e5 dxe5 14 fxe5 ♘d7 15 ♘e4 ♗xe4! 16 ♕xe4 ♘c5 17 ♗xc5 ♗xc5+ 18 ♔h1 ♕d4 and Black stands a little better (Jimenez-Lein, 1972). White should play 12 ♕e2.

2b) 10...♕c8 11 f5 ♘xd4 12 ♗xd4 exf5 13 ♕d3! and White obtains reasonable compensation for the pawn (Fischer-Larsen, 5th match game 1971).

3) 9...♘xd4 10 ♗xd4 b5 11 ♘xb5 ♗a6 12 c4 ♗xb5 13 cxb5 ♘xe4 14 ♕g4 ♘f6 15 ♕e2 ♘d7 and now White can gain the advantage with 16 ♖ac1.

10 f4

After this move Black can subject the e4-pawn to constant pressure. However, if White makes a waiting move (say, 10 a3) in order to support the e-pawn later with f2-f3, then 10...♘a5 is good for Black.

10 ...　　♘xd4
11 ♗xd4　　b5 (D)

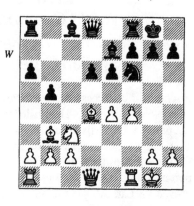

12 a3

Little can be achieved by such restrained play. Fischer apparently still wishes to play his favourite advance, f4-f5. However, the most suitable method to exploit White's opening advantage at this point, as shown by later practice, is 12 e5. After 12...dxe5 13 fxe5 ♘d7 14 ♘e4 ♗b7 15 ♘d6 ♗xd6 16 exd6 ♕g5 a difficult position arises with chances for both sides, but White's credentials are probably slightly better. An example from practice is 17 ♕e2 e5 18 ♗e3 ♕g6 19 ♖ad1 ♔h8 20 c3 ♗e4 21 ♕f2 and Black stood well (Hamman-Gligorić, Skopje 1972). However, 17 ♖f2! is stronger.

12 ...　　♗b7
13 ♕d3　　a5! (D)

The real point of Black's ninth move, undoubtedly the fruit of homework. Black has now definitely lost a tempo, but this is exactly the reason White runs into some difficulty. There

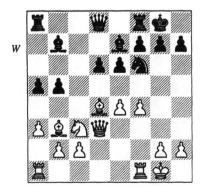

is no longer time to advance the f-pawn, so Fischer decides to push the e-pawn.

14 e5   dxe5
15 fxe5   ♘d7
16 ♘xb5

White must carry on. If 16 ♘e4, then after 16...♗xe4 17 ♕xe4 ♘c5, a position arises similar to that in variation 2a after Black's ninth move.

16 ...   ♘c5
17 ♗xc5

After this, Black has two mighty bishops raking the board. Although it is true that after 17 ♕e2 ♘xb3 18 cxb3 ♗a6 19 ♖ad1 ♕d5 20 a4 ♕xb3 White's position collapses, Olafsson's suggestion 17 ♕e3 keeps White's feet more firmly on the ground. The point is that White suffers no material loss after 17...♘xb3 18 ♕xb3 a4 19 ♕d3, although Black would keep good compensation for the pawn; e.g., 19...♕d5 20 ♖f2 ♖ac8 (prevents 21 c4 and threatens 21...♗a6) 21 ♘c3 ♕c6 and White's pawn preponderance on the queenside is of little significance.

Fischer preserves his 'Sicilian bishop' with the text-move, but he gets little joy from it. The black bishops will exert a paralysing effect.

17 ...   ♗xc5+
18 ♔h1   ♕g5 (D)

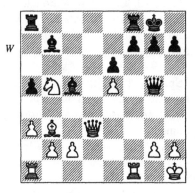

Initially it was thought that this move indicated Spassky's intention to play for a win, but a closer analysis shows that the alternative, exchanging queens, is no guarantee of an easy draw: 18...♕xd3 19 cxd3 and now:

1) 19...♗a6 20 ♘c7 ♗xd3 21 ♖fc1! with advantage (21...♖ab8 22 ♘xe6, or 21...♗e3 22 ♖c3 ♖ad8 23 ♖ad1).

2) 19...♗c6 21 ♖fc1 ♗xb5 21 ♖xc5 ♗xd3 22 ♖d1 with a small but lasting advantage for White.

19 ♕e2

A very passive move by Fischer's standards, which shows that he underestimated the dangers facing his position. Otherwise he would have chosen 19 ♕g3, to head for a draw; for example, 19...♕xg3 20 hxg3 and now:

1) 20...a4 21 ♗c4 ♖a5. Black now has the strong threat 22...♗a6 which indirectly threatens the pawn on e5. White can save himself with 22 b4 axb3 23 cxb3 ♗a6 24 a4.

2) 20...♗a6 21 ♗c4 ♗xb5 22 ♗xb5 ♗d4 23 c3 ♗xe5 and, although the situation is virtually balanced, Black stands just a little better because of his centre pawns.

19 ...   ♖ad8

Spassky thought about this for nineteen minutes. His judgement is correct and based on the following grounds:

First: White will be compelled to move his rook from the f-file due to the threat 20...♖d2, and thus White's pressure against f7 will be reduced.

Second: The bishop on b7 has the square a8 available in answer to a possible ♘b5-d6.

Third: The d-file which White obtains is of only secondary importance because the struggle will take place mainly on the kingside.

20 ♖ad1   ♖xd1
21 ♖xd1   h5 (D)

An almost thematic continuation. Black threatens to advance the pawn to h3 and thereby strengthen the grip his bishop-pair exerts on White's position. Nevertheless, there are good alternatives:

1) 21...♖d8, recommended by Nei. 22 ♘d6 is not possible now because of 22...♗xg2+ 23 ♔xg2 ♕xe5 and Black wins. Nei gives the continuation 22 ♖xd8+ ♕xd8 23 c3 ♕g5 24 ♘d4

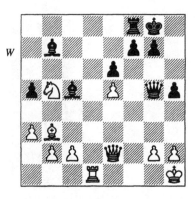

(24...♗xg2+ was threatened) 24...♕c1+ 25 ♗d1 ♗d5 with more than enough compensation for the pawn. However, it is an open question whether it does more than merely win back a pawn on d4 after 26 ♕c2 ♕f4 27 ♕e2.

2) 21...♗e3. This direct move with the dual threats 22...♕xe5 and 22...♗f4 puts White in great difficulties. If he tries to resist with 22 ♘d6 ♗c6 23 ♖f1 ♗f4 24 ♕f2 he faces 24...♕g4! (Olafsson) with the crushing threat 25...♕h3. More stubborn is 23 ♘c4 (instead of 23 ♖f1) 23...♗f4 24 ♔g1. After 24...a4 25 ♗a2, 25...h5 follows with even stronger effect than in the game.

22 ♘d6

Reshevsky rejects this move and feels that White should use the knight for defence with 22 ♘d4. With hindsight, there is certainly something to be said for it; for instance, after 22...h4 23 ♘f3 ♕f4 24 h3 White stands passively indeed, but there is no immediate way to exploit that situation. The text-move can be justified from a practical point of view: in many lines White has the possibility of sacrificing on f7, and the knight also has the possibility of returning to the defence via e4. On the other hand, the strongpoint on d6 can become shaky, as will become apparent.

22 ...   ♗a8
23 ♗c4

Fischer must have played this strong defensive move, which protects the queen on e2 and in general brings the bishop back into the game, purely by intuition. Attempts to re-exert pressure against f7 fail: 23 ♖f1 h4 24 ♘xf7 h3! (even stronger than 24...♖xf7 25 ♗xe6 h3) 25 ♘xg5 hxg2+ and mate next move.

23 ...   h4 (D)

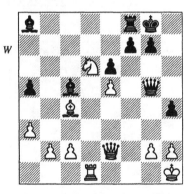

Once again 23...♗e3 comes into consideration. White would have no better than 24 ♗d3 ♗f4 25 ♗e4 ♕xe5 (but not 25...♕h4 26 g3 ♗xg3 27 ♗xa8 ♖xa8 28 ♕g2 and White wins) 26 g3! ♗xe4+ 27 ♕xe4 ♕xe4+ 28 ♘xe4 ♗e5 and Black's strong bishop

gives him the advantage in the endgame.

24 h3

Although not as bad as was generally thought, this move is clearly an example of superficial calculation. Other moves:

1) 24 ♖d3. This is refuted simply with 24...♗xg2+ 25 ♕xg2 ♕c1+, winning the exchange.

2) 24 ♘e4 ♕xe5 25 ♘xc5 ♕xc5 26 h3 (D).

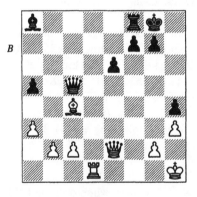

Opinions are divided on this position. Some find that Black has a great advantage, others that White does not stand much worse. Indeed, it is not easy to find the best plan for Black. After much searching, I think the solution lies in 26...♕f5! After 27 ♔g1 ♖c8 White is faced with the threat 28...♕c5+ and must make the concession of choosing a square for his bishop at this unsuitable moment. After either 28 ♗b3 ♗e4 or 28 ♗d3 ♕g5 followed by the advance of the e-pawn (with White's bishop no longer on the a2-g8 diagonal, the f7-square is no longer so weak), Black is clearly in a position to control matters.

24 ...   &e3!

At last, and now with even greater effect. Destruction is threatened with 25...&f4 and 25...♕g3. White has less to fear from 24...♕g3 25 ♘e4 (but not 25 ♖d3 &xg2+ 26 ♕xg2 ♕e1+ 27 ♔h2 ♕xe5+ and wins) 25...♕xe5 26 ♘xc5 ♕xc5 and the same position as in the above variation *B* arises, but with White having an extra move.

25 ♕g4   ♕xe5

Black correctly keeps the queens on the board. The ending after 25...♕xg4 26 hxg4 does not offer much:

1) 26...h3 27 &f1 &f4 28 ♘c4 and White keeps his head above water.

2) 26...&f4 (the knight is prevented from going to c4) 27 &e2! (much stronger than 27 ♖e1 h3 28 &f1 f6 with overwhelming play for Black) 27...&xe5 28 ♘c4 followed by 29 &f3 and the white position holds together.

26 ♕xh4 (D)

For the moment, White holds his extra pawn. 26 ♘xf7 is again incorrect since after 26...♔xf7 27 &xe6+ ♔f6! (not 27...♕xe6 28 ♖d7+) 28 ♖f1+ ♔e7 White has nothing for the piece.

26 ...   g5

With gain of tempo, this frees a square for the king so that the rook may be used for an attack along the half-open h-file. On the other hand, the position of the black king is weakened, which White can exploit. Also,

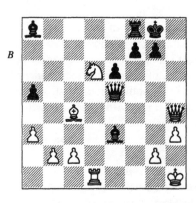

26...&g5 27 ♕e1 (not Nei's suggested 27 ♕d4 which leads to a very favourable ending for Black after 27...♕xd4 28 ♖xd4 &f6) achieves little, but Olafsson's recommendation, the bold pawn-grab 26...♕xb2! is very strong. Black meets the direct attack 27 ♘xf7 with the counteroffer 27...&xg2+! *(D)*.

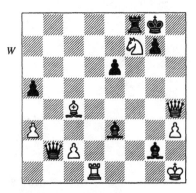

The bishop cannot be taken, but after 28 ♔h2 ♕xc2 29 ♕h8+ (the white knight is in the way!) 29...♔xf7 30 ♖d7+ ♔e8 31 ♖d8+ ♔xd8 32 ♕xf8+ ♔c7 White has no perpetual check and

the black king escapes to the queen-side.

What better move does White have after 26...♛xb2? The attacking attempt 27 ♗d3 is easily brushed aside with 27...♗h6. The best is 27 ♗b3!, defending c2, maintaining the threat 28 ♘xf7, and at the same time allowing the knight to spring to c4. However, Black has regained his pawn and can keep a solid positional advantage with 27...g5.

27 ♕g4   ♗c5

Black correctly saw that after 27...♖d8 White could force a draw with 28 ♘xf7. After 28...♖xd1+ 29 ♕xd1 Black can try:

1) 28...♚xf7 29 ♕d7+ with an immediate draw by perpetual check.

2) 28...♕g3?? 29 ♘h6+. All(!) commentators thought that White had a perpetual check here – all except Donner, who after initially making the same mistake, discovered that Black gets mated after 29...♚g7 30 ♕d7+.

3) 28...♕e4! 29 ♗f1 ♚xf7 30 ♕d7+ ♚f6 31 ♕d8+ ♚e5 32 ♕e7, and despite everything, Black cannot avoid a draw.

28 ♘b5

Fischer again takes his knight out of play and thereby lands in a hopeless situation. Instead, he can use the weakened position of the black king by showing that the knight was not really threatened after all: 28 b4!. After 28...axb4 (the point is that 28...♗xd6 29 ♖xd6 ♕xd6 30 ♕xg5+ leads to perpetual check) 29 axb4 ♗xb4 30 ♗e2

White has the opportunity to play the knight back to c4 and to further neutralise the position with ♗f3. As Black would have pawns on only one wing, his winning chances would be limited.

28 ...   ♚g7

Threatening the decisive ...♖f8-h8-h4. The knight must return to the defence.

29 ♘d4   ♖h8 *(D)*

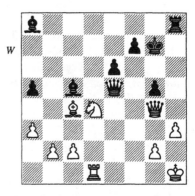

The first reports and analyses from Reykjavik all mentioned that Spassky had missed a win here. Not with 29...♗d6, when 30 ♘f5+ draws at once. The important alternative is 29...♖d8. Now 30 ♘xe6 fxe6 31 ♖xd8 ♕e1+ and 30 ♘f5+ ♚f6! don't work, so the knight must be defended. After 30 c3 Black has these possibilities:

1) 30...♖h8 (with the thought that now White can't exchange queens on c3, as he can in the game) and now:

1a) 31 ♗d3. The intention is to meet 31 ...♖h4 by the constantly recurring 32 ♘f5+. However, Black simply plays 31...♚g8 (Nei's suggestion of 31...♗b6 is also good, but 31...♔f8 is weaker because of 32 ♖f1 with counterattack) and the threat 32...♖h4 is even stronger than before.

1b) 31 ♖f1. First given by Smyslov in *64*. The idea is the same as in variation 1a but the execution is more refined. It is nevertheless hardly sufficient after 31...♖h4 32 ♘f5+ ♕xf5 33 ♖xf5 ♖xg4 34 ♖xc5 ♖xg2 35 ♖xa5 (the showy 35 ♗d5 leads to a lost pawn endgame after 35...♗xd5 36 ♖xd5 exd5 37 ♔xg2 a4!) 35...♗f3 36 b3 (Byrne's 36 ♗f1 ♖xb2+ is certainly not better) 36...♔g6 and penetration by the black king cannot be stopped (37 ♖a7 f6!).

1c) 31 ♗xe6! ♗xd4 32 cxd4 (this is where the advantage of c2-c3 shows) 32...♕xe6 33 ♕xg5+ ♕g6 34 ♕e5+ *(D)* and although three pawns are insufficient compensation for a piece in this position, an eventual win for Black is problematical.

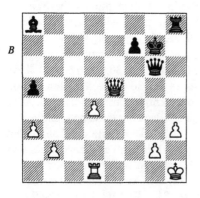

Olafsson now gives 34...♔h7. Nei gives 34...f6 35 ♕c7+ ♔h6 36 d5 ♖g8

37 ♕f4+ ♕g5 38 ♕f3 with good winning chances for Black.

2) 30...♗d6 31 ♔g1 ♕e3+ 32 ♔f1 (after 32 ♔h1 ♖h8 33 ♘f3 ♗f4 34 ♖d7 ♔g6 the threat 35...f5 is deadly) 32...♗g3 33 ♕e2 ♕f4+ 34 ♔g1 ♗h2+ 35 ♔h1 ♖h8 and now not 36 ♖f1 ♖xh3 37 ♖xf4 ♗xf4+ 38 ♔g1 ♗e3+ and wins, but 36 ♘xe6 fxe6 37 ♖d7+. Here the weakened position of the black king again plays a role.

3) 30...♕e3. Given by Donner. Black keeps the more direct attempts in reserve and maintains his grip on the position. It is difficult to find a defence to the threatened ...♖d8-h8-h4. White can just survive, however, by playing 31 ♗e2 with the neutralising threat 32 ♗f3. After 31...♗xd4 32 ♖xd4 f5! 33 ♕h5 ♖xd4 34 cxd4 g4 White is again obliged to offer a piece: 35 hxg4 ♕xe2 36 ♕g5+ ♔f7 37 gxf5. His drawing chances are better here than in variation 1c.

All things considered, there is no reason to fault Spassky's continuation. His mistake comes two moves later.

30 ♘f3   ♗xf3

30...♕f4 is an interesting try. After 31 ♕xf4 gxf4 32 ♗e2 Black has more than sufficient compensation for the pawn, and 31 ♕xg5+ ♕xg5 32 ♘xg5 seems no more attractive because after driving the knight back Black can capture on h3 with great force. However, White still has a way out:

1) 32...♖h5 33 ♘xe6+ fxe6 34 ♗xe6 and White has four pawns for the piece while h3 is defended.

2) 32...♔f6 33 ♖e1 (Donner) and White saves himself.

31 ♕xf3   ♗d6?

In slight time trouble, Spassky must have overlooked the spoiling answer to this. The many-sided 31...♖h4 is required to continue the attack. Whereas White can force the exchange of a pair of heavy pieces with 32 ♖f1 ♖f4 33 ♕e2, this would hardly stop the attack: 33...♖xf1+ 34 ♕xf1 ♗d6 35 ♔g1 (35 ♕g1 is even worse) 35...♕h2+ 36 ♔f2 ♗c5+ 37 ♔e1 ♕e5+ and Black wins two queenside pawns, obtaining a passed a-pawn, for if 38 ♕e2 ♕xb2 39 a4? ♕c1+ 40 ♕d1 ♗f2+ 41 ♔e2 ♕e3+ 42 ♔f1 ♗g3 43 ♕e2 ♕c1+ and mate. You can see how dangerous the black attack remains despite the reduced material.

32 ♕c3

This queen exchange removes all danger. The resulting ending is a dead draw. That the players still continued for so long indicates the fighting spirit that characterised the whole match.

32	...	♕xc3
33	bxc3	♗e5
34	♖d7	♔f6
35	♔g1	♗xc3
36	♗e2	♗e5
37	♔f1	♖c8
38	♗h5	♖c7
39	♖xc7	♗xc7
40	a4	♔e7
41	♔e2	f5
42	♔d3	♗e5
43	c4	♔d6
44	♗f7	♗g3
45	c5+	½-½

Game Eight
Fischer – Spassky
World Championship Match (10), Reykjavik 1972
Ruy Lopez, Breyer Variation

Perhaps influenced by Spassky's strong handling of the opening in the fourth game, Fischer decided to open with 1 c4 the next two times he had the white pieces. And with success: he won both games. Having thus built up a 5½-3½ lead, in the tenth game he returned to his old, trusted 1 e4. Spassky answered it classically, and after an interesting opening phase they went into a middlegame full of unclear combinational twists and turns. Fischer, as usual, pressed on very purposefully, and, when Spassky failed to play with absolute accuracy, he converted his small material advantage into victory in a virtuoso endgame performance.

The game is fascinating throughout all its phases, and in my opinion it is the best game of the entire match.

1	**e4**	**e5**

For the first time in the match – and not unexpectedly – Spassky plays an 'open' defence. Just as he usually replies to 1 d4 with an orthodox defence, so he often answers 1 e4 with 1...e5.

2	**♘f3**	**♘c6**
3	**♗b5**	**a6**
4	**♗a4**	

In game sixteen of this match, Fischer reverted to the Exchange Variation with which he had beaten Portisch, Jimenez, and Gligorić quickly and convincingly in the 1966 Havana Olympiad.

4	**...**	**♘f6**
5	**0-0**	**♗e7**
6	**♖e1**	**b5**
7	**♗b3** *(D)*	

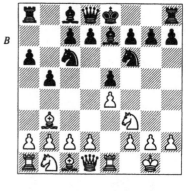

B

7	**...**	**d6**

In Santa Monica 1966, Spassky prepared the way for the Marshall Attack against Fischer with 7...0-0. The result was a draw after 35 moves: 8 c3 d5 9 exd5 ♘xd5 10 ♘xe5 ♘xe5 11 ♖xe5 c6 12 g3 ♘f6 13 d4 ♗d6 14 ♖e1

♗g4 15 ♕d3 c5 16 dxc5 ♗xc5 17 ♕xd8 ♖axd8 18 ♗f4 h6 19 ♘a3 g5 20 ♗e3 ♗xe3 21 ♖xe3 ♖d2 and Black's initiative endured into the endgame.

Spassky used the Marshall frequently as an attacking weapon in his younger years. Now he plays the Breyer Variation almost exclusively, as in this game.

8	c3	0-0
9	h3	♘b8
10	d4	♘bd7
11	♘bd2	

Fischer always used to play 11 ♘h4, an immediate attempt to question the efficacy of Black's time-consuming knight manoeuvre. According to Byrne, the game Byrne-Spassky in Moscow 1971 was probably Fischer's reason for trying something else this time. The then World Champion attained comfortable equality with Black in that game: 11...exd4 12 cxd4 ♘b6 13 ♘d2 c5 14 ♗c2 cxd4 15 ♘hf3 ♖e8 16 ♘xd4 ♗f8 17 b3 ♗b7, etc.

Fischer also once tried the other direct method against the Breyer, 11 c4, versus Portisch in Santa Monica 1966. It was a gripping game in all its phases, though it finally ended in a draw. After 11 c4 c6 12 c5 ♕c7 13 cxd6 ♗xd6 14 ♗g5 exd4 15 ♗xf6 gxf6 16 ♕xd4 ♘e5 17 ♘bd2 ♖d8 18 ♕e3 ♘d3! 19 ♕h6 ♗f4 20 ♕xf6 difficult complications arose.

11	...	♗b7
12	♗c2 (D)	
12	...	♖e8
13	b4	

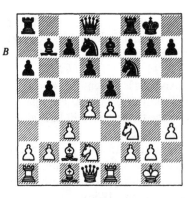

At this point White has the choice of bringing the ♘d2 to the kingside with 13 ♘f1 or beginning an immediate action on the queenside. The text-move initiates the latter plan.

13 ... ♗f8 (D)

A direct reaction with 13...a5 only leads to difficulties after 14 ♘b3 axb4 15 cxb4 ♖ab8 16 ♘a5 c6 (or 16...♗a8 17 d5) 17 ♘xb7 ♖xb7 18 ♗b3 and White has gained the pair of bishops at no cost (Suetin-Tringov, Titovo Uzice 1966).

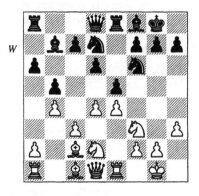

14 a4

After this game, this immediate attack became fashionable. Formerly, White always aimed for c3-c4.

14 ...   ♘b6

And this is currently the most common reply. Black tempts the a-pawn to advance farther and will later aim for ...c7-c5. Alternatives are:

1) 14...c5 15 bxc5 exd4 16 cxd4 dxc5 and White stands better, though it is not entirely clear (Balashov-Podgaets, Moscow 1966).

2) 14...d5. In principle Black's pieces are ideally placed to justify this advance. After 15 dxe5 ♘xe4 16 ♘xe4 dxe4 17 ♗g5! f6 18 ♗xe4 ♗xe4 19 ♖xe4 ♘xe5 20 ♖d4 ♘xf3+ 21 ♕xf3 ♕c8 White has not achieved much (Vasiukov-Zuidema, Wijk aan Zee 1973). More enterprising is 15 ♘xe5 dxe4 16 f4 as in Vasiukov-Kholmov, Dubna 1973. White stood a tiny bit better after 16...exf3 17 ♘dxf3 ♘xe5 18 ♘xe5 ♗d6 19 ♗f4.

3) 14...a5. This other way of forming a square of pawns seems strange at first sight. It was popular for a while until it was discovered that 15 bxa5 ♖xa5 16 ♖b1 leads to advantage for White in all variations; e.g.:

3a) 16...♗a6 17 d5 ♕a8 18 ♗a3 c5 19 dxc6 ♕xc6 20 ♗b4 (Belyavsky-A. Petrosian 1973).

3b) 16...♕a8 17 axb5 exd4 18 cxd4 ♘xe4 19 ♘xe4 ♗xe4 20 ♖xe4! ♖xe4 21 ♘g5 ♖h4 and now 22 g3! is the correct reply to maintain the advantage, according to Geller. Instead, White played 22 ♘xf7 ♔xf7 23 ♗g5

♖e4 24 ♕f3+ ♘f6 25 ♗xf6 ♖e1+ and Black just managed to save himself (Geller-Portisch 1973).

15 a5   ♘bd7
16 ♗b2

In Savon-Vogt, Skopje 1972, White let his opening advantage slip away entirely with 16 ♖b1 d5!. White must pay attention first of all to the centre.

16 ...   ♕b8

Black prepares ...c7-c5 by indirectly protecting the e-pawn. This does not work badly here, but later experiences brought Spassky around to playing 16...♖b8. A sharp struggle developed against Planinc (Amsterdam 1973) after some preparatory manoeuvring: 17 ♖b1 ♗a8 18 ♗a1 g6 19 c4 exd4 20 cxb5 axb5 21 ♘xd4 d5 22 ♘4f3 dxe4 23 ♘g5 e3! 24 ♗b3 and now, instead of 24...♗d5, Black could have played 24...exf2+ 25 ♔xf2 ♗d5, as given by Keene.

This variation does not seem unfavourable for Black. Nevertheless, Smejkal varied on the 19th move against Browne at Wijk aan Zee 1976 with 19...bxc4. White had some advantage after 20 dxe5 ♘xe5 21 ♘xe5 dxe5 22 ♗c3 ♗c6 23 ♕e2 ♗b5 24 ♘xc4 c5 25 bxc5 ♗xc5 26 ♗b3. Six months later, Karpov reached full equality against Browne, in Amsterdam 1976, with 25...♖c8! – a theoretical novelty on the 25th move – with the idea of capturing on c5 with the rook.

17 ♖b1 *(D)*

A very logical move. White covers b4 and at the same time places his

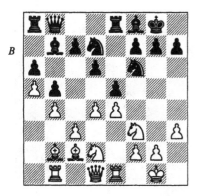

rook vis-à-vis the black queen. Yet it is not the most energetic continuation. White can get a big advantage with 17 c4!. The point is that he will not waste time recapturing after 17...bxc4 but will continue sharply with 18 ♗a4 and Black has difficulties: 18...c6 19 ♘xc4 ♕c7 20 dxe5 dxe5 21 ♕b3 (Savon-Mukhin, USSR 1973), or 19...exd4 20 ♕xd4 d5 21 exd5 ♖xe1+ 22 ♘xe1 ♘xd5 23 ♘d3 (Kavalek-Reshevsky, Chicago 1973). In both cases the black position is shaky.

17 ... c5
18 bxc5

A fundamental decision. In a game played not very much earlier, Fischer decided to close the centre with d4-d5, which focused the play entirely on the kingside. In that case he did not achieve very much; i.e., 18 d5 g6 19 ♗a3 (threatens 20 c4 with a spatial advantage on the queenside) 19...c4 20 ♘f1 ♘h5 and the thematic attacking push g2-g4 was no longer feasible.

18 ... dxc5
19 dxe5 ♘xe5

20 ♘xe5

In *64*, Polugaevsky recommends 20 c4, which would achieve excellent results after 20...♗d6 21 ♘h4. Better, however, is 20...♘xf3+ 21 ♕xf3 ♖e6 and Black does not stand badly.

20 ... ♕xe5
21 c4 ♕f4
22 ♗xf6 (D)

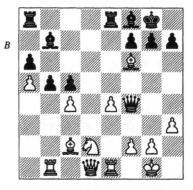

The most easy-going solution of the problems of the position. White gives up control of many dark squares and thus can no longer hope for advantage. Interesting and more enterprising is 22 e5; e.g.:

1) 22...♖ad8 23 exf6! *(D)* (the position is too sharp for the quiet 23 ♖e3, which threatens nothing and gives Black the chance to get an excellent square on d5 for his knight with 23...bxc4). Black now has a choice of captures:

1a) 23...♖xd2 24 ♕xd2! ♕xd2 25 ♖xe8. The brilliant point is 25...♕xc2 26 fxg7 ♕xb1+ 27 ♔h2 and Black is lost. White has only a few pieces left

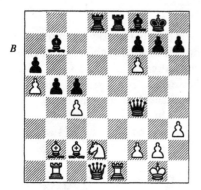

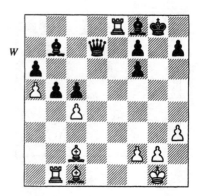

but their position makes mate unavoidable. Also 25...♗c6 loses immediately: 26 fxg7 ♗xe8 27 ♗xh7+ ♔xh7 28 gxf8♕, etc.

The only move is 25...gxf6. I originally thought that White must continue elegantly with 26 ♖be1 ♕xc2 27 ♖1e3 ♔g7 28 ♖g3+ ♔h6 29 ♗xf6, but it does not offer many chances; for example, 29...♕b1+ 30 ♔h2 ♗d6 31 ♗g7+ ♔h5 32 ♗e5 ♕e4! 33 f4 f6, followed by 34...♗xe5 and White has little chance of saving himself. 26 ♗c1 is stronger, simpler, and actually more aesthetic than the fantastic 26 ♖be1?. Again, 26...♕xc2 fails: 27 ♗h6 ♕xb1+ 28 ♔h2 with unstoppable mate. The only way to avoid this mate is 26...♕d7 *(D)*, but then White breathes new life into the attack with an exchange sacrifice:

27 ♖xf8+ ♔xf8 28 ♗h6+ ♔g8. The black king has to go back and is now awkwardly shut in. Initially I thought that White could take advantage of this with 29 ♖b3. Then there certainly are some terrible threats, but

letter-writers from three different countries, including S. Pederzoli (Italy) and M. Rayner (England), have pointed out to me that Black has a venomous riposte here: 29...♗e4!!. As a result of this tactical turn of events Black is able to utilise his bishop for his defence, something which White, of course, should prevent. First of all 29 ♖d1 is indicated. On 29...♕e7 a very strong continuation is 30 cxb5 axb5 31 ♗f5, for after 31...♗c6 32 a6 Black is powerless against the further advance of the a-pawn. Critical is 29...♕c7 and now certainly 30 ♖d3. After 30...♕xa5 31 ♖g3+ ♔h8 32 ♗g7+ ♔g8 33 ♗xf6+ ♔f8 34 ♗xh7 ♔e8 35 ♗f5 ♔f8 it looks as if White should have a quick decisive finish. However, closer examination shows that there is no mating attack here. Certainly 36 ♗g7+ ♔e7 37 ♖e3+ ♔d6 38 h4 is very strong, since it is not easy to see how Black can oppose the further advance of the h-pawn.

1b) 23...♖xe1+ 24 ♕xe1 ♕xd2 (stronger than 24...♖xd2 25 ♗c1 ♕g5

26 ♕f1 and Black does not get enough compensation for the exchange) 25 fxg7 (or 25 ♗e4 ♕xe1+ 26 ♖xe1 ♗xe4 27 ♖xe4 ♖d2 28 ♗e5 b4! and Black can hold the position thanks to the finesse 29 fxg7 ♖d1+ 30 ♔h2 ♗d6) 25...♕xe1+ (with queens on the board, the black king's shattered position would be a factor) 26 ♖xe1 ♗xg7 27 ♗xg7 ♔xg7 28 ♖e7 ♖d2! and Black can just hold the balance.

2) 22...♖ed8 23 ♖e3! (naturally, 23 exf6 is now pointless) 23...♘e8 24 ♕e2 and White has a great advantage.

3) 22...♘d7 and now both 23 ♗e4 ♗xe4 24 ♖xe4 ♕f5 25 ♕e2 and 23 ♘f3 ♖ad8 24 ♗c1 ♕xc4 25 ♗b3 are favourable for White.

It is clear that Black must look in variation 1 for any chance to maintain the balance. It is much easier for him after the text-move.

22 ... ♕xf6
23 cxb5 (D)

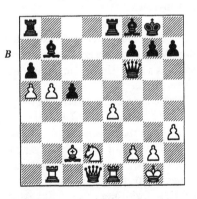

White is a pawn ahead for the moment but that is of minor importance here. Black has great influence over the whole board because of his control of the dark squares.

23 ... ♖ed8

It was clear which rook had to be moved, because after 23...♖ad8 24 ♕c1 ♕c3 25 bxa6 ♗xa6 White has the riposte 26 ♗a4! with great advantage.

Polugaevsky, however, thinks that 23...axb5 is Black's best. After 24 ♖xb5 ♗a6 White has two rook moves:

1) 25 ♖b6 ♕c3 and White is in big trouble. On 26 ♘b3 there can follow Polugaevsky's recommended 26...c4 or the strong 26...♖ed8 27 ♕c1 c4 28 ♖e3 ♕e5. The attempt to keep the position in balance by 26 ♖b3 ♕xa5 27 ♗d3 fails to 27...♖ed8 (28 ♕c2 c4 or 28 ♕e2 ♖xd3 29 ♖xd3 ♖d8).

2) 25 ♖b3. Surprisingly enough, this move holds the white position together. Black does indeed win a pawn after 25...c4 26 ♖f3 ♕d8 (or 26...♕d4) 27 ♘f1, but his advantage is not great.

24 ♕c1

Of course, the queen must get out of the pin.

24 ... ♕c3

The beginning of an ambitious plan. Other possibilities:

1) 24...♕f4. Aiming to exchange queens. After 25 ♘f3 ♕xc1 26 ♖excl axb5 27 ♖xb5 ♗a6 28 ♖b6 ♗e2 White has achieved nothing. Therefore 25 ♘c4!, with the intention of sacrificing the exchange, comes into consideration: 25...♕xc1 26 ♖exc1 axb5 27 ♖xb5 ♗a6 28 ♗a4 ♗xb5 29

♗xb5 with the positional threat of transferring the bishop to d5 via c6. In any case, White cannot lose.

2) 24...axb5. Later the same year, Smyslov played this move against Vasiukov at Polanica Zdroj. The continuation illustrates the chances for both sides: 25 ♖xb5 ♗a6 26 ♖b6 ♕c3 (The advantage over the text-move becomes clear: the black queen saves time by moving only when it is attacked. Polugaevsky's notes – written before the game in Poland was played – gives 26...♕f4 27 ♘f3 ♕xc1 28 ♖xc1 c4 and White keeps his advantage with 29 e5, although Black would not necessarily lose.) 27 ♘b3 g6! 28 e5 (if 28 ♖e3 ♕e5) 28...♗h6 29 ♕b1 c4 30 ♘c5 ♕xa5 (winning the pawn back, but now the initiative reverts to White) 31 ♘e4 ♗c8 32 ♘d6 ♖a6 33 ♖b8 ♗e6 34 ♖e4 ♗f8 35 ♖xd8 ♕xd8 36 ♘xc4 ♕c7 37 ♗d3 ♖c6 38 ♕f1 ♗f5 39 ♖f4 ♗e6 40 ♕e2 ♗g7 and in this equal position a draw was agreed.

25　♘f3　　　　♕xa5 (D)

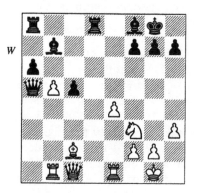

At this late moment it would be unfavourable for Black to capture on b5, as we see after 25...axb5 26 e5! (Less clear is 26 ♖xb5 ♗a6 27 e5, as given by Byrne. He continues his variation with 27...♕xe1+ 28 ♕xe1 ♗xb5 29 ♕b1 and now 29...♖xa5. But that allows White a winning attack with 30 ♗xh7+ ♔h8 31 ♘g5 ♗c4 32 ♗g8, etc. Instead, 29...♗c4! wins an important tempo; e.g., 30 ♗xh7+ ♔h8 31 ♘g5? ♗e7 32 ♗g8? ♗d3 33 ♘xf7+ ♔xg8 and Black comes out best) 26...g6 (not 26...b4 27 ♖e3 and the queen has no retreat) 27 ♖xb5 and Black is in trouble after both 27...♗xf3 28 ♖b3 ♕xa5 29 ♖xf3 and 27...♗a6 28 ♖b6 ♕xa5 29 ♕b2.

Another try to maintain the initiative is 25...c4. The threat is 26...♗a3; e.g., 26 b6 ♗a3 27 ♖e3 ♖d3! with advantage to Black. Olafsson, however, gives something more powerful: 26 bxa6 ♗xa6 27 e5 g6 28 e6 and White has an attack.

26　♗b3

Spassky must have underestimated this. White suddenly goes on the attack, and it is a surprisingly dangerous one.

26　...　　　　axb5

There is no useful alternative.

27　♕f4　　　　♖d7 (D)

An important decision. This move is objectively not worse than the simpler 27...c4, but the obscure subtlety required to justify it only makes Black's task more difficult. After 27...c4 his disadvantage would be minimal: 28 ♗xc4 bxc4 29 ♖xb7 f6

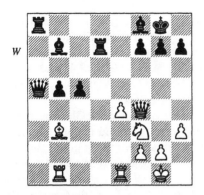

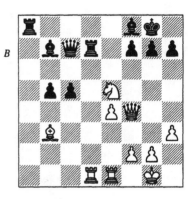

(not 29...♕h5 30 g4) 30 e5 (the only way to try to take advantage of the slightly weakened position of Black's king) 30...♕d5! 31 ♖c7 fxe5 and now:

1) 32 ♖xe5 ♖a1+ 33 ♔h2 ♗d6 and White must force a draw by perpetual check with 34 ♖xg7+ ♔xg7 35 ♕g5+ ♔f7 36 ♕f5+.

2) 32 ♘xe5 ♗d6 33 ♕xc4 (also 33 ♖xg7+ ♔xg7 34 ♕g5+ ♔h8 35 ♕f6+ only draws; but not 35 ♘g6+ hxg6 36 ♕xd5 ♗h2+ – Black always has this finesse in reserve.) 33...♕xc4 34 ♖xc4 ♗xe5 35 ♖xe5 ♖a1+ 36 ♔h2 ♖a2 and Black must be able to draw.

28 ♘e5

Attacking f7 with a piece for the third consecutive move.

28 ... ♕c7

After long detours the black queen returns to the defence. But now White comes up with a sublime continuation of the attack.

29 ♖bd1 *(D)*

Fischer had this in mind on the 26th move. 29...♖xd1 fails to 30 ♗xf7+ ♔h8 31 ♘g6+ hxg6 32 ♕h4 mate.

29 ... ♖e7

Spassky chooses the worst of the two possibilities, but that was difficult to appreciate in advance. The sensational 29...♖ad8 is necessary, adding yet another pin. As with the text-move, Black loses an exchange, but the difference is that a pair of rooks will be traded, and long variations show that this helps Black.

After the forcing continuation 30 ♗xf7+ ♖xf7 31 ♕xf7+ ♕xf7 32 ♘xf7 ♖xd1 33 ♖xd1 *(D)* the position becomes very complicated as White will always have a problem holding back Black's dangerous passed pawns. It is striking that not one of the authors of the many books on the match comes to a well-founded judgement at this important moment, although Olafsson comes very close with some study-like variations. Their beauty and depth are the reasons I give them here at length.

1) 33...b4. Nei considers this the best. Without giving variations he claims that Black has good drawing chances. It is insufficient, however,

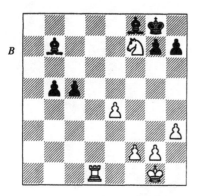

because of 34 ♘d6. White threatens to maintain the point d6 with 35 e5; Black can hardly avoid this threat, so he must eliminate it directly with 34...♗xd6 35 ♖xd6 ♗xe4. Black now threatens to win with 36...b3, so the rook must get behind the pawn immediately: 37 ♖b6. Now White threatens 38 ♖b5. Black is compelled to play 37...♗d3, after which his king is cut off by 38 ♖b7!. White now comes just in time: 38...♔f8 39 f3 ♔e8 40 ♔f2 ♔d8 41 ♔e3 and if 41...♔c8, 42 ♖xg7 is decisive.

2) 33...c4. This is Olafsson's drawing line, to which he adds an exclamation mark. He gives the following marvellous variation: 34 ♘d6 ♗c6 (here Black allows White to support d6; but not 34...♗a6 because of 35 ♖a1 b4 36 ♖xa6 c3 37 ♘c4! and White stops the pawns right at the gate) 35 e5 c3 36 ♖b1 (the requisite method of holding the pawns) 36...♗xd6 37 exd6 ♔f7 38 f3! (a subtle move; White prevents 38...c2 with the follow-up 39...♗e4) 38...♔e6 39 ♖b3 b4 (the

toughest; Black gives up his least advanced pawn in order to get his king into the game in time) 40 ♖xb4 ♔d5 41 ♖b1 ♔c4 42 ♔f2 c2 43 ♖c1 ♔d3 44 ♔e1 ♗d7 and White must be satisfied with a draw.

It is remarkable that Olafsson, having got that far, did not get the idea that White can win by giving up his rook for the dangerous passed pawn. The idea is 43 ♖g1 (instead of 43 ♖c1) 43...♔d3 44 f4 ♗d7 45 g4 g6 46 f5! gxf5 47 g5 and either the white passed pawn or candidate passed pawn will stroll through to queen.

3) 33...♗xe4!. The correct decision. Black directly stops the formation of the strongpoint on d6. Most commentators are satisfied to say here that White wins after 34 ♘g5; e.g., 34...♗f5 35 ♖d5 g6 36 g4, or 34...♗c2 35 ♖d8 ♗b3 36 ♘xh7 ♔xh7 37 ♖xf8 and the black passed pawns are not dangerous enough.

It is Olafsson once again who looks further than the rest by sacrificing, in total, a whole rook with 34...♗c2 35 ♖d8 b4!. His main variation runs: 36 ♘e6 ♔f7 37 ♘xf8 b3 38 ♖b8 c4 39 ♘d7 c3 *(D)*.

The passed pawns are exceedingly dangerous now, but Olafsson thinks that White can just keep matters in hand with 40 ♘e5+ ♔e6 41 ♘c4 ♗d1 (Threatening to win with the c pawn. At first I thought that Black could save himself with the indefatigable 41...♔d5 to rush the king to the aid of the passed pawns; but then White wins

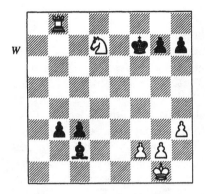

by attacking the c-pawn with his knight: 42 ♘b6+! ♔d4 43 ♘a4 followed by 44 ♖d8+.) 42 ♘a3 c2 43 ♘xc2 bxc2 44 ♖c8 ♔d5 45 ♔f1 ♔d4 46 ♔e1 ♔d3 47 ♖d8+ ♔c3 48 ♖xd1 and White wins the pawn endgame.

So far this is analysis by Olafsson. Some further elaboration is not inappropriate here. After 48...cxd1♕+ 49 ♔xd1 ♔d3 it is not so easy to drive the black king back. After 50 ♔e1 g5 51 ♔d1 ♔d4 52 ♔d2 h5 White has only one winning move. The game is drawn after 53 g3 g4! and also after 53 f3 h4 54 ♔e2 ♔e5 55 ♔e3 ♔f5 56 f4 g4! 57 hxg4+ ♔xg4 58 ♔e4 ♔g3 when both sides queen at the same time. However, the winning move is 53 g4! and Black cannot maintain the opposition; e.g.: 53...hxg4 54 hxg4 ♔e4 55 ♔e2 ♔f4 56 f3 ♔e5 57 ♔e3 or 53...h4 54 f3 ♔d5 55 ♔d3 ♔e5 56 ♔e3 ♔d5 57 f4.

In order to challenge Olafsson it is necessary to go further back in variation 3. On the 34th move the natural 34...♗f5 is dispatched with 35 ♖d5

without comment, but it is precisely this position that brings salvation for Black. He plays 35...h6!, forcing the exchange of his queen's bishop for the knight. After 36 ♖xf5 hxg5 White has no time for 37 ♖xg5, on account of 37...b4 and the queenside pawns cannot be stopped. So 37 ♔f1 and now Black, in turn, should not react too energetically, for after 37...b4 38 ♔e2 c4? 39 ♖xg5 b3 40 ♖b5 ♗e7 41 ♔d1 ♔f7 42 ♖b6, followed by 43 ♖c6, the black pawns are blockaded, after which White's material advantage on the kingside is decisive. The cautious 37...♗e7 is sufficient to hold the endgame; for instance: 38 ♔e2 g6 39 ♖d5 ♔f7 40 ♖d7 c4 and White doesn't have a single winning chance.

30	♗xf7+	♖xf7
31	♕xf7+	♕xf7
32	♘xf7	♗xe4

Spassky finds his best chance, despite his time trouble, and reduces White's pawn preponderance on the kingside. 32...c4, to immediately begin dangerous actions with the pawns, was tempting. But with three rooks on the board, the base at d6 after 33 ♘d6 ♗c6 34 e5 would be even stronger than in the variations after move 29 that begin with the trade of rooks.

33 ♖xe4

There is no time to weaken the position of the black king with 33 ♘h6+ gxh6 34 ♖xe4 because it will be difficult to stop the passed pawns after 34...b4.

| 33 | ... | ♔xf7 |

34 ♖d7+   ♔f6
35 ♖b7

Fischer plays the ending purposefully and instructively right from the start. One rook behind the passed pawns, the other operating from the flank – in short, the strategy that the player with the rooks must adopt in the struggle against two connected passed pawns.

35 ...   ♖a1+

Black again faced a difficult choice: on which side of the passed pawns must his rook stand? The game continuation shows that, due to the text-move, the position of his bishop becomes too insecure. The only drawing chance is 35...b4, keeping his rook on the back rank, as suggested by Larsen during the game. Byrne considers this insufficient because after 35...b4 36 ♔f1 ♖c8 37 ♖c4 ♖d8 38 ♔e2 ♔e6 39 ♖b5 Black's king cannot reach either d5 or d6 without losing a queenside pawn, so 'Fischer would proceed then to win just as in the game, by advancing his kingside pawns.'

How did Byrne actually envisage that? In the game, both of Fischer's rooks are positioned actively and so he can create a passed pawn on the kingside which, partly through tactical means, forces the decision. But if the rooks were to stand as passively as Byrne has them, there would be absolutely no chance of this.

Nei and Olafsson both give 36 ♖b6+, which is clearly much stronger.

White reduces his opponent's space because after 36...♔f5 Black is in a mating net – not with 37 ♖be6, as given by Olafsson, on account of 37...♖a1+ 38 ♔h2 ♗d6+ 39 g3 b3 and Black suddenly has all sorts of chances, but with the laconic 37 f3 (Nei), already threatening 38 h4, possibly followed by 39 ♖be6. The retreat 36...♔f7 is thus forced. Olafsson now continues his variation with 37 ♖ee6 c4 38 ♖ec6 c3 39 ♖b7+ ♔g8 40 g3, but as a winning plan this is rather deficient. White's rooks are indeed as active as possible, but the black pawns have advanced far enough to pose a permanent danger to White. Thus after 40...h5, 41...♖a2 is already threatened.

A more likely winning plan is given by Nei; after 37 f4 White will utilise his majority on the kingside under far more favourable conditions than in Byrne's variation. Whether this will succeed in overrunning Black's position if Black simply waits is an open question. It is hardly possible to analyse it to the end.

36 ♔h2   ♗d6+

Thus Black manages to post his bishop more actively but, as we will see, it does not stand very sturdily.

37 g3   b4
38 ♔g2   h5

It is too committal to play the bishop to a stronger square with 38...♗e5. Byrne gives 39 f4 ♗d4 40 g4 (the formation of the pawn duo is already almost decisive) 40...♖a2+ 41 ♔f1 ♖a3 42 h4 and there is no time to advance the b-pawn (42...b3 43 f5). Nei points out a method of playing the bishop to d4 by preparing it with 38...♗f5, but this isn't good enough either: 39 ♖h4 ♗e5 40 ♖h5+! (much stronger than 40 ♖xh7 ♗d4 as given by Nei) 40...♔e6 41 ♖b6+ ♗d6 (or 41...♔d5 42 f4) 42 ♖xc5. The rooks work together beautifully.

39 ♖b6   ♖d1
40 ♔f3 *(D)*

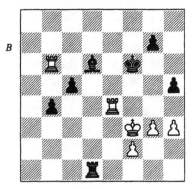

Fischer plays logically and perfectly. First he tied the black rook down, and now he will attack it while at the same time centralising his king. It is wrong to try to form the pawn duo f4-g4 directly with 40 f4 since Black can activate his king with 40...♔f5. Neither 41 ♖c4 ♖d2+ 42 ♔f3 ♖d3+ nor 41 ♔f3 ♖f1+ 42 ♔e2 ♔xe4 43 ♔xf1 ♔d5 is unfavourable for Black.

40 ...   ♔f7

The last move in time trouble, and an unfortunate one. Spassky meekly allows the formation of the pawn duo

f4-g4. 40...g5 was unanimously recommended afterwards, but it doesn't save Black either. White continues 41 ♔e2 ♖d5 42 g4 and after 42...hxg4 43 hxg4 Black is in virtual zugzwang. He must play 43...♔f7, but then White can improve the position of his rooks with 44 ♖b7+ ♔f6 45 ♖d7 to make the zugzwang complete. Tougher is 44...♔f8 in order to exchange a rook. But with the king cut off it is still hopeless; e.g., 45 ♖e6 ♖e5+ 46 ♖xe5 ♗xe5 47 ♔d3 ♗d4 48 f3 ♔e8 49 ♔c4 ♔f8 50 ♖d7 ♗f2 51 ♖d5 ♗e3 52 ♖e5 and Black's bishop must give up its protection of one of the two pawns.

41 ♔e2   ♖d5
42 f4   g6
43 g4

The pawn duo is formed.

43 ...   hxg4
44 hxg4   g5 *(D)*

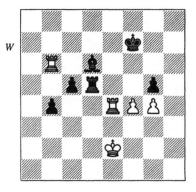

Spassky's seconds evidently found this to be his best chance. If he doesn't play it, then 45 ♖b5 is even stronger because Black would not have the square e5 to give check on if White's rook took the b-pawn; e.g., 44...♔f6 45 ♖b5 ♔f7 (or 45...g5 46 f5) 46 g5! (certainly not 46 ♖exb4? cxb4 47 ♖xd5 ♗xf4 and the endgame is a theoretical draw even if White wins the b-pawn) 46...♖f5 47 ♔e3 and Black is outmanoeuvred. If 47...♖d5 then 48 ♖exb4 wins, or if, for example, 47...♔g7 48 ♖b6 ♖d5 49 ♖e6 is hopeless. The black king is systematically driven back.

45 f5

Naturally White does not take the pawn. The protected passed pawn and the squares it gains are mighty possessions.

| 45 | ... | ♗e5 |
| 46 | ♖b5 | ♔f6 |

The bishop cannot go to d4 because White gets a mating attack with 47 ♖b7+ ♔f8 48 ♖e6.

| 47 | ♖exb4 | ♗d4 |

Black still has a vague hope: play the king to f4.

| 48 | ♖b6+ | ♔e5 |
| 49 | ♔f3! | |

Fischer winds it up very nicely. Mate in one is threatened.

49	...	♖d8
50	♖b8	♖d7
51	♖4b7	♖d6
52	♖b6	♖d7
53	♖g6	♔d5
54	♖xg5	♗e5
55	f6	♔d4
56	♖b1	1-0

If 58...♗xf6 59 ♖d1+ ♔c4 60 ♖xc5+.

Game Nine
Spassky – Fischer
World Championship Match (19),
Reykjavik 1972
Alekhine Defence

Undoubtedly the most dramatic game of the match was the thirteenth. Fischer chose the Alekhine Defence and Spassky, after treating it rather inaccurately, soon found he was forced to offer a pawn for vague attacking chances. Fischer, in turn, played superficially. Spassky's attacking chances became very real and for a long time it was unclear who had matters best in hand. It developed into a very unusual ending which Fischer finally decided in his favour.

Both players seemed to have been affected by that far from faultless game. The next two games, both finally drawn, were full of serious tactical and strategical mistakes. Then the weight of all that tension seemed to lift, and both combatants played freely again. The series of five draws that preceded the last decisive game contained chess of the highest level. Fischer continued to experiment in the opening, with Black as well as with White: a Najdorf in the fifteenth game without the capture on b2, a Pirc Defence in the seventeenth, and again an Alekhine Defence in the nineteenth.

The nineteenth game is discussed here. It is a textbook example of attack and defence balancing each other; as in the tenth game, one can identify mistakes only after deep analysis. It was also Spassky's final, mighty attempt to keep the world title from Fischer – the title which would bring Fischer to a state of total inertia.

1	e4	♘f6
2	e5	♘d5
3	d4	d6
4	♘f3	♗g4

An older continuation than the 4...g6 played in the thirteenth game of the match. It was popular for a while, until the latest experiences showed that White has several ways to get the advantage.

5	♗e2	e6
6	0-0	♗e7

7	h3	

Whether or not this move is played will prove to be important later.

7	...	♗h5 *(D)*

Black cannot very well capture, as shown by the game Vasiukov-Torre, Manila 1974 (via a different move order): 7...♗xf3 8 ♗xf3 ♘c6 9 c4 ♘b6 10 ♗xc6 bxc6 11 b3 0-0 12 ♘c3 a5?! 13 ♗e3 ♘d7 14 ♕h5! with great positional advantage.

8	c4	♘b6

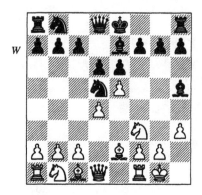

9 ♘c3

The capture on d6 used to be played here automatically. With the text-move, White intends to wait for Black to play ...♘b8-c6.

9 ...   0-0

9...dxe5 10 ♘xe5 ♗xe2 11 ♕xe2! ♕xd4 12 ♖d1 ♕c5 13 b4 ♕xb4 14 ♘b5 is too dangerous.

10 ♗e3   d5

The point of White's avoidance of exd6 on his ninth move is that this push would be more favourable for Black if there were no pawns on c7 and e5. 10...♘c6 is followed by 11 exd6 cxd6 12 d5 and White keeps an enduring advantage after either 12...♗xf3 13 ♗xf3 ♘e5 14 dxe6 fxe6 15 ♗g4 or 12...exd5 13 ♘xd5 ♘xd5 14 ♕xd5.

11 c5 (D)

This leads to a great advantage in space. Although experience has shown that White can certainly expect an advantage, a different move to gain the upper hand has been tried more recently; e.g., Sznapik-Schmidt, Polish Championship 1977, went 11 cxd5

♘xd5 12 ♕b3 ♘b6 13 ♖fd1 ♕c8 14 d5 ♘xd5 15 ♘xd5 exd5 16 ♖xd5 and, according to Sznapik, Black could have minimised his disadvantage by playing 16...♘c6.

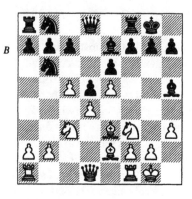

11 ...   ♗xf3
12 ♗xf3

In Gaprindashvili-Kushnir 1969, the game that originated this system (but without White's h3 and Black's ♗h5), White recaptured with the pawn, forcing the black knight to retreat. The white doubled pawn signifies no disadvantage, as appears from, among other games, Pokojowczyk-Schmidt, Poland 1976 (again, without h3 and ♗h5): 11 gxf3 ♘c8 12 f4 ♗h4 13 ♗d3 g6 (13...♘e7 is probably better. Then Enklaar's 14 ♗xh7+ is not at all convincing since White retains the bad bishop and Black is able to blockade the position. Better is 14 ♕h5 ♘f5 15 ♗xf5 g6 16 ♕g4 exf5 17 ♕f3) 14 f5! exf5 15 ♕f3 c6 16 ♔h1 ♔h8 17 ♖g1 ♘e7 18 ♕h3 ♘g8 19 ♗xf5! with advantage. After 19...gxf5 20 ♕g2

Black must return the piece to prevent mate.

12 ...   ♘c4
13 b3

After the match, the system used by Fischer understandably became popular. Geller particularly, one of Spassky's seconds in Reykjavik, made grateful use of improvements found during the match (see also the sixth match game); he introduced 13 ♗f4 against Hecht in Budapest 1973, and achieved quick success after 13...♘c6 14 b3 ♘4a5 15 ♕d2 b6 16 ♖ac1 bxc5 17 dxc5 ♗xc5? 18 ♘xd5 ♗d4 19 b4 exd5 20 bxa5 ♕d7 21 ♖xc6 ♕xc6 22 ♕xd4 ♖ad8 23 ♖c1 ♕b7 24 ♗g5, 1-0.

The latest example from practice is equally discouraging: 13 ♗f4 ♘c6 14 b3 ♘4a5 15 ♖c1 b6 16 ♘a4! (after 16 ♕d2 the improvement 16...bxc5 17 dxc5 ♖b8! 18 ♗xd5 exd5 19 ♘xd5 ♖b5! 20 b4 ♘xb4 21 ♘xb4 ♕xd2 22 ♗xd2 ♖xc5 is possible, with roughly equal play, as in Geller-Timman, Wijk aan Zee 1975) 16...♗g5 17 ♗xg5 ♕xg5 18 ♕d3 ♖ab8 19 ♗g4 ♕f4 20 ♖fd1 f5 21 exf6 ♖xf6 22 ♕e3 with advantage to White (Geller-Timman, Teesside 1975).

13 ...   ♘xe3
14 fxe3   b6 *(D)*

This manner of attacking the pawn chain is dubious. On the other method, 14...f6, White has two reactions (the direct solution with 15 exf6 ♗xf6 16 ♗g4 ♕e7 gains nothing):

1) 15 e4 dxe4! 16 ♗xe4 (or 16 ♘xe4 fxe5 17 dxe5 ♘c6) 16...♘c6!

17 ♗xc6 bxc6 18 ♕g4 f5 and Black certainly does not stand worse. His doubled pawn is compensated for by his majority on the kingside.

2) 15 ♗g4 and now:

2a) 15...♕d7 16 exf6 (This is best now that the black queen is on a less favourable square – as in the above variation, e7 is better. 16 e4 dxe4 17 exf6 gxf6! is not good) 16...♗xf6 17 b4 with freer play for White.

2b) 15...f5 16 ♗e2 and White moves the bishop to d3. Again he stands a little better.

Petrosian draws attention to the idea 14...♘c6, a typical Petrosian waiting move. White's best is 15 ♖b1 followed by 16 b4 (the immediate 15 b4 is premature because of 15...♘xb4 16 ♖b1 ♘c6 17 ♖xb7 ♘a5); e.g., 15...b6 16 b4 and 17 ♕a4 with advantage to White.

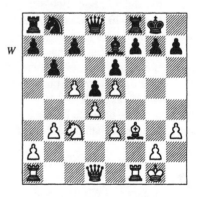

15 e4

A strong answer. 15 b4 promises nothing after 15...a5 16 a3 (16 ♕a4 ♘d7) 16...axb4 17 axb4 ♘c6!. White must play 15 e4 immediately or the pawn formation will become static.

15 ...   c6

He must keep the long diagonal closed since 15...bxc5 16 exd5 cxd4 17 dxe6! (this is much stronger than 17 d6 cxd6 18 ♗xa8 dxc3 with unclear play) 17...c6 18 exf7+ ♖xf7 19 ♘e4 gives White a great positional advantage.

16 b4

White need not fear ...a7-a5 now that Black has a pawn on c6, occupying a favourable square for Black's knight.

16 ...   bxc5

Fischer must have done a lot of deep calculation and evaluation here. He cannot free his game with 16...a5; e.g.,

1) 17 b5. This method of increasing the tension is inadequate; 17...bxc5 18 bxc6 cxd4 and now both 19 ♘xd5 and 19 exd5 dxc3 20 d6 ♘xc6! 21 dxe7 ♕xe7 are in Black's favour.

2) 17 a3, and White keeps a spatial advantage on the queenside. It is true that Black gets counterplay with 17...axb4 18 axb4 ♖xa1 19 ♕xa1 ♗g5, but White plays 20 ♖e1 with advantage. The black knight is still badly placed.

17 bxc5   ♕a5 (D)

The only possible follow-up to the previous move. If White were able to play 18 ♕a4 he would have the position well under control; for example, 17...♘d7 18 ♕a4 ♕c7 19 ♖ab1 ♖ab8 20 ♕a6 with enduring pressure.

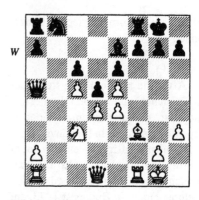

18 ♘xd5 (D)

This attractive piece sacrifice leads to enormous complications. However, White can keep a clear advantage by means of the quiet 18 ♕e1 (Olafsson), threatening 19 ♘xd5. Gligorić in his book gives 18...♗g5, but, as Olafsson remarks, after 19 exd5 cxd5 20 ♘xd5 ♕xe1 21 ♖axe1 exd5 22 ♗xd5 ♘a6, White does not continue with 23 ♖xf7 ♖xf7 24 ♗xa8 ♔f8 with an unclear position, but with 23 e6! and Black has no defence; e.g., 23...♖ad8 24 ♖f5 or 24 ♗c4 followed by 25 e7, or 23...fxe6 24 ♖xe6 ♖xf1+ (24...♘c7 25 ♖e8+ and mates) 25 ♔xf1 ♖f8+ 26 ♖f6+ and wins.

Remarkably, Black has no satisfactory response to 18 ♕e1. Olafsson further points out 18...♕b4 19 ♖ad1 a5. Black not only protects the queen with this move but also opens an escape route for his queen's rook. White, however, should not be discouraged; now he can sacrifice the bishop on d5: 20 exd5 cxd5 21 ♗xd5! exd5 22 ♘xd5 ♕b7 23 ♕e4 ♖a7 24 ♖b1 and White has overwhelming compensation for the piece.

After 18 ♕e1 Black therefore can do nothing except retreat the queen empty-handed: 18...♕d8. It is true that Black has prevented ♕d1-a4 in a roundabout way, but only extensive analysis is able to show this.

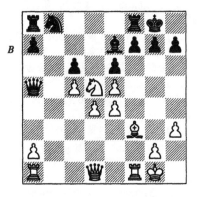

18 ...   ♗g5

Fischer did not hesitate at all with this reply, which cuts off the retreat of the white knight. Such a quick response does not necessarily imply that the player had been waiting for his opponent's previous move. In a game Botvinnik-Spassky, Moscow 1969, Botvinnik at one point played a subtle, unexpected move and Spassky replied immediately – 'so quickly,' wrote Botvinnik, 'that I came to the conclusion that Spassky wanted to avoid creating the impression that he had overlooked the move.'

One is unlikely to come to the same conclusion in this case. Finding a flashy move like 18 ♘xd5 is child's play for Fischer, as is the provoking of such a move.

His reply confronts White with a difficult choice: either to play for attack or to try to hold the extra pawn and if possible manoeuvre his knight to d6 via e3 and c4. I examine:

1) 19 ♕d3 ♘a6 (capturing on d5 is still not good, but now it is threatened) 20 ♕c4 (White must carry on because 20 ♘e3 leads to complications favourable to Black after 20...♖ad8; e.g., 21 ♘c4 ♕xc5 22 ♘d6 ♘b4. But the immediate 20...♘b4 is not so good because of 21 ♘c4 ♕xc5 22 ♕c3 ♗e3+ 23 ♕xe3 ♕xc4 24 ♗e2! ♘c2 25 ♗xc4 ♘xe3 26 ♖fc1 ♖fd8 27 ♔f2 and White stands a little better). After 20 ♕c4, inferior is 20...cxd5 21 exd5 exd5 22 ♗xd5 and the f-pawn goes too; White's three centre pawns give him great influence on the board (22...♕c7 23 e6!). The wonder is that Black need not capture the knight but can get satisfactory counterplay with 20...♕b5!. Exchanging queens with 21 ♕xb5 cxb5 does not solve White's problem of how to maintain his strong central position.

2) 19 ♕e2 ♘a6 20 ♘e3 ♕c3! 21 ♘c2 ♘b4 and Black wins the pawn back with advantage.

3) 19 ♕e1 ♕d8 and White lacks a useful move.

4) 19 h4. A striking attempt. White returns the pawn to temporarily limit the activity of Black's bishop. A sharp position with mutual chances arises after 19...♗xh4 20 ♕e2 (not 20 ♘e3

♕c3) 20...♘a6 21 ♘e3. In some cases Black can sacrifice his knight on c5 for three pawns.

19 ♗h5!

Spassky's decision to play for attack is fully justified, considering the previous variations, and was probably made when he played his last move. White has many chances and Black must defend carefully, as we shall see.

19 ... cxd5 (D)

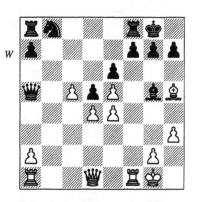

Bad is 19...g6 because White gets a decisive attack with 20 ♘f6+.

20 ♗xf7+

White pushes on energetically, but he overlooks an ingenious saving resource. Interpolating 20 exd5 before the sacrifice increases its strength:

1) 20...♘a6 (Nei). Black's idea is to save himself after 21 dxe6 fxe6 22 ♕g4 with 22...♗e3+ 23 ♔h1 ♘c7. The advance 21 d6 is nothing special after 21...g6. The white pawn mass looks impressive but can be destroyed at any moment by a countersacrifice, so it remains White's task to destroy

the black king's shelter: 21 ♗xf7+ ♖xf7 22 ♖xf7 ♔xf7 23 ♕h5+ ♔g8 24 ♕xg5. At the moment, White has three pawns for the piece and Black cannot satisfactorily oppose them with his badly placed knight; e.g., 24...♕c3 25 ♖d1 exd5 26 e6 ♘c7 27 ♕e5 and White controls the board.

2) 20...exd5 21 ♗xf7+ ♖xf7 22 ♖xf7 and now:

2a) 22...♘c6 23 ♕f3! (not 23 ♕h5 ♘xd4 24 ♖af1? ♗h6! – but not 24...♘e6? 25 ♖xg7+ ♘xg7 26 ♕f7+ and mate) 23...♕b4 24 ♖f1 ♕xd4+ 25 ♔h1 ♕xc5 26 ♖c7! and White is winning.

2b) 22...♕d2 23 ♕g4 (D) (the difference from the actual game is that here the d4-pawn is protected; 23 ♖c7 achieves nothing because of 23...♘a6 24 ♖b7 ♗e3+ 25 ♔h1 ♕xd4 26 ♕xd4 ♗xd4 27 ♖d1 ♘xc5 28 ♖c7 ♘a6!)

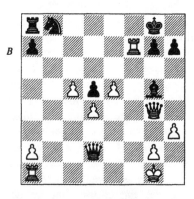

23...♘c6 (or 23...♔xf7 24 ♖f1+ ♔e7 25 ♕f5 and Black is paralysed despite his two extra pieces) 24 ♖d1!! ♕e3+ 25 ♔h1 ♔xf7 26 ♖f1+ and again the black king would be unsafe after 26...♔e7 27 ♕f5. Black must therefore return the piece with 26...♔g8. But after 27 ♕e6+ ♔h8 28 ♕xc6 ♖g8 29 ♕xd5 White retains the better prospects as he can disarm the attacking try 29...♗f4 with 30 ♕f3.

If 28...♖d8 (instead of 28...♖g8) 29 ♕b7! (much stronger than 29 ♕xd5 g6) and the white c-pawn is very dangerous; for example, 29...♕xd4 30 c6 ♕b6 (the same reply would follow 30...♕c4) 31 ♖b1 ♕xb7 32 ♖xb7! and wins.

Nevertheless, the text-move might also have led to a significant advantage, as deep research has shown me.

20	...	♖xf7
21	♖xf7	♕d2!

This brilliant defensive move forces a drawable endgame. Nearly all other moves lose quickly:

1) 21...♗e3+ 22 ♔h2 ♔xf7 23 ♕h5+ ♔e7 24 ♖f1 ♘d7 25 ♕f7+ ♔d8 26 c6 and wins.

2) 21...♘c6 22 ♕g4 (simpler than Olafsson's 22 ♕h5) 22...♔xf7 23 ♖f1+ ♔g8 24 ♕xe6+ and White will have no less than four pawns for the piece.

3) 21...♕c3 is the most reasonable alternative. Black ties the white queen to the protection of the queen's rook. Nei now gives 22 exd5 exd5 23 ♖b1 ♘c6 24 ♖bb7 ♗h6 25 ♕g4 ♕xd4+ 26 ♕xd4 ♘xd4 27 ♖xa7 with a complicated ending; as I see it, White has the better chances. Olafsson gives a far more convincing way to maintain the

advantage: 22 ♖f1!. The white rooks are connected so that the white queen can threaten to penetrate the black position destructively from either side: via a4, g4, or h5. After 22...♘c6 23 ♕g4! ♕xd4+ 24 ♔h1 ♕xe5 25 exd5 Black has no satisfactory way to recapture: if 25...exd5 26 ♖ae1 ♗e3 27 ♕f3 or 25...♕xd5 26 ♖ad1 ♕e5 27 ♖d6 (27 ♕f3 ♕xc5 and Black's f8-square is covered twice) and now:

3a) 27...♖f8 28 ♕xe6+ (surprisingly, 28 ♖xf8+ ♔xf8 29 ♕f3+ ♔e7 30 ♖xc6 ♕e1+ 31 ♔h2 ♗e3! gives Black dangerous threats, so White must take the perpetual check with 32 ♖c7+ ♔d8 33 ♕f8+ ♔xc7 34 ♕d6+, etc.) 28...♕xe6 29 ♖xf8+ ♔xf8 30 ♖xe6 and the endgame is advantageous for White;

3b) 27...♘e7 28 ♖xe6 ♕d5 (or 28...♕xc5 29 h4 and White wins) 29 ♖fe1 (threatening 30 ♖6e5) 29...♕f5 (29...h6 30 h4 wins) 30 ♕c4 ♔h8 (30...♕d5 31 ♕xd5 ♘xd5 32 ♖6e5 wins material) 31 ♖xe7 ♗xe7 32 ♖xe7 and White should win.

With the queens on the board, White has attacking chances because the black pieces are always hanging.

22 ♕xd2

There is nothing better; 22 ♖c7 ♘a6 23 ♖c6 ♘b4 24 ♖xe6 dxe4 leads to a sharp position in which Black would have the better chances.

22	...	♗xd2
23	♖af1	

The rooks are finally connected. It seems like a whole game has been played, but we are only just past move twenty!

23   ...   ♘c6 *(D)*

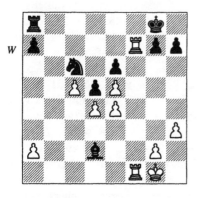

24   exd5

Spassky must have seen the forced draw position already. The play would have remained more complicated after 24 ♖c7, which Byrne and Nei consider more dangerous for Black. The point is that after 24...♘xd4 25 ♖ff7 ♗h6 26 exd5 exd5 27 ♖xa7 White reaches the same position as in the first line of variation 3 above (after Black's 21st move), a complicated position in which White nevertheless has the better chances. Byrne and Nei both note, however, that the white attempt 24 ♖c7 would achieve nothing after 24...♘d8 25 ♖e7 ♘c6 26 ♖xe6 ♘xd4 27 ♖e7 ♗e3+ 28 ♔h1 dxe4 29 ♖1f7 ♘e6! and Black has the advantage. But this variation gives Black no more than a draw if White decides to play his rook back to c7 on the 26th move. Moreover, White can undertake a well-founded winning attempt with 25

exd5 exd5 26 ♖d7, since the black knight would stand too passively. However, as Olafsson points out, 24 ♖c7 fails to an unexpected combination, namely 24...dxe4! 25 ♖xc6 e3, and all at once the e-pawn becomes incredibly dangerous. On 26 ♖xe6 there follows 26...e2 27 ♖b1 ♖f8! with the terrible threat 28...♖f1+ 29 ♖xf1 ♗e3+ and wins. Initially I thought that White had a stronger riposte in 26 ♖f4, but subsequent investigation showed me that White still does not come out of it well after 26...e2 27 ♖e4 e1♕+ 28 ♖xe1 ♗xe1 29 ♖xe6 ♖d8!.

White's passed pawns are not strong enough, because his king is too far away. After 30 ♖d6 ♖xd6 31 exd6 ♔f7 the block of pawns is going to be swept away by Black. Somewhat better is 30 c6, but then Black continues cold-bloodedly with 30...♔f7 31 c7 ♖c8 32 ♖c6 ♗a5 and the c-pawn falls. So Spassky had seen that he had to avoid this variation.

24   ...   exd5
25   ♖d7

The position still seems critical for Black, but Fischer quickly dispels that illusion.

25   ...   ♗e3+
26   ♔h1   ♗xd4

Capturing with the bishop improves the co-ordination of his minor pieces.

27   e6   ♗e5! *(D)*

Fischer's defence is hair-fine. The squares d6 and c7 are taken away from

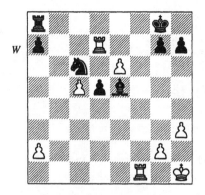

White and at the same time the e-pawn is cut off so that it may be captured.

28 ♖xd5   ♖e8
29 ♖fe1   ♖xe6
30 ♖d6!

A finesse without which Spassky would have to fight for the draw.

30 ...   ♔f7

The safest solution. White would be the only one with winning chances after the continuation 30...♖xd6 31 cxd6 ♔f8 32 ♖c1 ♘d8 33 ♖c8 ♔e8 34 ♖c7.

31 ♖xc6   ♖xc6
32 ♖xe5   ♔f6
33 ♖d5   ♔e6
34 ♖h5   h6
35 ♔h2   ♖a6
36 c6

Of course it was not possible to keep both queenside pawns.

36 ...   ♖xc6
37 ♖a5   a6
38 ♔g3   ♔f6
39 ♔f3   ♖c3+

½-½

Game Ten
Bronstein – Ljubojević
Interzonal Tournament, Petropolis 1973
Alekhine Defence

Bronstein and Ljubojević are representatives of different generations, but their styles have common elements: sharp, rich in ideas, and with a tendency toward the bizarre. Neither of them, in the end, had an important result in the 1973 Interzonal. When their game was played, however, Ljubojević was leading with 7½ out of 10 and Bronstein was somewhere in the middle with 5½. Knowing this, one must admire Ljubojević's courageous and admirable choice of opening. Although he had the black pieces, his play was razor-sharp from the beginning, and he certainly did not concern himself with trying for mere equality.

He found a worthy opponent in Bronstein. Grandmasters nowadays combat the Alekhine Defence almost exclusively with the quiet 3 ♘f3, which in most variations guarantees White a slight but tangible advantage. Bronstein, however, took off the velvet gloves and chose the Four Pawns Attack, the old main line of this opening, which promises extremely sharp positions with mutual chances.

This indeed proved to be the case. I have analysed the opening fairly extensively, not only because it is interesting and still little researched, but also because the game reached critical heights already in the opening stage.

1	e4	♘f6
2	e5	♘d5
3	d4	d6
4	c4	♘b6
5	f4	dxe5
6	fxe5	c5

This attempt to further sharpen a sharp variation stems from the Russian Argunov, who used it with success in the 1920's. Still, the most striking characteristic of the move is its riskiness. White gets a tremendous centre.

7	d5	e6
8	♘c3	

A healthy developing move which also covers the e4-square. 8 d6 is premature on account of 8...♕h4+ 9 g3 ♕e4+ 10 ♕e2 ♕xh1 11 ♘f3 ♘c6 12 ♘bd2 ♘d7! and White has no good way to win the black queen, as shown in the consultation game Nekrasov and Tokar against Argunov and Yudin, USSR 1931.

8	...	exd5
9	cxd5	c4

Mikenas' move. The alternative is 9...♕h4+ 10 g3 ♕d4. Practically all standard theoretical works, including the *Encyclopedia of Chess Openings* and Bagirov's book on the Alekhine Defence (revised edition, 1979), give 11 ♗b5+ ♗d7 12 ♕e2 as the refutation, citing the game Ljubojević-Moses, Dresden 1969, which went: 12...♘xd5 13 e6 fxe6 14 ♕xe6+ ♘e7 15 ♘f3 ♕f6 16 ♕e2 ♘c6 17 ♘e4 ♕e6 18 ♗c4 with great advantage for White. Adams points out in the *British Chess Magazine,* however, that all the theory books have forgotten an old game between Drogomiretsky and Kaiev from the semi-final of the All-Russian Championship, Sverdlovsk 1934, where Kaiev improved Black's play with 15...♕b4 *(D)* (instead of 15...♕f6).

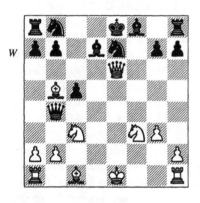

Black gets a decisive attack after 16 ♗xd7+ ♘xd7 17 ♘g5 0-0-0 18 ♘f7 ♘c6 19 ♘xh8? (19 ♘xd8 is a little better, although Black still has many chances after 19...♘xd8) 19...♘d4! 20 ♕e4 ♘f6 21 ♕g2 ♖e8+ 22 ♔d1 ♕c4 – he does not even bother taking the time to capture the knight on h8! Instead of helping his opponent to complete his development, White does

better to play energetically for attack with the (most often temporary) piece sacrifice 16 ♘e5! ♗xb5 17 ♗g5 and the complications are probably in White's favour.

Nevertheless, the question remains whether 11 ♗b5+ is a clear refutation of 9...♕h4+. White has a much more solid approach in 11 ♗f4. The ending after 11...g5 12 ♗g5 ♕xe5+ 13 ♕e2 is clearly better for White.

Now we return to the position after 9...c4 *(D).*

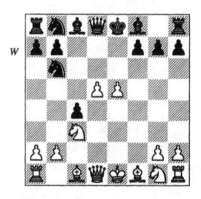

10 ♘f3

Once again, sound development above all. Estrin and Panov recommend 10 a3 to keep Black's king's bishop out of b4, but Black stands well after the simple 10...♗c5. Bagirov's recommendation, 10 d6, is again premature, because White will have difficulty defending the e-pawn after 10...♘c6; e.g., 11 ♘f3 ♗g4 or 11 ♗f4 g5. Finally, 10 ♕d4 also promises little after 10...♘c6 11 ♕e4 ♘b4 and now 12 a3 ♘4xd5 13 ♘xd5 ♕xd5 14

♕xd5 ♘xd5 15 ♗xc4 ♘c7 leads to a roughly equal ending (Ciocaltea-Ljubojević, Malaga 1971). That was the first time Ljubojević tried this system for Black.

10 ...   ♗g4 *(D)*

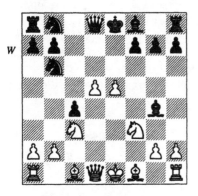

The alternative is 10...♗b4. Boleslavsky then gives 11 ♗xc4 ♘xc4 12 ♕a4+ ♘c6 13 dxc6 ♗xc3+ 14 bxc3 b5 15 ♕b4! a5 16 ♕c5 ♕d3 17 ♗g5 with very dangerous threats. Ree showed in the *Haagse Post*, however, that Black can offer an excellent pawn sacrifice with 11...♗xc3+ 12 bxc3 ♘xc4 13 ♕a4+ ♘d7! 14 ♕xc4 ♘b6 15 ♕b5+ ♕d7. Black is guaranteed equal play because of the opposite-colour bishops and his resulting pressure on the light squares.

White has better, however: 11 ♗g5!. Now 11...f6 12 exf6 gxf6 13 ♕e2+ would be disastrous for Black, while 11...♕xd5 12 ♕xd5 ♗xc3+ 13 bxc3 ♘xd5 14 0-0-0 brings no relief either.

11 ♕d4

A quiet continuation would not achieve so much this time because 11 ♗e2 would be followed by the annoying 11...♗c5 (but not 11...♗b4 12 0-0 0-0 because of 13 ♘g5! ♗xe2 14 ♕xe2 h6 15 e6! with a strong attack, as in Silyakov-Bagirov, Baku 1969).

The text is a many-sided move. The black queen's bishop is attacked, a later queen check on h4 is prevented, the c5-square is taken away from the king's bishop, and, finally, the c-pawn is attacked. White can also take the c-pawn immediately with 11 ♗xc4, but that gives him little chance of advantage after 11...♘xc4 12 ♕a4+ ♘d7 13 ♕xc4 ♗xf3 14 gxf3 ♘xe5 15 ♕e2 (or 15 ♕e4 ♕h4+!) and now not 15...♕e7 16 0-0! with advantage to White (Browne-Ničevski, Rovinj-Zagreb 1970), but 15...♕h4+ with good play for Black.

11 ...   ♗xf3
12 gxf3   ♗b4
13 ♗xc4   0-0
14 ♖g1

Before bringing his own king to safety, White launches an immediate attack, supported by his mighty pawn duo in the centre, against the enemy king. Remarkably, Ljubojević already had this position with White, at Čačak 1970. His opponent, Honfi, replied 14...♕c7 but was quickly mated after 15 e6 f6 16 ♗h6 ♕xc4 17 ♖xg7+ ♔h8 18 ♖g8+! ♔xg8 19 ♕g1+. Black's counterplay in this game was very feeble. As we shall see, Black can get all sorts of counter-chances against 14 ♖g1. Therefore in Gonzalez-Bryson,

Lucerne 1982, the staggering novelty 14 ♗h6!? was introduced. After the interesting continuation 14...♘8d7 15 ♖g1 g6 16 e6 ♘e5 17 ♗e2 ♗c5 18 ♕xe5 ♕h4+ 19 ♖g3 ♕xh6 White should have followed up with 20 d6!, which would have given him – with his mighty, far-advanced passed pawns – a winning game. In the German bible on Alekhine's Defence – I refer to the two-part work by Siebenhaar, Delnef and Ottstadt which altogether runs to more than 1,200 pages – 14...♘xc4 is given as an improvement on Black's play. In my opinion this is no more satisfactory after 15 ♕g4 g6 16 ♕xc4 ♗xc3+ 17 bxc3 ♖e8 18 0-0-0! (White does best to return the pawn immediately) 18...♖xe5 19 ♕d4 ♕f6 and now not 20 ♖he1, as given by the authors, but 20 f4 ♖f5 21 ♕xf6 ♖xf6 22 ♖he1 ♘d7 23 ♖e7, followed by 24 ♖de1, when Black has insuperable difficulties. The move 14 ♗h6 is probably really critical for Black.

14 ... g6

After the above-mentioned game Ljubojević must have asked himself what he would do if faced with the text-move. Bronstein's answer is exceptionally deep and beautiful.

15 ♗g5!

The introduction to a long-term rook sacrifice. Bronstein undoubtedly conceived the whole idea over the board, although this position had occurred earlier, in the correspondence game Gibbs-Stuart 1971/72. That game continued 15 ♗h6? whereupon Black

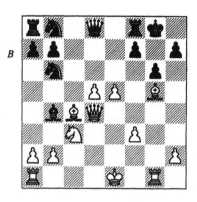

played a positional exchange sacrifice with 15...♘c6! 16 ♕e4 ♘xe5 and won smoothly after 17 ♗xf8 ♕xf8 18 ♗b5 ♕c5! 19 0-0-0 ♗xc3 20 bxc3 ♕xc3+ 21 ♕c2 ♕a1+ 22 ♔d2 ♘xf3+ 23 ♔e3 ♘xd5+! 24 ♔xf3 ♕f6+ 25 ♔g3 ♕g5+ 26 ♔f2 ♕h4+ 27 ♖g3 ♕xh2+ 28 ♖g2 ♕xg2+, etc.

15 ... ♕c7

The correct square for the queen. After 15...♕c8 16 ♗b3 ♗c5 17 ♕h4 ♗xg1 18 ♕h6, mate can only be deferred by 18...♗e3.

16 ♗b3 ♗c5
17 ♕f4 (D)

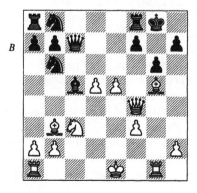

17 ...   ♗xg1

Black takes the rook, a much criticised decision. Hort gives this move a question mark in the *Encyclopedia of Chess Openings* – yes, we are still very much in the opening – as do Kotov, Blackstock, and Wade in their joint book *World Championship Interzonals 1973*. Zaitsev and Shashin were the first to criticise the capture of the rook. They give two variations in 64:

1) 17...♘8d7 18 d6 ♕c6 and now:

1a) 19 ♖g4? ♘xe5 20 ♕xe5 ♖ae8 21 ♗e7 ♗xd6 and Black wins.

1b) 19 ♘e4. This move was suggested by Ree during an informal analysis session with me when we first saw the game. The point is that Black runs out of moves after 19...♗xg1 20 ♗f6! ♘xf6 21 exf6 ♖fe8 22 ♕h6 ♖xe4+ 23 ♔f1 ♕b5+ 24 ♔xg1. Soon after this variation was published in *Schaakbulletin,* Marović found a hole in it. In the Yugoslav magazine *Sahovski Glasnik* he showed that Black has the much stronger 23rd move 23...♖e1+! He continues with 24 ♔g2 ♖e2+ 25 ♔xg1 ♕c5+ 26 ♔h1 ♖xh2+! 27 ♕xh2 ♕f5 with unclear play. I wonder whether he saw that 28 ♗xf7+ was possible – the bishop can be captured only on pain of mate. However, even after 28...♔h8 White has achieved little. The bishop will be forced to retreat when Black captures on f6, and thus 28 ♗xf7+ seems to be merely a wasted tempo for the win of a relatively unimportant pawn. White's best seems to be 28 ♕g3

♕xf6 29 ♖e1 with good compensation for the pawn.

1c) 19 0-0-0. Zaitsev and Shashin now give a line which superficially seems to give Black equal play; i.e., 19...♗xg1 20 ♖xg1 ♕c5 21 ♖e1 ♖ae8 22 ♗e7 ♖xe7. But Marović goes further and concludes that White clearly has the better chances after 23 dxe7 ♕xe7 24 e6! fxe6 25 ♖xe6 ♔h8 26 ♖xe7 ♖xf4 27 ♘d5 ♖xf3 28 ♘xb6 ♘xb6 29 ♖xb7. Let us underline this judgement: White is in fact winning. 27...♖d4 (instead of 27...♖xf3) would be tougher, but 28 a3 would best illustrate the helplessness of Black's position. While White quietly prepares to further strengthen his position, Black cannot free himself.

2) 17...♖e8. How treacherous the position is can be seen in the variation 18 d6 ♗xd6 19 ♘b5 ♗xe5 20 ♘xc7 ♗xc7+ 21 ♕e4 with the better ending for White, a variation originally given by Ree and myself and unquestioningly adopted by Kotov, Blackstock, and Wade in their book. However, it fails to consider an important finesse for Black. Adams gives 18 d6? ♗xd6 19 ♘b5 *(D)* and now:

19...♖xe5+!! 20 ♕xe5 ♗b4+ and Black wins.

Therefore, after 17...♖e8 White must resort to 18 ♗f6, the move analysed by Zaitsev and Shashin. After 18...♘8d7 there can follow:

2a) 19 d6 (Zaitsev and Shashin). However, Black comes out of it well after 19...♘xe5 (not 19...♕xd6? 20

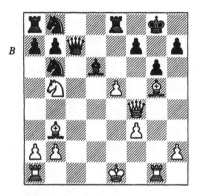

♗xf7+ ♔xf7 21 ♗e7+! winning the
queen) 20 ♔f1 ♗xd6 21 ♘b5 ♕c6 22
♘xd6 ♕xd6 23 ♖d1 ♕c6 24 ♗xe5
♕b5+ 25 ♔f2 ♕xe5 26 ♗xf7+ ♔g7.
O'Kelly tries to improve White's play
with 20 dxc7, but after 20...♘d3+ 21
♔f1 ♘xf4 22 ♖g4 ♘e6! 23 ♘e4 ♗e7
24 ♖c1 White by no means has the
better of it, as O'Kelly thinks; Black
plays simply 24...♖ac8 with good
chances.

2b) 19 ♘e4! *(D)*. Very refined.

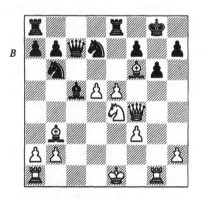

The subtle point came to light in
Marjanović-Filipowicz, Yugoslavia

1974: 19...♘xe5 20 ♖xg6+!! with a
crushing attack. 19...♖xe5 is better,
but White clearly has the better prospects after 20 ♗xe5 ♘xe5 21 ♔e2.

In short, neither of Black's two alternatives, 17...♘8d7 and 17...♖e8,
lead to satisfactory play. Even so, is
either of them a relatively better try
than the text-move? If you look at the
game superficially you might tend to
think so, but analysis proves that the
opposite is true.

18 d6

Black won quickly after 18 ♔e2? in
Gheorghiu-Ljubojević, Manila 1973:
18...♕c5! 19 ♖xg1 ♕xg1 20 ♗f6
♕g2+ 21 ♔e3 ♕xb2 22 ♔d3 ♘8d7
23 ♘e4 ♖ac8 24 ♕h6 ♘xe5+ 25 ♔e3
♖c3+ and White resigned.

It is remarkable that this short game
was played after Petropolis, puzzling
that Gheorghiu, who also played in the
Interzonal tournament, would deviate
from Bronstein's play, and surprising,
too, that Ljubojević would risk losing
with the same variation twice in a row.
All this rather confused some commentators: Adams wrote that Gheorghiu-Ljubojević was also played at
Petropolis, and thus he created the impression that Bronstein had improved
White's play later in the tournament.
Bagirov, though correctly locating the
game in Manila, asserted that the Interzonal had been held later, and thus
he too implied that Bronstein had prepared his novelty. But there is really
no doubt that Bronstein had thought
it all out over the board. Gheorghiu

probably remembered the line incorrectly and Ljubojević, the eternal optimist, probably wanted to try the system once more.

18 ...   ♛c8

It was difficult to foresee that this is the wrong square for the queen. Besides the text-move, I analyse the following possibilities:

1) 18...♛c6. A suggestion of the Danish analyst Bo Richter Larsen. After 19 ♗f6 ♘8d7 20 ♛h6 ♘xf6 21 exf6 ♖fe8+ White has nothing better than 22 ♘e4, after which the play is similar to that in variation 1b above (after Black's 17th move). 19 0-0-0 is much stronger. White wins at least a whole rook back while maintaining a great positional advantage by 19...♗c5 20 e6 ♘8d7 21 e7!.

2) 18...♛c5. The commentators either did not mention this move or dismissed it with 19 ♘e4 ♛e3+ 20 ♛xe3 ♗xe3+ 21 ♗xe3 with satisfactory play for White; if 19...♛b4+ 20 ♔f1 and White wins. But why should Black panic and give check? After the centralising 19...♛d4, it seems White generally does not have such dangerous threats against the black king. If 20 ♘f6+ ♔h8, and 20 ♖d1 ♛xb2 21 ♘f6+ ♔h8 22 ♛h4 ♛xh2 also leads nowhere.

After 18...♛c5 19 ♘e4 ♛d4, the indicated move is 20 ♔f1 so that after the virtually forced 20...♛xb2 White has a choice of places to put his rook. The best is 21 ♖e1 with the idea of indirectly protecting the e-pawn after

21...♛xh2 22 ♛g4. Black then loses his bishop, and White has sufficient compensation for the exchange after, e.g., 22...h5 23 ♛xg1 ♛xg1+ 24 ♔xg1 ♘8d7. I think the reason Ljubojević repeated the variation against Gheorghiu was that he had found 19...♛d4! and felt that the resulting possibilities were sharp enough and not onesidedly in White's favour. A correct assumption, as later became apparent. Against Grünfeld at the Riga Interzonal 1979, after 20 ♖d1 Ljubojević did indeed play 20...♛xb2 and won relatively quickly after 21 e6 ♘8d7 22 e7 ♛xh2 23 exf8♛+ ♖xf8 24 ♛xh2 ♗xh2 25 ♘f6+ ♔g7 26 ♘xd7 ♘xd7 27 ♗e7 ♖b8 28 ♔f2 ♗e5 29 ♖c1 ♘c5 30 ♖d1 ♗f6 31 ♗xf6+ ♔xf6 32 ♗c4 ♖d8 33 ♔g3 a6 34 ♗f1 ♔e5 35 f4+ ♔e6 36 ♗c4+ ♔f6 37 ♔f3 b5 and White resigned.

Meanwhile this variation has again been developed further. In order to pursue this, I again consulted the 'Alekhine bible'. Instead of 21 e6 White should play 21 ♘f6+ ♔h8 22 ♖d2. More than four pages, full of analysis, then follow in the book. The best move seems to me to be 22...♛a1+. In a game Grünfeld-Wiemer, Tecklenburg 1984 (so Grünfeld tried it again!) this was followed by 23 ♔e2 ♘c6! 24 ♛h4 h5 25 e6? ♘d4+ 26 ♖xd4 ♛xd4 and Black had a won game. The Grünfeld variation has not brought very much success. Siebenhaar *et al* give 25 ♘g4 as better, after which the wild suggestion 25...f5 is probably good.

But according to the authors White can play better earlier on, namely 23 ♗d1. This move was recommended by J. Weidemann as long ago as 1983. A striking variation is 23...♘8d7 24 ♕h4 ♕xe5+ 25 ♔f1 h5 26 ♘xh5 gxh5 27 ♕xh5+ ♔g8 28 ♖g2 with a winning attack. However, in the position after 23 ♗d1 Black has an amazing escape which I found in 1991 during my preparations for the Candidates match against Hübner: 23...♗e3!! 24 ♕xe3 ♘c4 and White cannot very well avoid exchanging queens, after which it becomes quite difficult to continue the attack.

19 ♔e2 (D)

Bronstein errs too. His unconcern for the safety of his king might have cost him dearly. 19 0-0-0 is indicated, as Bronstein gave after the game. White would then be unable to make immediate use of his knight in the attack against the black king with ♘e4, but, remarkably enough, Black would still not have time to set up a watertight defence. Bronstein's variation continues 19...♗c5 20 e6 fxe6 21 ♕e5 ♖e8 22 ♗h6 ♕d7 23 ♘e4 and White wins. 19...♕c5 is tougher, but even then Black has hardly any survival chances after 20 e6 ♘8d7 (the standard move to cover f6 in this position) 21 exf7+ ♔g7 22 ♔b1 (threatening 23 ♘e4) 22...♕e5 23 ♖xg1, and White already has two pawns for the exchange.

19 ... ♗c5

This gains nothing. It should have been the easiest thing in the world for

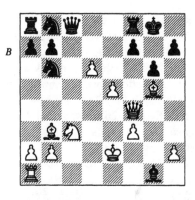

Ljubojević to find the strong reply 19...♕c5!. Bronstein gives that move himself, with the variations 20 e6 ♘8d7 and 20 ♘e4 ♕b5+, in both cases with clear advantage for Black, says Bronstein. But in the second variation (20 ♘e4 ♕b5+), I don't think White should be worried if he continues with 21 ♔d2; e.g., 21...♘c4+ 22 ♔e1! (not 22 ♔c3 ♕xe5+ 23 ♕xe5 ♘xe5 24 ♖xg1 ♖c8+ and wins) and now, although everything looks very promising for Black, what should he play? After 22...♗e3 23 ♘f6+ ♔h8 23 ♕h4 the bishop on e3 is only in the way (of 24...♕xe5+).

The best seems to be 22...♕xe5, although White keeps clear compensation for the exchange after 23 ♗xc4 ♕xf4 24 ♗xf4.

20 ♘e4

Now everything goes according to White's desires.

20 ... ♘8d7

The most obvious. Yet 20...♘6d7 would have made heavier demands on White's attacking ability. O'Kelly comes up with two variations, one showing how not to continue, the other an (alleged) route to victory:

1) 21 ♖c1 (this move was given with a question mark) 21...b6 22 ♗f6 ♘xf6 23 ♘xf6+ ♔g7 24 ♘h5+ gxh5 25 ♕f6+ ♔g8 26 e6 ♕e8! and White must take a draw since 27 e7 is answered by 27...♘d7.

2) 21 ♗f6 (given an exclamation mark) 21...♘xf6 22 ♘xf6+ ♔g7 23 ♘h5+ gxh5 24 ♕f6+ ♔g8 25 e6 ♕e8 26 ♕g5+ ♔h8 27 ♕xc5 ♘d7 28 ♕d4+ f6 29 e7 ♖g8 30 ♗xg8 ♕xg8 31 ♔f2 and wins.

A rather unconvincing business. How does White actually win? Not by attack, for the black king is safe enough. Admittedly, White's far-advanced passed pawns keep the opponent from making use of his material advantage, but beyond that, there is little to say.

In variation 2 it makes sense for White first to force a further weakening of the black king's position with 23 ♕h4 instead of rushing ahead with the showy knight sacrifice. Then 23...♖h8 fails to 24 ♘h5+ ♔g8 25 ♗xf7+ and mate, so 23...h6 is the only possibility. Now White indeed offers the knight with 24 ♘h5+, but now Black can't take it on account of mate after 24...gxh5 25 ♕f6+ ♔g8 (or 25...♔h7 26 ♗c2+ ♔g8 27 ♕xh6) 26 ♕g6+ ♔h8 27 ♕xh6+ ♔g8 28 ♗c2. Black must contort himself to avoid direct mate; i.e., 24...♔h7 25 ♕f6 ♖g8 26 ♕xf7+ ♔h8 *(D)*.

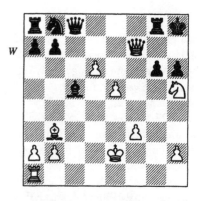

Strangely enough, there is no clear win for White here: 27 ♘f6 fails to 27...♖g7, and after 27 ♕f6+ ♔h7 28 ♗xg8+ ♕xg8 29 ♕e7+ ♔h8 30 ♘f6 Black escapes with perpetual check after 30...♕c4+.

So, after 20...♘6d7, how does White win? The attentive reader must have seen it by now: White plays the move rejected by O'Kelly in variation 1, 21 ♖c1!. Now after 21...b6 22 ♗f6 ♘xf6 23 ♘xf6+ ♔g7 White continues 24 ♕h4! (instead of 24 ♘h5) 24...h6 25 ♘h5+ ♔h7 26 ♕f6 ♖g8 27 ♕xf7+ ♔h8 28 ♕f6+ ♔h7 29 ♗xg8+ ♕xg8 30 ♕e7+ ♔h8 31 ♘f6 and wins as Black now has no saving check on c4. Earlier, Black's possible queen check on a6 never had any point because White could have met it with ♗c4.

21 ♖c1   ♕c6 *(D)*

Threatens to start checking on b5, but White's following move removes any possible sting from that.

22 ♖xc5

White gets a proud knight on f6 by means of this exchange sacrifice.

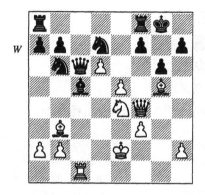

22	...	♘xc5
23	♘f6+	♔h8
24	♕h4	

Black is lots of material ahead, but he cannot prevent loss. He tries a few last checks.

| 24 | ... | ♕b5+ |
| 25 | ♔e3! | |

The crowning point of White's attacking play. Black's only reasonable check is 25...♕d3+, but after 26 ♔f2 he has no more to say; e.g., 26...h5 27 ♘xh5 gxh5 28 ♗f6+ ♔g8 29 ♕g5+ and mate.

Note that the immediate 25 ♔f2 (instead of 25 ♔e3) only draws after 25...♘d3+ 26 ♔g1 ♕c5+ 27 ♔h1 h5 28 ♘xh5 ♕f2 29 ♘g3+ ♔g8 30 ♗f6 and Black has perpetual check with 30...♕xf3+. The move 26 ♔g2 (instead of 26 ♔g1) is not better; Black

has such a great advantage in material that he can afford 26...♘e1+.

And 25 ♔e1 is even worse because of 25...♕b4+, forcing the exchange of queens.

| 25 | ... | h5 |
| 26 | ♘xh5 | ♕xb3+ |

Black must give back quite a lot of material in order to prevent immediate mate.

| 27 | axb3 | ♘d5+ |
| 28 | ♔d4 | |

The king is a strong piece.

28	...	♘e6+
29	♔xd5	♘xg5
30	♘f6+	♔g7
31	♕xg5	

Now White has the material advantage. Ljubojević continued playing until the time control since Bronstein was in serious time trouble. The rest is not interesting.

31	...	♖fc8
32	e6	fxe6+
33	♔xe6	♖f8
34	d7	a5
35	♘g4	♖a6+
36	♔e5	♖f5+
37	♕xf5	gxf5
38	d8♕	fxg4
39	♕d7+	♔h6
40	♕xb7	♖g6
41	f4	1-0

Game Eleven
Karpov – Spassky
Semi-final Candidates Match (9),
Leningrad 1974
Sicilian Defence, Scheveningen Variation

When Spassky, with the black pieces, won the first game of his 1974 semi-final match against Karpov, almost every expert considered Spassky the clear favourite. This was due primarily to the manner in which he won – that is, unmistakably in the powerful style of his best years. But surprisingly, we saw little of the old Spassky again. After a short draw in the second game, Karpov hit back hard in the third. It was only the second time in his life that Karpov opened with 1 d4 and not 1 e4 – curiously, Fischer, too, regularly found alternatives to his favourite 1 e4 in his match against Spassky. When Karpov had built up a 2-1 lead with five draws after eight games, he again opened with the king's pawn. And with what virtuosity!

'His play is dry, but very good,' declared Hort after the game. Hort was present in Leningrad during the match, as I was. Nearly all the grandmasters in the press room were deeply impressed. This is undoubtedly one of Karpov's best games and is very typical of his style, although it is not to be found in his book of fifty of his own games. The contours of the future World Champion were already becoming clear.

1	e4	c5
2	♘f3	d6
3	d4	cxd4
4	♘xd4	♘f6
5	♘c3	e6
6	♗e2	

In this match, Karpov employed the modest 6 ♗e2 for the first time in his life. In five earlier games he tried the sharp Keres Attack with success: he won all five, including a famous one against Hort in Moscow 1971.

6	...	♗e7
7	0-0	0-0

8	f4	♘c6
9	♗e3	♗d7 *(D)*

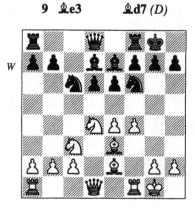

W

In the first game, Spassky succeeded with the then almost unknown
move 9...e5. After 10 ♘b3 a5 11 a4
♘b4 12 ♗f3 ♗e6 13 ♔h1 ♕c7 14 ♖f2
♖fd8 15 ♖d2 ♗c4 16 ♘b5?! ♗xb5 17
axb5 a4 18 ♘c1 d5! complications
favouring Black arose. Geller, one of
Karpov's seconds during the 1974
match, strengthened White's play a
few months later in a game against
Spassky: 12 ♔h1 ♕c7 13 ♖c1! and
White clearly had the better play after
13...♗e6 14 ♘d2 exf4 15 ♘b5 ♕d8
16 ♗xf4.

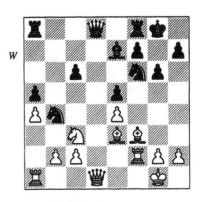

10	♘b3	a5
11	a4	♘b4
12	♗f3	♗c6

An interesting novelty that could
be an important improvement over
12...e5. After that move White gained
the advantage with 13 ♔h1 ♗c6 14
fxe5! dxe5 15 ♕e2 ♕c7 16 ♕f2 ♘d7
17 ♖ad1 in Geller-Polugaevsky, 1973.

| 13 | ♘d4 | g6 |

An idea connected with the previous move: Black will give up the
bishop-pair in return for a strong central position.

14	♖f2	e5
15	♘xc6	bxc6
16	fxe5	

A good move which Karpov must
have played with pleasure. He has a
great preference for positions with
fixed pawn structures.

| 16 | ... | dxe5 (D) |
| 17 | ♕f1 | |

White concentrates his pieces on
the f-file, not the d-file. If he could

now also play his king's bishop to c4,
the f7-square would be fatally weak.

| 17 | ... | ♕c8 |
| 18 | h3 (D) | |

A typical Karpov move. There was
no actual threat of 18...♘g4, because
of the reply 19 ♗xg4 ♕xg4 20 ♕c4,
but, just to make sure, he removes any
possibility of it. Perhaps he is dream-
ing of getting his bishop to c4 and
doesn't want to have to exchange it on
g4.

18 ♖d1 should also be considered.

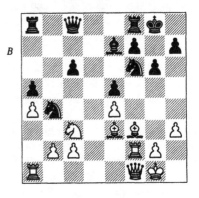

| 18 | ... | ♘d7 |

And this is typical of the way Spassky played against Fischer two years earlier. In the eighth game of the 1972 match, Spassky played an incomprehensible tactical blunder with 19...♘f6-d7 (Fischer-Spassky: 1 c4 c5 2 ♘c3 ♘c6 3 ♘f3 ♘f6 4 g3 g6 5 ♗g2 ♗g7 6 0-0 0-0 7 d4 cxd4 8 ♘xd4 ♘xd4 9 ♕xd4 d6 10 ♗g5 ♗e6 11 ♕f4 ♕a5 12 ♖ac1 ♖ab8 13 b3 ♖fc8 14 ♕d2 a6 15 ♗e3 b5 16 ♗a7 bxc4 17 ♗xb8 ♖xb8 18 bxc4 ♗xc4 19 ♖fd1 ♘d7). Now in the ninth game of this match, he commits an equally incomprehensible positional blunder with 18...♘f6-d7.

The exchange of White's bad light-squared bishop for the knight leads to a strategically ruinous position. The correct plan for Black is to force the exchange of White's other bishop; for example, 18...♔g7 (the immediate 18...h5 is not bad either) 19 ♖c1 (Intending to bring the bishop to c4. Perhaps 19 ♖d1 is better, but if 19 ♕c4 ♕a6.) 19...h5 20 ♗e2 ♘h7 and now 21 ♗c4 is answered by the advance ...f7-f5, and other moves are answered by 21...♗g5.

In *64*, Tal gives the line 18...♕e6 19 ♖c1 ♖ad8 20 ♗e2 ♖d4 for Black. He must have done this analysis in a great hurry, because we had both concluded in the press room during the game that this attempt to keep the bishop out of c4 was inadequate on account of 21 b3 ♘xe4 (what else?) 22 ♗xd4 exd4 23 ♘xe4 (better than 23 ♗c4 ♘xf2! 24 ♗xe6 fxe6) 23...♕xe4 24 ♗d3 or 24

♗c4, and Black does not have enough compensation for the sacrificed exchange.

After 18...♔g7 (or 18...h5) 19 ♘b1 (to regroup), then Black can reply 19...♕e6.

19 ♗g4

Tal writes that Furman predicted Karpov's moves here and on the 24th move. Indeed, Karpov's old teacher always joined in the analysis when his pupil stood well, and at such times it was impossible to remove the smile from his face.

The text-move is actually very easy to find: it is the only way to prevent Black's positional threat 19...♗c5.

19	...	h5
20	♗xd7	♕xd7
21	♕c4	

A consequence of White's 19th move. Black would have nothing to complain about if he could play his queen to e6.

| 21 | ... | ♗h4 |
| 22 | ♖d2 | ♕e7 *(D)* |

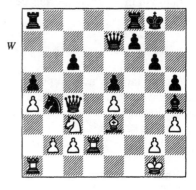

A nice move, as now 23 ♗c5 ♕g5 24 ♖d7 is nothing due to 24...♘xc2 25 ♖f1 ♘e3 26 ♗xe3 ♕xe3+ 27 ♔h1 ♔h8!; for example, 28 ♖dxf7 ♖xf7 29 ♕xf7 ♖g8!. Of course, Karpov does not have to enter this line.

23 ♖f1   ♖fd8

Already the decisive mistake. The black rook will have to return later to protect the kingside. 23...♖ad8 is correct, not with the idea of offering the queen after 24 ♗c5 ♖xd2 25 ♗xe7 ♗xe7, which is refuted by 26 ♖f2 ♖d4 27 ♕e2, but to play 24...♕b7! (Hort), when White has nothing better than to exchange a pair of rooks. But even then White's advantage is unmistakable.

24 ♘b1!

The other move prophesied by Furman. Now even the knight on b4 will be driven back, and the black position goes rapidly downhill.

24 ...   ♕b7
25 ♔h2

A strong quiet move.

25 ...   ♔g7
26 c3   ♘a6
27 ♖e2

Only Karpov's 18th move was deserving of some criticism; all his other moves are extraordinarily strong. The text-move maximises the pressure on Black's position.

27 ...   ♖f8
28 ♘d2   ♗d8
29 ♘f3   f6
30 ♖d2   ♗e7
31 ♕e6   ♖ad8

32 ♖xd8   ♗xd8 *(D)*

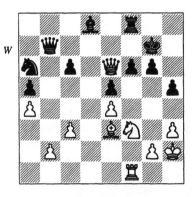

While we in the press room were occupying ourselves with the spectacular 33 ♘xe5, which we thought nicely decides matters after 33...♕c7! (Timman) 34 ♗f4 ♘c5 35 ♕c4 fxe5 36 ♗h6+ ♔xh6 37 ♖xf8 ♘d7 38 ♖h8+ ♔g5 39 ♕e6! ♘f6 40 g3! (Tal), or 37...♗e7 38 ♕f7 ♕d6 39 ♖h8+ ♔g5 40 ♖e8 ♗d8 41 h4+! ♔xh4 42 ♖xd8 ♕xd8 43 ♕xg6 (Hort), Karpov mercilessly made his final, prosaic moves.

Later, our rushed analysis was indeed shown to be faulty. Black wins with 43...♕g5 in the last position (after 43 ♕xg6). The right way is 40 ♕f2 (instead of 40 ♖e8) with the crushing threat 41 h4+ ♔g4 42 ♕g3 mate. After the forced 40...♕d3, White wins with 41 h4+ ♔g4 42 ♖g8 ♕xe4 43 ♕g3+ ♔f5 44 ♕xg6+ ♔f4 45 ♕f7+.

33 ♖d1   ♘b8
34 ♗c5   ♖h8
35 ♖xd8   1-0

If 35...♖xd8 36 ♗e7.

Game Twelve
Korchnoi – Karpov
Final Candidates Match (11),
Moscow 1974
Queen's Indian Defence

The Karpov-Korchnoi match, the finals of the 1974 candidates series – only later did it become clear that it was actually for the World Championship – was greeted by only lukewarm enthusiasm by the chess world. Karpov won two games with White right in the opening; both times Korchnoi had deviated from his favourite French Defence. Then Korchnoi won a game with White. Karpov won another game when Korchnoi cooked his own goose in a horrible manner, and Karpov's second loss came when he underestimated the dangers in a very clearly drawn position. And it rained draws.

Yet there were no boring games, although the combinational possibilities only rarely surfaced. One of these games is the eleventh.

The opening followed a traditional path and both players then undertook traditional manoeuvres. Analysis shows that much hidden beauty did not come to the fore; the game seemed to follow a gradual progression to an ending which, at first, both players were trying to win. Korchnoi finally turned out to be the only one with chances. Karpov, slippery as an eel, managed to trade down to a rook endgame which seemed to be only a draw despite Korchnoi's two extra pawns.

	1	d4	♘f6
	2	♘f3	e6
	3	g3	b6

Black had the alternative 3...b5 available, to prevent White from forming a centre with c2-c4. Karpov, however, has a small opening repertoire which he understands very thoroughly and from which he seldom deviates.

	4	♗g2	♗b7
	5	c4	♗e7
	6	♘c3	

Earlier, 6 0-0 used to be played exclusively. The text conceals a finesse which would appear after 6...♘e4 7 ♗d2. In the variation 7...♗f6 8 ♕c2 ♘xd2 9 ♕xd2 White can answer the advance 9...c5 with 10 d5 because after 10...♗xc3+ 11 ♕xc3 Black's g-pawn is unprotected.

| | 6 | ... | 0-0 |
| | 7 | ♕d3 (D) | |

An unusual square for the queen. In the fifth game White placed his queen on c2, which Karpov answered with 7...c5. That advance is unattractive here, so Black is compelled to look for another way to challenge the centre.

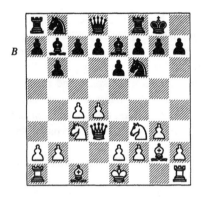

7 ...   d5

More or less forced because of the threatened e2-e4. Later, Karpov also took to answering 7 0-0 with 7...d5. As Ree points out in the *Haagse Post*, this was Botvinnik's method of playing for a win with Black in the queen's Indian. The former World Champion would then meet 8 ♘e5 by 8...♕c8 – but White can gain the advantage with 9 cxd5 exd5 10 ♗g5.

The present World Champion approaches it differently; after 7 0-0 d5 8 ♘e5 he plays 8...♘a6, a move first used in Smejkal-Byrne, Biel 1976. It introduces an important area of opening theory, since the position can also be reached via the English or the Catalan.

8 cxd5   ♘xd5

Seen in the light of the above comments, 8...exd5 is a worthy alternative. White doesn't have many choices other than 9 ♘e5, and then 9...c5 can be played, possibly followed by ♘b8-a6-c7.

9 ♘xd5   exd5

10 0-0   ♘d7
11 ♗f4

The next time Korchnoi had White, he deviated with 11 ♖d1. The idea was probably to answer 11 ...c5 with 12 dxc5 bxc5 and immediately fianchetto the queen's bishop with 13 b3 and 14 ♗b2. After 11...♖e8 12 ♗e3 ♗d6 13 ♖ac1 a5 14 ♕c2 c6 Black certainly did not stand worse.

11 ...   c5
12 dxc5   bxc5

Black would not have enough compensation for the positional disadvantage of the isolated pawn after 12...♘xc5 13 ♕d1. After the text-move he has a reasonable version of the hanging centre.

13 ♖fd1   ♘f6
14 ♕c2   ♕b6
15 ♘d2

White reveals his plans. After an undefined build-up typical of his style, Korchnoi is ready for 16 e4, which Black opposes with his following move.

15 ...   ♖fe8
16 ♕b3 (D)

This move received unanimous praise. Polugaevsky, in his notes in *64*, called it Korchnoi's best move of the first half of the match.

White indirectly increases the pressure on d5; for instance, 16...♖ad8 is prevented. This is a good tactic in this sort of position. The player opposing the hanging pawns must work mainly with pin-pricks to entice an early ...c5-c4 or ...d5-d4 or to create disharmony

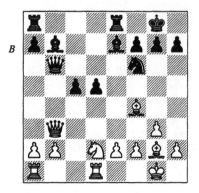

among the enemy pieces. The player with the hanging pawns must try to be ready for the crucial advance of one of the pawns at the most unexpected moment.

16 ...　　　♛a6

An understandable response. Black must play this sooner or later. For instance, after 16...♗f8 17 e3 h6 18 h4 Black has little other than 18...♛a6. Then 19 ♖ac1 with the threat 20 ♗f1 c4 21 ♞xc4 comes into consideration, so Black, just as in the game, should play 19...♗c6.

Polugaevsky shows also that Black cannot profit from the position of the white queen's bishop; e.g., 16...♞h5 17 ♗e5 ♗f8 18 ♗xd5 ♗xd5 19 ♛xd5 ♖ad8 20 ♛e4 ♛e6 21 ♞f3 f6 22 ♛h4 followed by 23 ♗c3 with advantage.

17 e3

17 ♞f1 comes strongly into consideration, in order to increase the pressure on d5 via e3. Polugaevsky says then 17...♗c6 18 ♛c2 ♖ac8 19 ♞e3 d4 20 ♗xc6 ♛xc6 21 ♞c4 ♞d5 gives Black counterplay. In my opinion,

White has a small but enduring positional plus. After 22 ♗d2 the position is more-or-less characteristic of many positions with hanging pawns; Black clearly has more space and pressure against e2, but White has a nice blockade and the good bishop, while he can comfortably protect the e-pawn and aim for e2-e4.

Korchnoi, however, continues cautiously.

17 ...　　　♗c6
18 ♛c2 (D)

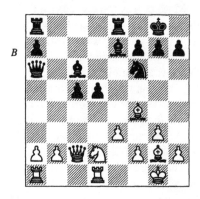

The queen returns to its post, not entirely empty-handed. The black queen and queen's bishop are a little more vulnerable than before. In seven moves they will again stand on b6 and b7.

18 ...　　　♗a4

It is clear that Karpov still does not know what to do with his position. The text-move loses at least a tempo, since the ensuing pawn move is certainly not disadvantageous for White.

Polugaevsky writes that the black position was already ripe for a pawn advance: 18...d4. After 19 ♗xc6 ♕xc6 20 exd4 ♘d5 *(D)* he looks at two variations:

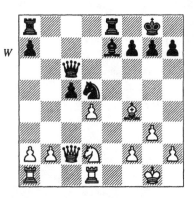

1) 21 ♗e3 ♘xe3 22 fxe3 ♗g5 23 ♘f1 ♗xe3+ 24 ♘xe3 ♖xe3 25 ♕xc5 ♕e4 or 25...♕h6 and Black has compensation for the pawn. One must certainly agree with this. White's open king position guarantees Black a draw. The Russian also mentions that this direct attempt is not even necessary and that 21...♖ac8 with the intention 21 ♘f1 c4 is possible. This is also correct, but it seems to me that 21 ♗e3 hardly comes into consideration. The main variation is:

2) 21 dxc5 ♘xf4 22 gxf4 ♗xc5. At first sight it seems that Black has quite sufficient compensation for the pawn with his strong bishop and the ragged white king position, but he will experience some annoyance with the pin on the c-file. 23 ♖ac1 ♖ac8 24 ♘b3 ♕f3! achieves nothing for White, but it is not so easy after 23 ♘b3. Polugaevsky gives 23...♖e6 since White's

king is in a sticky position; e.g., 24 ♕xc5 ♖g6+ 25 ♔f1 ♕a6+ 26 ♔e1 ♖e8+ 27 ♔d2 ♖c6 28 ♕h5 ♖d6+ 29 ♔c1 ♕c4+ and the white king cannot escape. However, after the better 24 f5 ♖e4 25 h3 ♖c4 26 ♕d3 the question is whether Black has sufficient compensation. His initiative is exhausted, and on 26...♗b6 27 ♖ac1 consolidates. Therefore, after 23 ♘b3, the indicated move is 23...♕f3, aiming for perpetual check with 24...♕g4+.

In any case, we may conclude that this was a good moment to dissolve the hanging pawns. But it was not yet necessary, since Black had moves to strengthen his position: 18...♖ac8, 18...♖ad8, 18...h6, etc.

The text shows, besides Karpov's uncertainty of the value of his position, an unbridled optimism. Karpov seems to think he can do whatever he pleases. In the next few moves, Korchnoi firmly strengthens his position and gets a dangerous initiative.

19	b3	♗c6
20	♖ac1	♗f8
21	♘f3	

One of the results of Black's unenterprising play becomes clear; White is ready to transfer his queen's bishop to the long diagonal.

| 21 | ... | ♗b7 |

Polugaevsky thinks Black could still have kept White's bishop off the long diagonal with 21...♘d7. In *Schaakbulletin 84*, Enklaar writes that this attempt is refuted by 22 ♘d4 ♗b7 23 ♕f5, but this is hardly convincing after the simple 23...♘f6. Polugaevsky's variation continues with 23 ♘f5 ♕e6 24 ♗h3 ♕c6, but now Black is squeezed in a bottleneck: the white knight comes back with great force (25 ♘d4) and Black's prospects are gloomy.

22	♗e5	♘e4
23	♗a1	♖ad8
24	♘e5	♕b6 (D)

This offers the possibility of a complicated combinational twist, but one which would not have turned out badly for Black. His position is not enviable, but Karpov is often at his very best when he really stands badly and is threatened by genuine danger.

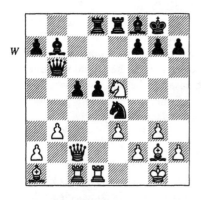

25 ♗xe4

The critical moment of the game. White's pieces are optimally placed and he has a subtle way of trying to take advantage of this immediately: 25 b4. According to Flohr in *Schach-Echo*, Karpov declared after the game that he had not feared that sharp move because he had the simple answer

25...♖c8 available. This shows a certain underestimation of the strength of White's position, since after 25 b4 ♖c8 26 ♗xe4 dxe4 27 ♘d7 White wins a pawn. If he were actually faced with the problem of 25 b4, the future World Champion would probably have solved it in another way, by accepting the challenge with 25...cxb4. After 26 ♕c7 Black has the following possibilities:

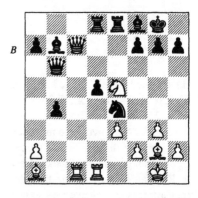

1) 26...♕xc7 27 ♖xc7 ♘c3 28 ♗xc3 bxc3 29 ♘xf7. Enklaar does not agree with Polugaevsky's assessment that White would now stand better, on account of 29...♖b8, after which he thinks that Black perhaps even has the advantage in view of his dangerous passed c-pawn and the fact that the white knight is out of play. However, White can eliminate these two perils with a single stroke: 30 ♘g5. The threat is 31 ♖xb7, and at the same time the c-pawn is hanging. There is not much else than 30...h6, after which White continues with 31 ♖xb7 hxg5

32 ♗xd5+ ♔h8 33 ♖xb8 ♖xb8 34 ♗e4 and retains good winning chances. On the other hand, 31 ♘h3 would be bad because of 31...♖bc8! 32 ♖xb7 c2 and White loses the exchange.

2) 26...♖e7. This move is not mentioned in any annotation, but it is an interesting attempt to fight back. The point is that after 27 ♕xb6 axb6 28 ♗xe4 f6 Black wins the piece back. White can then maintain a solid central position with 29 f4. Undoubtedly he has a big positional advantage here after, e.g., 29...♖ee8 (not 29...fxe5 30 ♗xe5 ♖ee8 31 ♗c7 etc.) 30 ♗c2! fxe5 31 ♗xe5 ♗c5 32 ♔f2, followed by 33 ♗b3. Therefore Black should play as sharply as possible in order to retain counter-chances: 29...fxe5 30 ♗xe5 ♖xe5! 31 fxe5 ♗c5 32 ♔g2 ♔f7 and now it is Black who will gain a central position. The weak pawn on e5 and the bishop pair constitute no mean compensation for the exchange.

However, White can improve on this variation. Dvoretsky gives 29 ♗xh7+! ♔xh7 30 ♘d3 and White wins a pawn without Black getting any compensation for it.

3) 26...f6. This is Black's best chance. Polugaevsky now gives the variation 27 ♕f7+ ♔h8 28 ♘d7 ♕b5 29 ♘xf6! ♘xf6 30 ♗xf6 ♕d7 31 ♖c7 ♕xf7 32 ♖xf7 gxf6 33 ♖xb7 with a big endgame advantage for White. This looks gloomy indeed for Black. However, he can play better: 28...♕d6! (instead of 28...♕b5) 29 ♘xf8 ♖e7. Undoubtedly White has the advantage

after 30 ♘g6+ hxg6 31 ♕xg6, but after 31...a5 Black is not without counterplay.

One can conclude, overall, that 25 b4 would definitely have led to an advantage for White. One cannot say that about the text-move. White gives up the bishop-pair in the hope of winning the c-pawn. The whole plan is called into question by a hidden finesse available to Black in a few moves; but, besides that, Black's solid position is certainly not worse.

Korchnoi, however, seems to have a different opinion about this. Compare his first match game against Petrosian in 1977. The opening moves were 1 c4 e6 2 g3 d5 3 ♗g2 ♘f6 4 ♘f3 ♗e7 5 0-0 0-0 6 d4 dxc4 7 ♘e5 ♘c6.

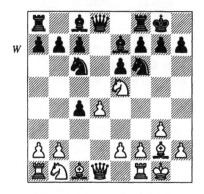

Here Korchnoi decided on the surprising 8 ♗xc6!? bxc6 9 ♘c3. The game continued 9...c5 10 dxc5 ♗xc5 11 ♕a4 ♘d5 12 ♘e4 ♘b6 13 ♕c2 ♗e7 14 ♘xc4 ♘xc4 15 ♕xc4 ♕d5 16 ♕c2 ♗b7 17 f3 ♕d4+ 18 ♔g2 and now Petrosian simplified with 18...♗xe4

19 ♕xe4 ♕xe4 20 fxe4 ♖fb8 21 b3
♗d6 22 ♗f4 ½-½.

Most experts discovered later that
Black could have obtained the advantage with 18...♖ad8, because the pair
of bishops was more important in that
position than Black's shattered queenside pawns. Korchnoi showed how
much he disagreed with this by telling
Ree, his second, that he had seriously
considered preventing Petrosian's
drawing simplification by playing 18
♘f2 instead of 18 ♔g2.

It would have been interesting to
see how Korchnoi would have done
against Fischer with the positions he
had against Karpov and Petrosian. Fischer, like no other player, knew how to
prove the strength of the bishop-pair
in all sorts of positions!

25 ...   dxe4
26 ♕c4

The Dutch player J. Krans points
out here the possibility of 26 ♘d7 in
order to exchange the bishop on f8.
On account of the chance that Black
has two moves later in the game,
viewed objectively this is probably the
best continuation. The position with
opposite-coloured bishops and major
pieces offers little chance of an advantage; on the other hand, White runs no
risk at all.

It is understandable that Korchnoi,
in ambitious mood as he was, re-
frained from 26 ♘d7. Less understandable is the fact that all the
commentators who mention Polugaevsky's discovery two moves later

pass this moment by (myself included,
in my original notes).

26 ...   ♕c7
27 b4 *(D)*

The consequence of the previous
move. The black position seems precarious because 27...♖xd1+ 28 ♖xd1
♖xe5 29 ♗xe5 ♕xe5 fails to 30 ♖d7.

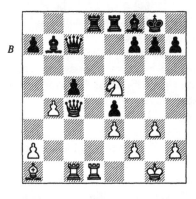

27 ...   ♖xd1+?

Missing the chance to show that the
white initiative is not so strong after
all, and for the first time to gain the
advantage based on the strength of his
defensive pieces: 27...♗d6! 28 ♘g4
cxb4! *(D)*.

This extremely subtle continuation
was overlooked by the grandmasters
in the press room and was discovered
only later by Polugaevsky in his analysis. The amazing point is 29 ♕d4
♗e5. Although many pieces are hanging, White has no fully satisfactory
way out. The best is 30 ♖xc7 ♖xd4 31
♖xd4 ♗xc7 32 ♖d7 (32 ♖xb4 ♗c8 is
even worse for White); still, Black
keeps an advantage with 32...♗c8 33

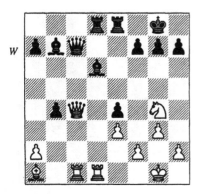

♘h6+! hxg6 34 ♖xc7 ♗h3. The white king is held more tightly in a potential mating net than the black king is.

Keene and Hartston, in their joint book on the match, mention that Korchnoi had seen 27...♗d6 when he was calculating 25 ♗xe4 but had assumed that Karpov would not find it. Personally, I do not attach much weight to this sort of pronouncement right after a game. Korchnoi very possibly did see the move: he is well-known for his highly developed powers of calculating sharp variations. But it seems to me an unnecessarily great risk to have assumed that Karpov would not see the same continuation two moves later – the more so since Korchnoi had an excellent alternative. The move 25 b4 would certainly have given his opponent very difficult problems.

Korchnoi's comment to the two English chess players is analogous to Karpov's telling Flohr that he had not feared 25 b4. The great tension of such a serious match does not permit one to show any sign of weakness which

might come to the attention of the enemy camp. One simply does not admit that one's powers failed at a particular moment or weakened to such an extent that a critical continuation was overlooked.

28 ♖xd1   ♗c8
29 bxc5   ♗e6

Black cannot take the minor exchange because his back rank is too weak: 29...♖xe5 30 ♗xe5 ♕xe5 31 ♖d8, and now Ree says the counterattack fails after 31...♕a1+ 32 ♔g2 ♗g4 33 ♕d4! (introducing the twist ♖xf8+ and ♕d8 mate into the position) 33...♗f3+ 34 ♔h3 ♕f1+ 35 ♔h4 g5+ (Black averts the mate of his own king but allows White's to escape) 36 ♔xg5 ♕h3 37 ♕d6! ♕g4+ 38 ♔f6 ♕g7+ 39 ♔f5 ♕g4+ 40 ♔e5 and the white king will escape from the checks, after which the c-pawn will decide the game in his favour.

30 ♕a4

Korchnoi continually works with little twists to keep his pawn advantage, at least temporarily.

30 ...   ♖c8
31 ♗d4   f6 (D)

If the knight now goes to c4 it will block the c-file. But Korchnoi finds yet another little something.

32 ♕a6   ♗d5

White can definitely keep the c-pawn after this. Much stronger is 32...♖e8! with the point that White loses his knight after 33 ♕c6 ♖e7. So he has nothing better than 34 ♘c4, and with 34...♗xc5 Black finally wins

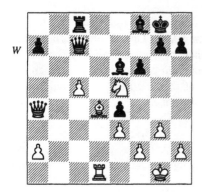
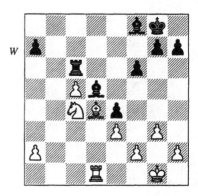

back the pawn with no problems. 'Roughly equal chances,' according to Polugaevsky; but, in my view, the better chances are more likely Black's, since he has the safer king position. It is important that 35 ♕b5, with the point 35...♖c8? 36 ♗xc5 ♕xc5 37 ♖d8+ and wins, achieves nothing because of 35...♖d8, and Black's position has already been strengthened.

33 ♘c4

White has finally reached what he had in mind: a solid extra pawn. Black cannot capture the c-pawn because of the same twist as in the previous note: 33...♗xc5 34 ♗xc5 ♕xc5 35 ♖xd5 ♕xc4 36 ♖d8+ , etc.

Another try to hold the pawn is 33 ♗b2, which would lead to a convincing result after 33...♕xc5 34 ♗a3!, but Black can parry the attack simply with 33...♕b7.

33 ...   ♕c6
34 ♕xc6   ♖xc6 (D)
35 ♖c1

Polugaevsky here gives a method to prevent Black's rook from exerting

pressure along the a-file: 35 ♘a5. The rook must then retreat since 35...♖a6 fails to 36 ♗c3, after which the c-pawn walks through unhindered. After 35...♖c7 36 ♘b3 White has consolidated his extra pawn, but without having real winning chances. It is true that Black cannot win the pawn back directly with 36...♗xb3 37 axb3 ♗xc5 because in the bishop ending after the continuation 38 ♖c1 ♗b6 39 ♖xc7 ♗xc7 40 ♗xa7 ♗d6 41 ♗d4 ♗b4 42 f3 f5 White really does have winning chances. Not, however, by walking his king over to the queenside, because then he can make no progress: 43 ♔f2 ♔f7 44 fxe4 fxe4 45 ♔e2 g6 46 ♔d1 ♔e6 47 ♔c2 ♔d5, and Black comes just in time. If 48 ♗c3, then 48...♗d6 49 ♗d2 ♗e5 follows. The b-pawn cannot advance because Black's king gets to c4. The winning attempt, therefore, is 43 ♔g2 ♔f7 44 fxe4 fxe4 45 ♔h3; White plans to penetrate the kingside in order to attack e4 and thus divert the black bishop from b4; for example, 45...h5 46 ♔h4! ♔g6 47 g4

♗e7+ 48 ♔h3 and White will gain ground.

There is no hurry to win the pawn back, of course. Black keeps the balance with the simple 36...♔f7, and White has nothing better than to position himself so as not to lose the c-pawn.

35	...	♔f7
36	a3	♖a6
37	♖c3	♔e6
38	♘d2	♔d7
39	f3 *(D)*	

With both players short of time, Korchnoi forces his opponent to make a small fundamental decision.

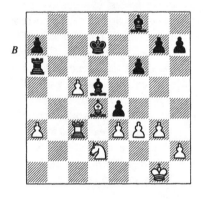

39 ... exf3

This adds some dynamism to the position, but it gives up space Black could have held with 39...f5. With this choice Karpov shows that he is not intent on simply insuring a draw.

40 ♔f2 ♖a5

Why not 40...♖a4 to prevent e3-e4? Enklaar explains in *Schaakbulletin* that the text-move is directed against 41 ♘xf3 and the plan of transferring the knight to d3. He gives the variation 41...♗xf3 42 ♔xf3 ♔c6 43 ♔e4 ♗xc5 44 ♔f5 ♔d6 (Enklaar actually gives 44...♔d5, but then White has the extra possibility 45 ♗xc5 ♖xc5 46 e4+ followed by the exchange of rooks) 45 ♖xc5 ♖xc5 46 ♗xc5+ ♔xc5 47 ♔e6 ♔c4 48 ♔f7 ♔b3 49 ♔xg7 ♔xa3 50 ♔xf6, and after the respective pawn marches, a queen endgame arises which Enklaar judges is drawn. In my view, however, it is won for White because of the bad position of the black king. Instead of this line, Black has a far more sober continuation: 41...♔c6 42 ♘e1 ♗e4 and now he can capture the knight without risk if it moves to d3, as he could also if the rook were on a4.

An acceptable explanation is that Black had one move to play before the time control and that 40...♖a5 was careless. After 40...♖a4 White would certainly not stand better any longer.

41 e4 ♗c6

The sealed move. All interim reports said that Korchnoi would be a pawn ahead with slight winning chances, according to Flohr in *Schach-Echo*. But, he added, Karpov had said after adjournment that he considered the position favourable for Black and would be playing for a win. 'A little fairy tale from the Moscow woods,' concluded the commentator jokingly – a childish way to treat a pronouncement by a man about to become the World Champion.

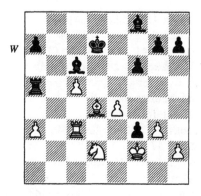

It is typical of Karpov's play, and one of his strong trumps, that in positions where he can get the worst of it or already stands clearly worse, he continues indefatigably, neither permitting a further worsening of his position nor losing sight of his possible winning chances. This is part of the profile of a real fighter at the highest level. A typical example was his game against Adorjan at Las Palmas 1977. The Hungarian grandmaster had the advantage from the opening, but he could not consolidate his advantage against the fast-moving World Champion and twice ran into time trouble. Just before the end, during his second bout of time trouble, he had a draw in hand but misplayed it, and Karpov finally won. I watched the post-mortem. At one point, when he was still in difficulties, the World Champion could have simplified to a drawn pawn-down endgame.

'Why didn't you play it then?' asked Adorjan 'Didn't you see it?' Karpov replied, 'I saw it, but why should I play it? If I keep the position as it is, I don't see how I can lose.'

Holding a position when one stands better is an art – or rather a technique – that many modern grandmasters have mastered. But the power to hold a position that is slightly worse is possessed only by the absolute greatest. Among them, Fischer was a shining example. In a lost position against Matulović in the 1971 Interzonal tournament, for instance, he avoided a draw by repetition of moves.

The third player worthy of adding to this list is Korchnoi. Very often he has been willing to allow his position to become critical in order to keep an extra pawn. In this game, his position at adjournment is not critical and his extra pawn hardly matters. He would not have doubted for a moment that he had good reason to play for a win. And had anyone told him afterwards what Karpov had thought about the position, he would have reacted with little more than a vague laugh. This is what makes their games against each other so hard, despite the often simplified positions.

42 ♔xf3   ♚e6

In his book *Anatoly Karpov, His Road to the World Championship*, Botvinnik writes that Karpov can head for a draw here with 42...♖a4 43 ♚e3 g6! 44 ♝xf6 ♖xa3 and adds:

'In this level position, Karpov plays for a win; dangerous tactics when a pawn down.' Didn't Botvinnik himself use to do that in his days of glory?

43 ♔e3

Karpov's remark after the game is characteristic: that 43 ♘c4 followed by 44 ♘d6 is the safest way to the draw here.

43 ...	♖a4
44 ♖b3	g6
45 ♔d3	a6

Preventing 46 ♘c4.

| 46 ♗e3 | ♗b5+ |
| 47 ♔c2 | f5 *(D)* |

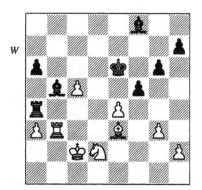

But this is much too optimistic. Black opens the position at a time when White is ready for action and thus White gets chances to realise his extra pawn. The position would remain balanced after 47...♗g7.

It is striking that Botvinnik is the only commentator who more-or-less approved of the text-move, on the grounds that Black must somehow put his initiative to use. This necessity, however, seems totally absent.

48 exf5+

White thus effortlessly rids himself of a weak pawn.

| 48 ... | gxf5 |

Flohr recommends 48...♔xf5, but after 49 ♗f2 Black would face the same problems as in the game.

| 49 ♗f2 | ♗g7 |

Karpov, apparently realising that he had played too adventurously, offered a draw here. Korchnoi; according to Flohr, answered only with a shrug of his shoulders.

50 ♖e3+	♔d7
51 ♖f3	♔e6
52 ♖e3+	♔d7
53 ♖f3	♔e6

White's repetition of moves not only wins time on the clock but also demonstrates that, at the moment, he is the only player who can choose whether to play for a win or a draw.

54 ♔b3

After this king move, Black's rook finds itself frequently in a compromised position. All this is a consequence of Black's 47th move.

54 ...	h5
55 ♖e3+	♔d7
56 ♘f3	

White's winning attempt is now beginning to gain momentum.

| 56 ... | ♗f6 |

Karpov continues as if nothing much was going on. It is high time to aim for further pawn exchanges to free the black rook. Better is 56...f4 and then 57...♗f6 only if White's rook retreats with 57 ♖e1. The difference is that now White will be able to move his rook laterally after the knight reaches a more active post than f3.

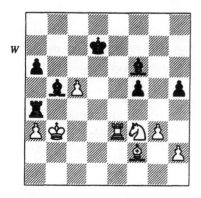

57 ℤe1

But after this, White's winning chances are minimal. Korchnoi was probably tempted by the positional threat 58 ♗d4, but this can be adequately countered. The commentators unanimously gave the strong 57 ♘e5+ here. Black has only one reasonable square for the king: c8 (not 57...♔c7 58 ♘g6 and Black cannot offer the exchange of rooks with 58...ℤe4 due to 59 ℤxe4 fxe4 60 ♘f4). After 57...♔c8 58 ♘f7 f4, Polugaevsky, who probably spent little time on the analysis of this position, continues with 59 ♘d6+ ♔d7 60 gxf4 ℤxf4 61 ♗g3 with winning chances for White.

This piece of shoddy analysis was gratuitously repeated by Botvinnik and was also printed in *Chess Informant*, in *Three Matches of Karpov* and in *The Games of Anatoly Karpov*. Once again we see how little trouble is taken with the games of today's top players.

Enklaar shows that Black can easily draw by placing his bishop on the square vacated by the black rook: 61...♗a4+ 62 ♔a2 ℤf1 and Black certainly does not stand worse.

There is, of course, no reason to tempt the rook to improve its position with gain of tempo. After 57 ♘e5+ ♔c8 58 ♘f7 f4 59 ℤf3 fxg3 60 ♗xg3 there would be real winning chances for White – for the first and last time in the game!

57 ...   f4
58 ♘e5+

One move too late, says Botvinnik, and he gives the variation 58 ♗d4 ♗xd4 59 ℤd1 ♔c6 (if 59...♗e2, 60 ℤd2 or 59...fxg3 60 ♘xd4 ♔c7 61 hxg3) 60 ℤxd4 ℤxd4 61 ♘xd4+ ♔xc5 62 ♘e6+, etc. However, as Ree noted in his comments for a Dutch news service, Black easily holds the draw with 59...fxg3 60 ♘xd4 ♔c8 61 hxg3 ℤc4 62 ♘xb5 axb5 63 ℤd5 h4, and on 64 gxh4 ℤxh4 65 ℤd6 the rook goes right back with 65...ℤc4.

It is remarkable that Botvinnik overlooked this fairly simple possibility. Having taken it upon himself to write a book on Karpov's rise to the top, he would have been expected to pay a great deal of attention to the analysis. As it turns out, unfortunately, there is no evidence of that kind of attention in the book.

58 ...   ♔c8 (D)
59 ♘f7   fxg3

This is the same position that would have arisen if Black had continued 56...f4. In principle, it would now be favourable for White to recapture with

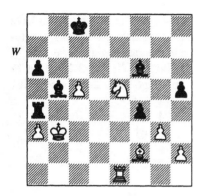

the bishop to hinder a possible exchange of kingside pawns, but if 60 ♗xg3 then 60...h4 gains space for Black.

60 ♘d6+   ♚d7
61 hxg3

If 61 ♗xg3 then again 61...h4 followed by 62...♖g4. Not, however, 61...♗d4? as given by Enklaar, because the pawn endgame arising after 62 ♖e4! ♗xc5 63 ♖xa4 ♗xa4+ 64 ♚xa4 ♗xd6 65 ♗xd6 ♚xd6 66 ♚a5 is won for White: 66...h4 67 ♚xa6 ♚c6 68 h3! ♚c7 69 ♚b5 and White catches the h-pawn while the black king cannot get back to f8 in time.

61 ...   ♖g4
62 ♘xb5   axb5
63 ♖h1

This looks awkward. Now, however, in a rook endgame in which he is two pawns down, Karpov demonstrates his great skill in defending bad endgames.

63 ...   ♚c6!
64 ♖xh5   ♗d4
65 ♗xd4   ♖xd4

The black pieces are very well placed. White cannot win because of his weak a-pawn.

66 ♖g5   ♖e4
67 g4   ♖a4 *(D)*

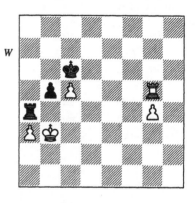

68 ♚b2

After the game Karpov showed that 68 ♖g8 also leads to a draw after the continuation 68...♚xc5 69 g5 ♖g4 70 g6 ♖g3+ 71 ♚c2 ♚c4 72 g7 ♖g2+ 73 ♚d1 ♚b3 74 a4 ♖g1+ 75 ♚d2 ♖g2+ 76 ♚d3 ♖g3+ 77 ♚e4 and now the white king is far enough from the queenside for Black to give up his rook: 77...bxa4 78 ♖b8+ ♚c2 79 g8♛ ♖xg8 80 ♖xg8 a3, etc.

Botvinnik gives another way to draw: 70...♚c6 (instead of 70...♖g3+) 71 ♚c3 ♚b7 72 ♚d3 ♖a4 73 ♚e3 ♖xa3+ 74 ♚f4 ♖a1 75 ♖e8 ♖g1 76 ♖e6 ♚c7 77 ♚f5 ♚d7 78 ♖e5 b4 79 ♚f6 (79 ♖b5 ♚e7) 79...♖f1+ 80 ♚g7 ♚c6.

Finally, Enklaar adds yet a third drawing method: 70...♚b6 71 ♚c3 ♚b7 72 ♚d3 b4; however, this needs to be carried further: 73 axb4 ♖xb4 74 ♖f8 ♖g4 75 ♖f6 ♔c7 76 ♔e3 ♔d7 77 ♔f3 ♖g1 78 ♔f4 ♔e7 and Black is just in time.

It is striking that White has no real winning chances at all despite his two extra pawns. A rare case.

68	...	♖f4
69	♔c2	♖f3
70	♔b2	♖f2+
71	♔c3	♖f3+
72	♔d4	♖f4+
73	♔e5	♖a4
74	♖g8	

Although a draw would still have been unavoidable, a sharper conclusion to the game would have been 74 ♔e6 ♖xa3 75 ♖e5 ♖g3 76 g5 b4 77 ♔f7 b3 78 g6 b2 79 ♖e1 ♔xc5 80 ♖b1 ♖g2 81 g7 ♖f2+.

74	...	♖xa3
75	g5	♔xc5
76	g6	♖g3
77	♖c8+	♔b4
78	♔f6	♖f3+
79	♔e6	♖g3
80	♔f7	♔a3
81	g7	½-½

Game Thirteen
Gulko – Timman
International Tournament, Sombor 1974
French Defence, Winawer Variation

When I was awarded the Grandmaster title during the 1974 FIDE Congress, a new world opened up for me. Previously I had grabbed with both hands every conceivable opportunity to play in tournaments, even in Russia, where one receives rubles that cannot be converted into another currency. Now a fairly varied assortment of attractive tournaments awaited me. I made a quick selection and decided that I would spend a few months travelling from tournament to tournament. The journey began in the United States, continued in Yugoslavia, and finally I arrived in Venice. One night, after having played in four tournaments in as many months, a large part of my money was stolen in a bar in Florence, so I decided, after due consideration, to go home. I had just enough money left for the return trip.

The game against Gulko was played in the second round of the tournament in Sombor, Yugoslavia. Later it became clear that this game was a struggle between the tournament winners. The play well reflected my lifestyle at that time: exciting, adventurous, and full of surprises.

Almost four years later I met Gulko again in Yugoslavia, in Nikšić. The tournament here was incomparably stronger than in Sombor, but we too had made progress. Once again we shared the first prize. For both of us it signified a milestone in our chess careers. I was very impressed with the fresh, imaginative play of the likeable Muscovite and did not doubt that he would become one of the world's top players. Things turned out differently. A year afterwards, on 15 May 1979, he applied for an exit visa to go to Israel. No reply came from the Soviet authorities, but, together with his wife – one of the best female players in the Soviet Union – Gulko was removed from the national rating list. He was no longer permitted to play in tournaments of any importance.

When I saw him again in Moscow on 24 April 1981 he was in a bad way. He had just come from the Emigration Office, where he had finally been given a reply to his application: a negative reply. With this reply, officialdom won – at least for the time being – the unequal struggle against an incorruptible, imaginative chess player.

| 1 | e4 | e6 | 3 | ♘c3 | ♝b4 |
| 2 | d4 | d5 | 4 | ♝d2 | |

An old variation in which White temporarily offers two pawns. Boleslavsky had a particular preference for it in the 1950's.

4   ...   dxe4
5   ♕g4   ♕xd4
6   0-0-0   h5

This move brought the variation into disuse. The queen must move to another square at an inopportune moment for White.

7   ♕h4 *(D)*

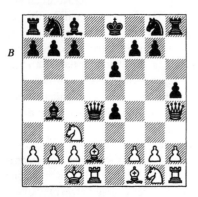

A suggestion by Keres which had never appeared in practice, although, as Gulko told me, he had played the move in a number of speed games. The usual move is 7 ♕g3, but Black has the better chances after 7...♗d6 8 ♗f4 h4! 9 ♕g5 (9 ♕g4 ♘f6) 9...♕f6 10 ♕xf6 ♘xf6 11 ♗xd6 cxd6 12 ♘b5 ♘a6 (Lundquist-Uhlmann, Marianske Lazne 1961).

7   ...   ♗e7
8   ♗g5   ♕e5

Theory is 8...♕c5 9 ♘xe4 ♗xg5+ 10 ♘xg5 ♘c6 with better play for

Black. I think this judgement is incorrect as after 11 ♘1f3 ♘f6 12 ♕f4! Black has great difficulty protecting his c-pawn; e.g., 12...e5 13 ♖e1, or 12...♕e7 13 ♗b5, or, finally, 12...♕b6 13 ♗c4. In all cases White has excellent attacking chances for the pawn.

9   ♘xe4   f6! *(D)*

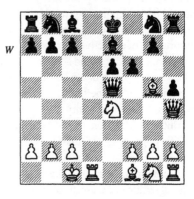

The point of the previous move. If White withdraws the bishop, then 10...g5 follows and the knight on e4 cannot be saved. After some thought, Gulko decides to make a virtue of necessity and boldly offers a piece.

10   ♘f3!   fxg5

In exchange for the piece, White, of course, has a tremendous advantage in development and fine attacking chances, especially due to the open centre. I put my faith in my pair of bishops and my partial control of the dark squares. Later, however, I was a little unhappy that I had permitted such a storm to break over my head.

The alternative is 10...♕f5, to offer the exchange of queens with 11...♕g4 and enter the endgame a solid pawn ahead. White cannot prevent this with 11 h3 because Black then uses the won tempo with 10...fxg5 11 ♘exg5 ♗d6, again with the threat of exchanging queens. White is not without chances after 11 ♗d3 ♕g4 12 ♗e3, due to his centralised pieces and advantage in development; but Black's compact pawn structure makes it difficult to find compensation.

11 ♘exg5   ♕f6

Now it is not possible to aim for the exchange of queens with 11...♕f5 because White mates prettily with 12 ♗d3 ♕g4 13 ♗g6+ ♔f8 14 ♘h7+ ♖xh7 15 ♖d8+ and mate next move.

12 ♗b5+!

The correct way for White to make use of his chances. After 12 ♗c4 ♘c6 13 ♖he1 ♘d8 Black is indeed somewhat cramped, but there are no really vulnerable points.

12 ...   c6

This takes the c6-square from the knight, but there is no decent alternative, as the following shows: 12...♗d7 (12...♘c6 13 ♕e4 ♗d7 leads to variation 1) 13 ♕e4! and now:

1) 13...♘c6 14 ♖xd7! ♔xd7 15 ♗xc6+ bxc6 16 ♘e5+ ♔c8 17 ♘gf7, and although Black is a full rook up, his position is in ruins.

2) 13...♗xb5 14 ♕xb7 ♗c6 15 ♕c8+ ♗d8 16 ♖xd8+ (this game is all sacrifices) 16...♕xd8 17 ♕xe6+ and Black either loses his entire material advantage after 17...♘e7 18 ♕f7+ ♔d7 19 ♖d1+ ♔c8 20 ♖xd8+ ♔xd8

21 ♘e5 with a continuing White attack, or gets mated after 17...♕e7 18 ♕c8+ ♕d8 19 ♖e1+ ♘e7 20 ♖xe7+ (the final sacrifice) 20...♔xe7 21 ♕e6+ ♔f8 22 ♕f7 mate.

These variations give a good picture of how strongly the white pieces combine in the attack.

13 ♗c4   b5

A necessary move. Black prepares to develop his knight via a6 so that it may support the threatened e6-point from c7 and may possibly go to d5. The immediate 13...♘a6 fails because the black position is too weakened after 14 ♗xa6 bxa6. Gulko then intended 15 ♕c4 e5 16 ♖d2! with the threat 17 ♘xe5, and things remain extremely difficult for Black after, say, 16...♘h6 17 ♖e1 with continuing heavy pressure.

14 ♗xb5 *(D)*

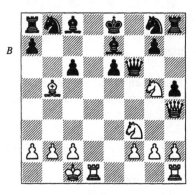

I must honestly admit that I had completely overlooked this move; or, to put it less strongly, I had not considered that White would slow his attack to win this pawn. It is easy to understand that, in practice, you do not worry at all about the loss of a pawn when you are in a precarious defensive position fending off an opponent who is a full piece down. It is even one of the principles of defence to return material at the right moment. In this case it occurred unconsciously.

Anyway, I had come to the conclusion that 14 ♗b3 ♘a6 15 ♕e4 e5 offered sufficient defensive chances because of the threat ...♘a6-c5.

14 ...   e5

I was not at all shocked by my oversight and played the text-move fairly quickly. But not too quickly: as I indicated in the notes to the 19th game of the Spassky-Fischer match (game 9 in this book), a too-quick response can be a sign of shock – to your opponent and to yourself. I did not like 14...cxb5 15 ♕e4 ♕f5 16 ♕xa8 ♗xg5+ 17 ♘xg5 ♕xg5+ 18 ♖d2! ♕f4 19 ♖hd1, and White has strong attacking possibilities.

15 ♗c4

Back to an excellent post, but with his next move Black can make strong use of the won tempo.

15 ...   ♗g4

With the threat 16...♗xf3. Black now takes the initiative for a while.

16 ♕g3   ♘d7! *(D)*

This required careful calculation.

Just as he could have done on the previous move, Black can exchange queens here, but after 16...♕f4+ 17 ♕xf4 exf4 18 ♖he1 his king remains

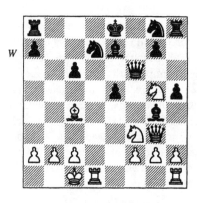

in a wasp's nest while White's pieces combine perfectly; e.g.:

1) 18...♘f6 19 ♗f7+ ♔f8 20 ♘e5 ♗f5 21 ♗e6! ♗xe6 22 ♘g6+ and the black position collapses.

2) 18...♘h6 19 ♘e6 ♗xe6 20 ♖xe6 and Black is tied hand and foot.

3) 18...♘d7. Perhaps the best. After 19 ♘f7 Black can return the exchange with 19...♖h6. But with 19 ♖d4 White can maintain the pressure.

17 ♘f7

This seems promising for White, but now we see the point of Black's last move.

17 ...   ♘h6
18 ♘xh8   ♘f5

The white queen is trapped. Gulko, however, still finds a way out.

19 ♗f7+

Also winning the queen. Black's king has no good flight square: if 19...♔d8 then simply 20 ♕xe5, or 19...♔f8 20 ♘g6+ ♔xf7 21 ♘fxe5+ ♘xe5 22 ♘xe5+ ♔e8 23 ♘xg4 with win of material.

19 ...   ♕xf7

20	♘xf7	♘xg3
21	hxg3	♔xf7 *(D)*

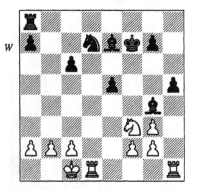

The dust has settled and Black has more or less emerged the victor. White is not without chances, however, since Black has three isolated pawns and White therefore has good squares for his knight.

At this stage, each player had only about twenty minutes left. It is not usual for so many complications to occur in only twenty-one moves, and the nervous tension they have generated is evident in the next part of the game.

22 ♖he1

Better is 22 ♖xd7 ♗xd7 23 ♘xe5+ ♔e6 24 ♘xd7 ♔xd7 25 ♖xh5. White would then have three pawns for the piece, but no really strong majority on either wing (note the doubled pawns).

22	...	♗f6
23	♖d6	♖c8
24	♘d2	

White strives purposefully to hold the initiative.

24	...	♔e7
25	♖d3	♗f5

The first of a series of inferior moves. Although this does not give his advantage away, the square chosen for the bishop is not the most desirable one. 25...♗e6 is better.

26 ♖b3

White also does not take full advantage of his chances. The next move shows that the text loses a tempo.

26	...	♖c7
27	♖a3	♔f7
28	♖a5	g6 *(D)*

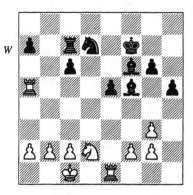

Anticipating a possible f2-f4.

29 ♘c4   ♔g7

But this is really an important tempo loss. The correct 29...♗e6 gives Black the clearly better play.

30 ♘d6

Suddenly threatening to win a rook in broad daylight.

30 ...   ♔f8

31 ♘xf5   gxf5

White has finally achieved something concrete. Black's bishop-pair has been liquidated and his pawns are hanging. But what now?

32 ♖h1

The wrong method. White wins a relatively unimportant pawn in exchange for two tempi. It is better to direct his attention toward the queenside with 32 ♖e3. After 32...♗e7 the play remains sharp but probably balanced; but not 32...♗g5+ 33 f4.

32	...	♔f7
33	♖xh5	♔g6
34	♖h1	e4

Black has won valuable time. His pieces co-operate excellently.

35 b3

White, in his haste, prevents Black from manoeuvring his knight to c4, but in so doing he further weakens his position. Better is 35 ♖d1 ♘b6 36 ♖a6 with a playable game.

35	...	♗d4
36	f3	

Black thus gets a winning passed pawn, but the alternative 36 ♖f1 ♘e5 was just as unattractive.

36	...	♗c3
37	♖a4	♘b6
38	♖a6	♖d7

White has just managed to save his rook, but the text-move now cuts off his king and threatens to walk the passed pawn through unchallenged. Less clear is 38...e3 39 ♔d1 and the white king reaches e2.

39 ♖d1

In desperation White sacrifices the exchange. There was no alternative, of course.

39	...	♗b2+
40	♔xb2	♖xd1
41	♖xa7 *(D)*	

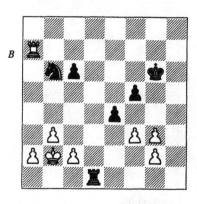

41	...	♘d5

The sealed move. The line I had in mind does not throw the win away, but it makes it considerably more difficult. In my exhaustion, it escaped me that 41...♔f6 wins outright. After 42 fxe4 fxe4 43 ♖h7 ♘d5 (clearer than 43...e3, when White starts checking on the h-file and Black's king will be unable to penetrate the third rank because of White's doubled g-pawns, and if the king attacks the rook, White puts it behind the e-pawn; e.g., 44 ♖h6+ ♔f5 45 ♖h5+ ♔g4 46 ♖e5 ♖e1 – or 46...♘d5 47 c4 – 47 a4 and the win, if there still is one, is much more difficult) 44 ♖h6+ ♔e5 45 ♖h5+ ♔d4 46 ♖h6 e3 47 ♖e6 and now Black has two ways to win: the prosaic 47...♖d2 48 ♔c1 ♘b4 and the charming 47...♘c3 48 ♖d6+ ♔e5 49 ♖xd1 ♘xd1+ 50 ♔c1 ♘f2 51 c3 (otherwise ...♔d4-c3) 51...♔f5 52 a4 ♔g4 53 a5 ♔xg3 54 a6

♘d3+ 55 ♔c2 e2 56 a7 e1♕ 57 a8♕
♕e2+ and mates.

42 c4   e3

The point of the last move. Black
wins the rook for a few pawns.

43 cxd5   e2
44 ♖e7   e1♕
45 ♖xe1   ♖xe1
46 dxc6   ♖e6

The game is not without interest.
Black reduces the white pawn advantage to four, but now the b-pawn advances with tempo.

47 b4   ♖xc6
48 b5   ♖e6

The second-best square for the
rook. Centralisation is in itself to be
recommended, but 48...♖d6 is more
suitable for this purpose. The position
is still a win – by a hair.

49 ♔c3   ♔f6 (D)

The king must of course be brought
more into play before Black can start
grabbing pawns.

50 ♔d4   ♔e7
51 a4

Loses without a chance. White
should continue his centralisation
with 51 ♔d5, but even then Black's
win is not very difficult after 51...♖e2

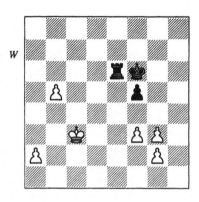

W

52 a4 ♔d7 53 a5 ♖xg2 54 ♔e5 ♖xg3
55 f4 ♖b3 with an elementary win.

51 ...   ♔d6
52 a5   ♖e5!

The simplest. The white king's route
to the kingside is definitely cut off.

53 ♔c4   ♖c5+
54 ♔b4   ♖c2

The rest is not difficult.

55 g4   fxg4
56 fxg4   ♖xg2
57 a6   ♖xg4+
58 ♔a5   ♔c7
59 b6+   ♔c6
60 a7   ♔b7
61 ♔b5   ♖g6
62 ♔c5   ♖h6

0-1

Game Fourteen
Gligorić – Portisch
Hoogoven Tournament, Wijk aan Zee 1975
Nimzo-Indian Defence

'I always watch their games with excitement, mainly because it is a battle of ideas. They do not just play moves, there is something more involved – they know how to raise their play to the highest level of classical chess.' So wrote Kavalek in his introduction to this game in the tournament book. The praise is high but not out of place. It is no accident that two games between these players are found in the present book.

This time Portisch is the winner. He employs a carefully nurtured improvement on a game between them which Gligorić had won fourteen years earlier. The novelty has the desired effect; although Black seems to become rather cramped, in fact he slowly but surely gathers all the positional trumps. At one point he accelerates this process – unnecessarily, as Kavalek showed afterwards. The resulting endgame contains unusually subtle manoeuvres. Gligorić soon goes wrong and Portisch finishes the job with merciless precision.

1	d4	♘f6
2	c4	e6
3	♘c3	♗b4
4	e3	b6
5	♘e2	♗a6

In a later round in this tournament I tried the controversial 5...♘e4 against Donner. He answered with the surprising 6 ♕c2 f5 7 g3! and after 7...♘xc3 8 ♘xc3 ♗b7 9 d5 b5? he could have gained a great advantage with 10 ♗d2! (instead of 10 ♗g2). Probably 6...♗b7 (instead of 6...f5) is more accurate.

6	♘g3	♗xc3+
7	bxc3	d5
8	cxd5	

An unusual but not unknown move which probably does not offer much.

| 8 | ... | ♗xf1 |
| 9 | ♔xf1 | ♕xd5 |

Capturing with the e-pawn would give White the position he wants after 10 f3.

| 10 | ♕d3 | ♘bd7 |

The game mentioned in the introduction, Gligorić-Portisch, Torremolinos 1961, continued 10...♘c6 11 e4 ♕d7 12 ♗g5 ♘g8 13 ♔e2 f6 14 ♗c1 ♘ge7 with equal chances (Gligorić). A possible improvement is 12 ♗a3.

With the text-move Black achieves a more harmonious development of his pieces.

| 11 | e4 | ♕a5 |

The point of the previous move.

| 12 | e5 | *(D)* |

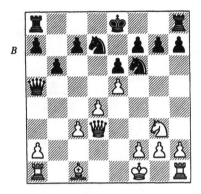

Typical of the opportunistic play of which Gligorić showed several glimpses in this Hoogoven tournament. (Compare Gligorić-Hort, for example: 1 d4 d5 2 c4 c6 3 ♘f3 ♘f6 4 ♘c3 dxc4 5 a4 ♘a6 6 e4 ♗g4 7 e5? ♘d7 8 ♗xc4 e6 9 0-0 ♗e7 10 h3 ♗h5 11 a5 ♘b4 12 ♘e4 0-0 13 ♗f4 ♘d5 14 ♗h2 ♗b4 and Black stood excellently.) Here too it gives him little satisfaction. The simple 12 f3 followed by 13 ♔f2 is better, with roughly equal play.

12	...	♘d5
13	c4	♘b4
14	♕b3	♘c6
15	♗b2	0-0
16	♗c3	♕a6
17	♕b5	

At first sight White seems to have a lot of play. The exchange of queens with 17...♕xb5 18 cxb5 ♘e7 19 ♗b4 ♖fe8 20 ♗xe7 ♖xe7 21 ♔e2 gives him comfortable pressure, and otherwise it seems Black will be driven back. This is an illusion, however; White must lose time getting his h-rook into

play, time which Black gratefully uses to direct his solid mass of pieces against the weakened White centre.

17	...	♕b7
18	♖e1	

Threatening the push 19 d5.

| 18 | ... | ♖fd8 *(D)* |

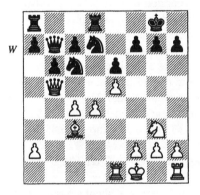

A nice line-up. If 19 d5, then 19...exd5 20 cxd5 ♘e7 21 e6 ♕xd5!. White's actions are not dangerous so long as his king's rook is not participating, which explains the next move.

19	h4	♘f8
20	♖e4	♘e7
21	h5	♘f5

White is kept busy. Now his pawn structure gets a little worse.

22	♖f4	♘xg3+
23	fxg3	c5
24	♖hh4	cxd4
25	♖xd4	h6

A little dubious. White gets a point to hit at, as we will soon see.

| 26 | ♕b1 | |

The queen was indeed a little out of play.

26	...	♖xd4
27	♖xd4	♕c7
28	♕e4	♖c8
29	♗b4	♘d7
30	♗d6	♕c6
31	♕e2 *(D)*	

Exchanging queens would have disastrous consequences. White's bishop, after all, is reasonably placed only for attacking purposes.

By refusing the exchange, White prepares a subtle action which would seem to find its best expression after a slow move like 31...a6 (intending 32...b5) and now: 32 g4! b5 33 g5 hxg5 (or 33...bxc4 34 gxh6 gxh6 35 ♖g4+, etc.) 34 ♕g4 bxc4 35 ♕xg5 ♕b5 36 ♖g4 ♕b1+ 37 ♔f2 ♕h7 38 ♖xc4 and White has all the play.

In America, at about the same time, the analyst Lubosh Kavalek found the same variation independently, but he also found in it a winning method for Black. He writes in his book (*Wijk aan Zee Grandmaster Chess Tournament 1975*, published by R.H.M. Press) that after 33 g5! White suddenly becomes a tiger; Kavalek gives the variation 33...hxg5 34 ♕g4 bxc4 35 ♕xg5 ♕b5 36 ♖g4! ♕b1+ (the same as my analysis) and all ends well for the white king. However, Kavalek produces the powerful move 34...♕b6! (instead of 34...bxc4) and White has no defence; e.g., 35 c5! ♘xc5 36 ♕xg5 ♘b3!!. Lubosh gives other variations too, but this is sufficient; he has examined the position very thoroughly and analysed it sharply.

With the next move Black sacrifices a pawn, which required sharp, intuitive calculation.

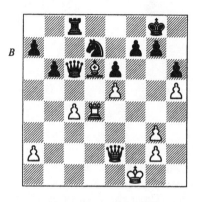

B

31	...	b5

At the cost of a pawn Black's forces will penetrate White's camp. Perhaps 31...a6 is more precise, as indicated above, but Portisch's decision is an excellent practical one.

32	cxb5	♕c1+
33	♖d1	♕g5
34	g4	♘b6
35	♔g1	♖c4 *(D)*

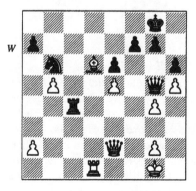

W

All three black pieces have suddenly left their modest rearward positions and have landed on vital squares.

36 &b8   ♖xg4
37 &xa7   ♘d5
38 ♖xd5

Forced, because Black's threats are getting serious.

38 ...   exd5
39 e6

Again the best.

39 ...   ♖e4

Black must watch out, as we can see from 39...fxe6? 40 ♕xe6+ ♔h8 41 ♕e8+ ♔h7 42 ♕g6+! ♕xg6 43 hxg6+ ♔xg6 44 b6 ♖b4 45 a4 and Black can just manage to draw.

40 exf7+   ♔xf7
41 ♕f3+   ♔g8
42 &f2

White must of course attend to his safety.

42 ...   ♕c1+
43 ♔h2   ♕f4+

Although this endgame should not have led to a win for Black, it is his best chance.

44 ♕xf4   ♖xf4 *(D)*
45 &c5?

White immediately makes the decisive mistake – something of a surprise, since the time-trouble phase is over. With the most natural move, 45 ♔g3, White keeps the choice of a square for his bishop open while bringing the king closer to the e5 square, where it is generally headed anyway, and thus he would keep the draw in hand. Hans Böhm and I finally completed the

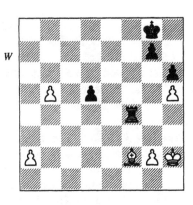

hellish task of examining this whole thing. The variations run 45 ♔g3 ♖a4 46 b6 *(D)* and now:

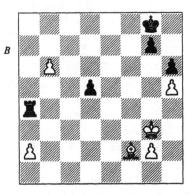

1) 46...♖xa2 47 &d4!. The difference from the game shows primarily in this variation. If 47...♖d2 48 &e5, or if 47...♖a4 48 &c5. In neither case can Black stop the dangerous march of the white king to e5.

2) 46...♔f7 is more accurate. The black king rushes to the centre while the rook is keeping the white bishop out of d4. Now is the time for White to play 47 &c5, after which Black must

manoeuvre very delicately: 47...♖xa2 48 ♔f4 ♔e6 49 ♗d4 ♖a4 50 ♔e3 ♔f7 51 ♗c5 (51 ♗c3 loses quickly to 51...♖a3 52 ♔d4 ♖b3 53 ♗a5 ♖b5, etc.) 51...♖c4! 52 ♗d6 ♖c3+ and now:

2a) 53 ♔d4 ♖b3 and White now has three options:

2a1) 54 ♗c5 ♔e6. The culmination of the manoeuvres principally devised by Hans Böhm. White is in *zugzwang* and is out-manoeuvred after 55 g4 ♖f3 56 ♗b4 ♖f4+ 57 ♔c5 ♖c4+ 58 ♔b5 ♔d7 59 ♗a5 ♔c8 60 ♔a6 ♔b8.

2a2) 54 ♗c7 ♖b5 (the white king cannot be permitted to reach c5) 55 ♔e5 ♔e7 56 ♔f5 (an idea of Tabe Bas: 56 ♗d6+ ♔d7 57 ♗f8 is refuted by 57...d4+ and 58...♖g5) 56...♔d7 57 ♔g6 d4 58 ♗f4 ♖xb6 59 ♔xg7 d3 60 g4 ♖b4 61 ♗xh6 ♖xg4+ 62 ♔f7 ♖h4 63 ♔g6 ♖h2 and Black is going to win the endgame by one tempo, as can be verified without much difficulty.

Dvoretsky thought that White can get a draw in this variation with 57 g4 d4+ 58 ♔e4. Initially I thought that this was correct, until I found a conclusive winning line for Black. It runs as follows: 58...♔c6 59 ♔xd4 ♖g5 60 ♗d8 ♖xg4+ 61 ♔e5 g6 62 hxg6 ♖xg6 and, because the white king is cut off, the h-pawn runs through. Only with a bishop on f2 and a king on f3 would White hold the draw.

2a3) 54 ♔c5. In this line the prettiest variations may arise: 54...d4! 55 ♗f4. In passing it should be noted that 55 ♔xd4 ♖xb6 loses. This position is only drawn if White's g-pawn, advanced to g4, can be protected by the king. In order to do this the white king must reach e4 in time, but this occurs in practically no variation. Returning to the position after 55 ♗f4: 55...d3 (on 55...♔e6 there may follow 56 g4 with the idea of 57 g5) 56 ♔c6 (now there is no time for 56 g4 due to 56...♖b2 and 57...d2) 56...♔e6 57 b7 ♔f5 58 ♗e3 ♔g4! 59 ♗b6 d2 60 b8♕ d1♕.

Originally I thought that this amazing position was definitive for the assessment of White's drawing chances after 45 ♔g3. Black escapes from White's checks in the nick of time: 61 ♕c8+ ♔xh5 62 ♕f5+ g5 63 ♕f7+ (the quiet 63 ♗c5 does not help after the even more quiet 63...♖d3!!) 63...♔g4 64 ♕e6+ ♔g3 65 ♕h3+ ♔f4 66 ♗c7+ ♔e4 67 ♕e6+ ♔d3 etc.

A fantastic overall concept, but Black can win more prosaically. Dvoretsky gives the variation 56...♖b2 (instead of 56...♔e6) 57 b7 d2! 58 ♗xd2 ♖c2+ 59 ♔b6 ♖xd2 60 b8♕ ♖b2+ with liquidation to a won pawn ending.

Therefore White must pursue his hopes of a draw in another direction.

2b) 53 ♔f4 ♖b3 54 ♗c5 ♔e6 55 g4!. Not 55 ♗d4 ♖b4 56 ♔e3 ♔f5! and White is driven back, as Hübner showed. But now Black cannot make further progress. Hans Böhm, who still tried to show that Black was winning, could hardly produce anything else; e.g., 55...♖c3 56 ♗f8 ♖c4+ 57 ♔f3 ♔f7 58 ♗d6, etc.

3) 46...♖c4. A last try by Böhm. Black wants to take both central squares, c5 and d4, from the bishop, but risks only danger after 47 ♗e1.

45	...	♖a4
46	b6	♖xa2
47	♔g3	♖c2! (D)

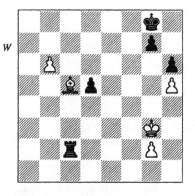

The difference from the variations with 45 ♔g3 now becomes clear. If 48 ♗d4 ♖c4 49 ♗e5 ♖b4 with an easy win.

48	♗d6	♖b2
49	♗c5	♔f7
50	♔f4	♔e6
51	g4	

The same losing line as in 2b above arises after 51 ♗d4 ♖b4 52 ♔e3 ♔f5.

51	...	♖b1
52	♔e3	♖f1
53	♔d4	♖f4+
54	♔d3	♖f7 (D)

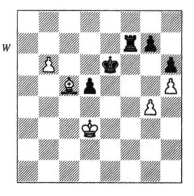

A simple, efficient winning plan: b7 and g7 are held under control simultaneously.

55	♔d4	♖b7
56	♔e3	♔e5
57	♔d3	

If 57 ♗d4+ ♔d6, etc.

| 57 | ... | ♔f4 |

0-1

Game Fifteen
Geller – Spassky
Alekhine Memorial Tournament, Moscow 1975
Sicilian Defence, Closed System

Geller had a great year in 1975. Although he was already over fifty, he won the very strong Alexander Memorial in Teesside with open-minded, fresh play. An even stronger tournament began in Moscow a month later. All the prominent Russian players except Karpov competed; for Korchnoi, it would prove to be his last tournament on Russian soil. Geller won again, half a point ahead of Spassky – a very respectable result for the latter when you consider that the Soviet Chess Federation had not allowed him to play outside his home country for more than a year.

The decisive game of the tournament began with an absorbing trench-warfare type of positional battle which culminated in a hair-raising time scramble in which Spassky made the last mistake.

1	e4	c5
2	♘f3	e6
3	d3	

Geller rarely chooses a quiet system.

3	...	♘c6
4	g3	d6

One may call this a slight inaccuracy, and we will soon see why.

5	♗g2	g6
6	0-0	♗g7
7	c3	e5
8	a3	

Usually this is the move when Black has played ...♘ge7 instead of ...d6. Under the present circumstances, 8 ♘h4 should definitely be considered; for example, 8...♘ge7 9 f4 exf4 10 gxf4 f5 11 exf5 ♘xf5 12 ♖e1+ ♔f8 13 ♘f3 and Black is in difficulties. The difference is that in the set-up without 4...d6 Black can answer 8 ♘h4 with the immediate 8...d5, profiting by the decentralised position of the white knight.

8	...	♘f6

Remarkably, Spassky once again plays inaccurately. The text-move delays the advance ...f7-f5, a vital move for Black in many situations. Very satisfactory play can be obtained with 8...♘ge7; e.g., 9 b4 0-0 10 ♗e3 b6 11 ♕d2 ♗a6! 12 ♖d1 ♕c7 13 ♗h6 ♖ad8 14 ♗xg7 ♔xg7 15 d4 d5 and Black even has the advantage since White's knight is still not developed (Kavalek-Timman, Teesside 1975). Developing the bishop on e3 is perhaps not the best, but also 10 ♗b2 b5! followed by 11...a5 gives Black no problems. The correct treatment of this system must probably begin with 10 ♘bd2.

9 b4   0-0
10 b5 *(D)*

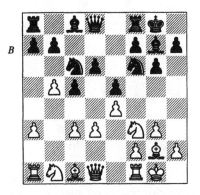

With Black's king's knight on e7, this advance would only have given Black the initiative after 10...♘a5 11 c4 f5, but here White gains space on the queenside. The d5-square, which Black has voluntarily surrendered, will thus become a sensitive weakness.

10 ...   ♘e7
11 a4   a6
12 ♘a3   axb5
13 ♘xb5   ♘c6
14 ♗g5!   h6
15 ♗xf6

As far as I know, this exchanging idea was first tried in Andriessen-Timman, Dutch Championship 1971: 1 c4 g6 2 ♘c3 c5 3 ♘f3 ♗g7 4 g3 ♘c6 5 ♗g2 e6 6 0-0 ♘ge7 7 d3 0-0 8 ♗f4 e5 and now instead of retreating to d2 White played 9 ♗g5 h6 10 ♗xe7 followed by 11 ♘d2 and preparation for b2-b4. Later, the same idea was used

by no less than Petrosian in an important game against Radulov in the last round of the 1973 IBM tournament: after 1 c4 c5 2 ♘f3 ♘c6 3 ♘c3 e5 4 g3 g6 5 a3 ♗g7 6 ♗g2 ♘ge7 7 ♖b1 a5 8 d3 0-0 9 ♗g5, Black did not allow the exchange but reacted with 9...f6, whereupon Petrosian, having provoked a small concession, retreated the bishop to d2.

What Geller does in this game is in principle much the same, even though at the moment the diagonal of his king's bishop is closed: simply put, he wants to get rid of his so that it will not be in the way of his knights as they manoeuvre and operate on the flanks. The loss of the dark squares does not weigh very heavily since in some instances there is the attractive possibility of exchanging the light-squared bishops and having a knight against Black's bad bishop. Tarrasch's positional rule applies, which is, freely translated, 'It isn't what's removed from the board that matters, but what remains.'

15 ...   ♗xf6
16 ♘d2 *(D)*

The first results of the white strategy becomes visible: White threatens 17 ♘c4 ♗e7 18 f4 to take the initiative all over the board. This cannot be stopped by 16...♗e6 because after 17 ♘c4 ♗xc4 18 dxc4 ♗e7 19 f4 White's shattered pawns on the queenside are no disadvantage as the c3-pawn controls important squares, as Botvinnik has shown in similar cases.

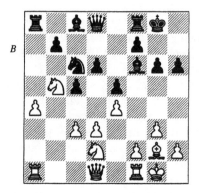

Spassky finds the only satisfactory answer.

16   ...   ♘a7!

The exchange of knights would considerably lighten Black's task, as here one may speak of a pair of knights in tones normally reserved for bishops.

17   ♘a3

The active 17 ♘c4 seems good at first sight, but it would lead to advantage only if Black had to give up the a-file after 17...♘xb5 18 axb5. He does not have to give it up, however: 18...♗e6! with the point 19 ♖xa8 ♕xa8 20 ♘xd6? ♖d8 and Black wins.

17   ...   ♘c6
18   ♖b1   ♗g7
19   ♘2c4   ♖a6

Protecting the square b6 and indirectly the pawn on d6.

20   ♘e3   ♘e7
21   ♘ac4   ♗d7 (D)

Black has thus succeeded in finding a strong square for his queen's bishop, but this has not closed all the holes in his position.

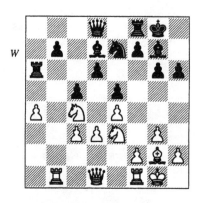

22   a5   ♗c6
23   ♘d5   h5
24   ♕b3

In combination with the following move, this is a sharp attempt to add tactical complications to what has been mainly a strategical game.

24   ...   ♗h6
25   f4 (D)

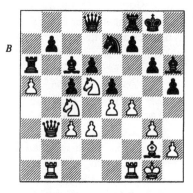

The time-trouble phase must have been starting about now. I am always amazed when a player decides to go into action at just such a time. We will see later that White is throwing his strategical advantage away, but this was determined only by dry analysis after the game.

25   ...   exf4
26   gxf4   ♗xd5!

Very sharply seen. Geller probably thought he had taken all the force out of this exchange by attacking the b-pawn on his 24th move, but Spassky has weighed the loss of this pawn and the consequent disintegration of his whole queenside against the strong f5-square he gets for his knight and from which he can unleash a strong offensive on the kingside. The board will be split in two!

27   exd5   ♘f5
28   ♗e4

White appreciates the strength of the strongpoint f5 and defers the capture on b7, which would give Black the chance for a promising exchange sacrifice: 28 ♕xb7 ♖xa5 29 ♘xa5 ♕xa5 and now 30 ♕b2 (to be able to defend important weak points from d2 or c2) 30...c4!, or 30 ♕b3 ♕d8 and Black's queen threatens to penetrate into the kingside. The position is still not entirely clear, of course, but it is understandable that White, having earlier created weaknesses in the enemy camp in a fine manner, is not willing to accept a complete reversal of roles.

28   ...   ♗xf4

The hand-to-hand fighting begins.

29   ♗xf5   ♕g5+
30   ♔h1   ♕xf5
31   ♕xb7 *(D)*

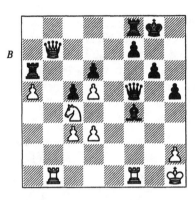

The high point of the struggle has been reached. The black rook cannot retreat, and protecting it doesn't help, for 31...♖fa8 is answered by 32 ♘xd6.

31   ...   ♖e8?

This looks very strong, since White can't take the rook in view of Black's mating attack, but in fact it's a rather useless demonstration which only weakens f7. Too bad, because his courageously begun counter-offensive could have yielded a draw with

1) 31...♕xd3!. This move is far from obvious: instead of protecting or moving away an attacked piece, he puts still another one en prise. On the other hand, the d-pawn was a vital element that held White's position together, as the following two variations show:

1a) 32 ♕xa6 ♕xd5+ 33 ♔g1 ♕g5+ and if White wishes to avoid the repetition of moves with 34 ♔h1 ♕d5+ he must allow 34 ♔f2 ♖e8 (now indeed) and his king has little chance of surviving.

1b) 32 ♖xf4. The main variation.

White not only captures an important attacking piece but also protects both the d-pawn and the knight. One can certainly call it a miracle that Black has sufficient counterplay despite his large material deficit: 32...♖a7! *(D)* and now:

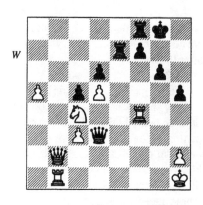

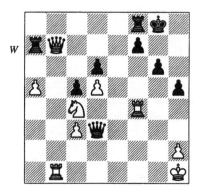

1b1) 33 ♕xa7 ♕xb1+ 34 ♔g2 ♕c2+ and White does best to accept the perpetual if he does not want to lose his knight.

1b2) 33 ♕b2. This move appears to consolidate the white position because 33...♕xd5+ is refuted by 34 ♕g2. But after 33...♖e7! *(D)* the disorganisation of the white forces is clear.

What should White do? The chief threat is 34...♖e2 intending to mate by 35...♕xd5+. White can prevent the execution of the first part of the threat only through heavy material loss, and the second part only with 34 ♘b6, which is also his most important try. Black must now demonstrate that his strongest threat is not 34...♖e2, which

is met by 35 ♕c1 ♕h3 36 ♕g1 with consolidation, but 34...♖fe8. White's only answer is 35 ♖bf1, which obviously leads to perpetual check after 35...♖e2 36 ♕c1 (not 36 ♕b1 ♖xh2+ 37 ♔xh2 ♖e2+, etc.) 36...♖d2! 37 ♖4f2 ♕e4+ 38 ♔g1 ♕g4+, as in all other variations too. It is amazing that the 'doomed' rook on a6 should play such a leading role in this analysis.

So much for the drawing line for Black that I found myself. In *Chess Informant* Volume 20 Marjanović gives two other ways for Black to reach the safe haven of a draw. The first is very complicated, the second actually staggeringly simple.

2) 31...♖aa8 32 ♘xd6 ♕xd3 33 ♖xf4 ♖ab8 34 ♕xb8 ♕xd5+ 35 ♘e4 (the alternative 35 ♖e4 gives Black the opportunity, after 35...♖xb8 36 ♖xb8+ ♔h7 37 a6 ♕xd6 38 a7 ♕d1+ 39 ♔g2 ♕d2+, to force a draw by perpetual check) 35...♖xb8 36 ♖xb8+ ♔g7 37 a6 ♕e5 38 a7 ♕xf4 39 ♘d2 ♕xd2 40 a8♕ ♕e1+ and Black forces a draw by perpetual check. This variation is not

entirely watertight, for White can try 37 ♖b2 (instead of 37 a6), though in view of the undefended position of the white king this attempt to win has little chance of success.

It is also interesting to examine exactly how the perpetual check comes about in the final position.

After 41 ♔g2 ♕e2+ 42 ♔g3 ♕e1+ 43 ♔f4 Black cannot allow the white king to escape to e5 and the territory behind the black c-pawn, because the presence of that pawn would hinder Black in giving check. Correct is 43...g5+!, after which the white king remains imprisoned on the kingside.

3) 31...♖a7. This direct rook sacrifice is the most convincing way to obtain a draw. White has to capture the rook, and then after 32 ♕xa7 ♕xd5+ 33 ♔g1 ♕g5+ 34 ♔f2 ♕h4+ 35 ♔e2 ♕g4+ he is unable to run away from the checks.

This last variation is actually so simple that the question arises as to whether Spassky was perhaps playing for a win in the mutual time-scramble. To be honest, I don't think so. Spassky once told me that if you are in good form the thought of offering only a draw should be alien to you.

It seems likely to me that the former World Champion, for lack of time to calculate concrete variations, instinctively chose a move that looked very active.

32   ♖f2!

A sober defensive move. If Black now continues 32...♕xd3, which was probably intended, then 33 ♖bf1! settles the matter. The white pieces are joined again!

32   ...   g5 (D)

Black is still trying to get all he can out of the position, and he almost succeeds. The text-move protects his bishop and allows his queen to move freely again.

33   ♖g1?

Superficially, there seems nothing wrong with this move. It pins the g-pawn and thus again restricts the black queen's movements. Nevertheless it is a serious mistake which throws away White's winning advantage. The cold-blooded 33 ♕xa6 is correct. Black then can capture the pawns in two different ways. The least promising is 33...♕xd3, for after 34 ♖bf1 ♕xd5+ 35 ♔g1 Black has no more play. So he must try 33...♕xd5+. After 34 ♔g1 ♕xd3, I analyse:

1) 35 ♖bf1. Initially I thought that this was the move that consolidates the material advantage. However, Gerding

(Haren) rightly points out that Black in fact wins with 35...♗e3!. The white queen cannot come to the rescue of the defence.

2) 35 ♕b5. The best move. After 35...♖e2 36 ♖xe2 ♕xe2 White gives a knight back with 37 ♕b2 in order to get a strong passed a-pawn.

33 ...   ♖ea8?

Time trouble is affecting both players. The imperturbable 33...h4! is necessary, instead of the somewhat panicky text-move. Suddenly we see the disadvantage of White's last move: his rook on g1 takes an important square away from the king, so Black can calmly leave his rook on a6. If White then still tries to justify his previous move, he quickly ends up in a hopeless position, as can be seen after 33...h4 34 ♘b6 ♖xa5 *(D)* and now:

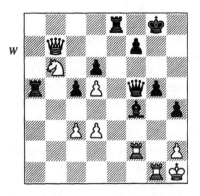

1) 35 ♕c6 with the intention of meeting 35...♖e3 with 36 ♕xd6, with good prospects for White. Black has a better rook move, however: 35...♖b8 (threatening 36...♖a6 to win a piece)

36 ♕c7 ♖xb6 37 ♕xb6 ♕xd5+ 38 ♖fg2 ♖a2 and Black wins.

2) 35 ♕d7 ♕xd7 36 ♘xd7 ♔h8! 37 ♘f6 ♖f8! (the only good square for the rook; for example, 37...♖b8 38 ♘h5! ♗e3 39 ♖xf7 ♗xg1 40 ♘f6 with unstoppable mate) 38 ♖xf4 (the only try to get something out of it) 38...gxf4 39 ♔g2 (White can create mating threats only with the king's help) 39...♖a2+ (Black makes no progress with 39...♔g7 after 40 ♘d7 followed by 41 ♔f3+) 40 ♔f3 ♖xh2 41 ♖g4 h3 42 ♔xf4 ♖f2+ 43 ♔g5. White finally threatens mate. However, Black has the sobering 43...♖g2 and wins. Ulf Andersson and I worked out this extremely adventurous variation together. We would very much have liked to see the inventive white play bear fruit, but it was not to be.

The conclusion is that 34 ♘b6 loses. After 33...h4 White must try 34 ♖gf1 *(D)*. This is the correct square for the white rook, as we also saw in the notes to White's 32nd move. This gives Black a free tempo for ...h5-h4, but the situation is not critical for White. Again he threatens to capture the rook on a6.

Now Black cannot continue his counterattack, since 34...♕h3 fails to 35 ♖g2! ♖e2 36 ♖xg5+! and White decisively goes on the attack. The variation continues 36...♔f8 37 ♕b8+ ♔e7 38 ♕c7+ ♔f6 39 ♕d8+ ♖e7 40 ♖g2 and White wins.

Black is therefore forced to head for an endgame with 34...♕c8. White

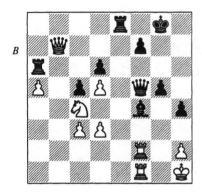

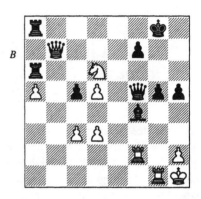

then maintains some winning chances because of his strong a-pawn which is conveniently protected by the knight. But Black also has strong pawns, protected by the bishop, and an exchange sacrifice on a5 is a possibility.

34 ♘xd6 (D)

Already the fatal blow. White not only wins an important pawn, but the knight, which was posted soundly but not very actively on the queenside, now enters the skirmishes on the kingside with tempo.

34 ... ♖xd6

In desperation Black sacrifices the exchange without getting anything for it. 34...♕f6 is only worse, however;

Black's position would collapse very quickly after 35 ♘e4.

35 ♕xa8+ ♔h7

36 c4

Protects the d-pawn in a natural way.

36 ... ♖f6

37 ♕b7 ♕h3

After 37...♕xd3 the simplest win is 38 ♕e7 with the threat 39 ♖xf4. Black sets a final trap with the text: he threatens 38...♗xh2 with at least a draw.

38 ♕b2

A simple preventive measure.

38 ... ♗e5

39 ♕e2 1-0

(Black lost on time)

Game Sixteen
Ljubojević – Andersson
Hoogoven Tournament, Wijk aan Zee 1976
Sicilian Defence, Scheveningen Variation

Kavalek once mentioned, with a mixture of astonishment and admiration, how remarkable it is that Andersson and Ljubojević can walk to the tournament hall together laughing and joking and then, across the chess board, face each other in a life-and-death struggle. That they do is fortunate, for otherwise the chess world would be poorer by a lot of interesting games.

At Wijk aan Zee 1976 Ljubojević started tremendously with three wins in a row. This is the third. A clash of styles is clearly apparent here. The actual course of the game is extremely original, and the hidden possibilities that show up in the analysis add extra refreshment. Seldom have I analysed a game with so much pleasure and devotion.

1	e4	c5
2	♘f3	e6
3	d4	cxd4
4	♘xd4	♘c6
5	♘c3	

Unusual for Ljubojević. I have never seen him use any system against the Taimanov system other than the build-up of the Maroczy wall with 5 ♘b5 d6 6 c4, which he handles in his own highly refined manner.

5	...	♛c7
6	♗e2	a6
7	0-0	♘f6
8	♗e3	♗e7

The game thus enters the paths of the Scheveningen Variation. The character of the Taimanov system can be maintained with 8...♗b4, but nearly all the lines arising from 9 ♘xc6 bxc6 10 ♘a4 are slightly better for White.

9	f4	d6
10	♛e1	0-0
11	♛g3	♗d7
12	e5 *(D)*	

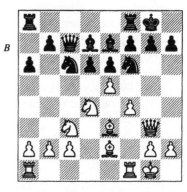

A new idea which has had repeated success in recent years. The first time was in Geller-Timman, Hilversum 1973 (with the added moves ♖ad1 for

White and ...b7-b5 for Black). I remember being very surprised, but I
quickly realised that Black faced a
hopeless task. After the picturesque
continuation 13 e5 ♘e8 14 ♘e4 dxe5
15 fxe5 ♘xe5 16 ♗f4 f6 17 ♗g4 I
managed to survive to the 70th move
by sacrificing the e6-pawn.

The second time it was played was
in Tal-Hartston, Hastings 1973/74.
The difference from the diagram position was the added moves ♔g1-h1 and
...b7-b5, which did not seem to be a
great improvement for Black. As the
Hoogoven chess player J. Mensch
showed in *Schaakbulletin* 81/82, accepting the pawn offer is a precarious
business here too: 13 e5 dxe5 14 fxe5
♘xe5 15 ♗h6! ♘e8 16 ♗f4 f6 17 ♗g4
or 16...♗d6 17 ♗xb5!, and in either
case White wins the pawn back with
advantage. Hartston did not accept the
pawn sacrifice, and this soon proved
fatal: 14...♘xd4 (instead of 14...♘xe5)
15 ♗xd4 ♘e8 16 ♗d3 ♗c6 17 ♕h3
g6 18 ♖ae1 ♖d8 19 ♕e3 ♖d7 20 ♗b6
♕c8 21 ♘e4 ♗xe4 22 ♗xe4 h5 23
♕h6 ♘g7 24 ♖xf7!.

In his game as White against Karpov at Nice 1974, Hartston showed
that he had learned something from
his encounter with Tal. For unclear
reasons he did not play Tal's 13 e5, but
first 13 a3 and after 13...♖ab8? only
then 14 e5. Karpov did not take the
pawn and ended up, as I did against
Geller, with a dismal position. The more
so with a rook on b8, taking the pawn
would have led to the same reaction

as in the present game: 14...dxe5 15
fxe5 ♘xe5 16 ♗f4 (Mensch's variation does not work now as the black
b-pawn is sufficiently protected after
16 ♗h6 ♘e8 17 ♗f4 ♗d6) 16...♗d6
17 ♖ad1 and the threat of 18 ♘b3 is
very unpleasant.

The fourth instance of this pawn
sacrifice that I know of is a game Ma-
tulović-Janošević, with the additional
moves a2-a3 and ...b7-b5. There it was
a real pawn sacrifice – as it is here in
Ljubojević-Andersson – and Janoše-
vić was wrong not to accept it.

In the present encounter, Andersson
manages to show that the white action
is premature. And a good thing, too.
My first reaction when I played over
this game was, 'If this is good, then
Black can't play the Sicilian anymore.'
The game of chess has not yet reached
that point.

    12 **...**   **dxe5**
    13 **fxe5**   **♘xe5**
Naturally.
    14 **♗f4**   **♗d6**
    15 **♖ad1**

A quiet but very pregnant move.
The simple threat is 16 ♘b3, after
which the various pins would cost
Black material. He therefore frees the
c7-square for the bishop.
    15 **...**   **♕b8**
The only move. Other methods to
solve the problem of the pins fail; e.g.,
15...♘d5 16 ♘f5! exf5 17 ♘xd5 ♕c5+
18 ♗e3 ♕c6 19 ♘f6+ ♔h8 20 ♘xd7
with complete destruction, or the fantastic 15...♘f3+ 16 ♖xf3 e5 17 ♗h6

♘h5 18 ♕g5 exd4 19 ♘d5 ♕c5 20 ♘f6+ and wins.

16   ♖d3! *(D)*

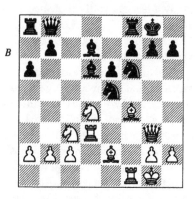

A sparkling idea. I don't know how much of this Ljubojević had prepared at home, but even if this manoeuvre was not found over the board, it is impossible for me to suppress my admiration for its originality. The main threat is 17 ♖e3.

16   ...   ♘e8

The bishop on d6 needed more protection so that the attacked knight on e5 could be moved away in answer to 17 ♖e3. White therefore tries another approach.

17   ♘e4   ♗c7

18   ♖c3 *(D)*

Attacks the bishop again! This seems to be awkward for Black since 18...f6 19 ♗g4 is anything but attractive.

18   ...   ♘c6!

Andersson, like no other player, knows which pieces to retreat and where to retreat them to. The other way to interpose a piece against the

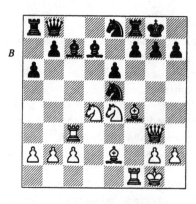

rook is bad: after 18...♗c6 19 ♘g5 the black kingside is short of defenders; e.g., 19...h6 20 ♘gxe6 fxe6 21 ♘xe6 ♖xf4 22 ♖xf4 ♘f7 23 ♘xc7 ♕xc7 and Black wouldn't feel too bad if White didn't have a nice forced win: 24 ♗c4 ♕b6+ (24...♘ed6 25 ♖xf7, etc.) 25 ♖e3! ♘ed6 26 ♗xf7+ ♘xf7 27 ♖xf7 ♔xf7 28 ♕f2+ ♔g8 29 ♖e8+ and wins the queen. There are still some technical difficulties because of 29...♖xe8 30 ♕xb6 ♖e2, but White can force the rook back with 31 ♕d8+ ♔f7 32 ♕c7+ and perhaps a few more checks. So 19...h6 is no good. The question is whether there is a playable move. The only one I can find is 19...♗d6, to continue firmly protecting the knight on e5 after White's impending knight sacrifice on e6. But then White wins in another pretty way: 20 ♕h3 h6 21 ♘dxe6 fxe6 22 ♕xe6+ followed by 23 ♗xe5.

Andersson, it seems, did not even consider the move 18...♗c6. After the game he showed it to Ree with a brief comment which suggested that it was not an alternative at that point. A matter of pure intuition.

19 ♗xc7   ♘xd4

Not 19...♛xc7 because of 20 ♘f6+ ♔h8 21 ♛xc7 ♘xc7 22 ♘xd7 ♘xd4 23 ♖xc7 ♘xe2+ 24 ♔f2 with the win of the exchange.

20 ♗d3

The best square for the bishop, directed toward the kingside where the storm will soon break.

20 ...   ♛a7

21 ♘c5

This shows that White still has the initiative. It is remarkable that he can complete the whole game without moving his king to h1.

21 ...   ♗b5?

This mistake has no disastrous consequences, but it does show an underestimation of White's possibilities. With 21...♘xc7 22 ♛xc7 ♗b5 Black can hold the extra pawn and White would have little initiative for it; e.g., 23 ♖f4 ♗xd3 24 ♖xd4 ♖ac8 followed by retreating the bishop to the kingside.

In *Schach-Archiv* Pachman gives a really lovely hidden drawing possibility for White after 21...♘xc7 *(D)*:

22 ♗xh7+ ♔xh7 23 ♛xg7+! ♔xg7 24 ♖g3+ and White checks freely on g3 and h3. I doubt that the players saw this combination, and I doubt that Andersson avoided 21...♘xc7 because of it.

Black can also try to hold his extra pawn with 21...♘f5, but then White's compensation takes on a more concrete form after 22 ♗xf5 exf5 23 ♗e5

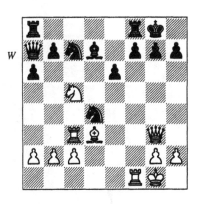

b6 24 ♘xd7 ♛xd7 25 ♖d3. The knight will never be able to reach the dream square e4.

22 ♗e5

With a really nice hidden point, which is seen in the variation 22...♗xd3 23 ♗xd4 ♗xf1 24 ♘xe6 fxe6 25 ♗xa7 ♖xa7 and now 26 ♛b8 wins the rook.

22 ...   ♘c6

23 ♗xh7+! *(D)*

Beautiful! This is what it's all about – the manoeuvres on the queenside were merely diversionary. White unleashes his attack just when the black pieces are all bunched together rather uselessly on the queenside. Nevertheless, Black doesn't have too much to worry about, as we shall see.

23 ...   ♔xh7

24 ♖f4

Again a very good move. White is obviously playing to win. Kavalek says White still has the draw in hand with 24 ♗xg7 ♘xg7 (24...♖g8? 25 ♛h4+ ♔xg7 26 ♛g5+ ♔f8 27 ♖xf7+ ♔xf7 28 ♖f3+ ♘f6 29 ♖xf6+ ♔e8 30

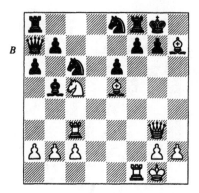

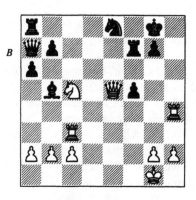

🜚xe6+ and mate next move) 25 ♕xg7+ ♔xg7 26 🜚g3+ with perpetual check.

24 ...   f6

Alternatives were:

1) 24...f5. This is also a move that creates a chance not considered by Ulf. Yet it is not easy to refute. After 25 🜚h4+ ♔g8 26 ♕g6, play branches once again:

1a) 26...♘xe5 27 ♕xe6+ 🜚f7 (not 27...♘f7 28 🜚ch3 and Black cannot stop the mate even though he can take the knight with check) 28 ♕xe5 *(D)* (now not 28 🜚ch3, however, because then Black can indeed save himself: 28...♕xc5+ 29 ♔h1 ♘g6 30 ♕xg6 ♔f8 31 ♕e6 ♘f6 and Black has won the game of cat and mouse).

Now Black has hardly any moves. He can still try 28...🜚d8, but the threatened penetration of the rook need not bother White, as we see in the line 29 🜚ch3 🜚d1+ 30 ♔f2 🜚f1+ 31 ♔g3 f4+ 32 ♔g4 ♘f6+ 33 ♔g5 and the white king escapes while his colleague faces mate in a few moves.

In his column 'Game of the Month' which appears in many chess magazines the world over, Gligorić refers to an analysis by chess enthusiasts from Bosanski Shamac in Yugoslavia. In the last variation they continue with 29...🜚f6! (instead of 29...🜚d1+) with the intention, after the too hasty 30 ♕e7, of giving mate with 30...🜚d1+ 31 ♔f2 🜚f1+ 32 ♔g3 ♕b8+ and mate. The move 29...🜚f6 has no further threat, however, so White can take the time to play a quiet move: 30 c4!. Besides the threat to capture the bishop, this move also threatens the now crushing 31 ♕e7. I see no satisfactory defence for Black.

1b) 26...🜚f6. An interesting attempt to defend which was suggested by the German player K. Werner. The idea is that after 27 ♗xf6 ♘xf6 White cannot follow up with 28 🜚ch3 because of 28...♕xc5+ 29 ♔h1 ♔f8 30 🜚h8+ ♔e7 31 ♕xg7+ ♔d6 32 🜚xa8 ♕xc2 and Black has the advantage. Stronger, therefore, is 28 a4!, in order on 28...♗e2 to continue with 29 b4.

The transfer of the other rook to the kingside cannot then be avoided. Also 28...♖d8, in order to begin a counter-attack after 29 axb5 ♖d1+ 30 ♔f2 axb5, is not quite sufficient on account of 31 ♔g3 ♕b8+ 32 ♔h3 ♖h1 33 g3 and the white king is safe. Incidentally, it is important that White first plays 28 a4. It would be precipitate to play 28 b4 because of 28...♘xb4! 29 ♖xb4 ♖c8 and Black captures on c5 without coming to any harm.

2) 24...♘xe5 25 ♖h4+ ♔g8 26 ♕xe5 ♕b6. This defensive method was recommended by Velimirović. After 27 ♖ch3 f6 the pawn on e6 is covered and the king makes his escape under fairly safe circumstances. However, it is again much stronger firstly to attack the bishop: 27 a4!. On 27...f6 White now has the strong move 28 ♕e3.

After 24...♘xe5 25 ♖h4+ ♔g8 26 ♕xe5 ♕b6 27 a4 Cvetković in *Chess Informant* recommends 27...♗xa4! with the assessment that Black stands clearly better after 28 ♖xa4 ♕xb2. This is correct, and 27...♗xa4 is indeed Black's best chance, but White in turn should react with 28 ♕e4 (28 ♖ch3 f6 29 ♕xe6+ ♕xe6 30 ♘xe6 ♗d7) 28...f6 29 ♕xa4 ♕xb2 30 ♕d4! and the dominant position of the white pieces guarantees more than adequate compensation for the two pawns. The main threat is 31 ♖h8+ ♔xh8 32 ♖h3+, winning the queen.

25 ♖h4+ ♔g8
26 ♕h3

Threatening mate in three. The white knight plays a useful role in the attack even though it's still pinned.

26 ...   ♘d8 (D)

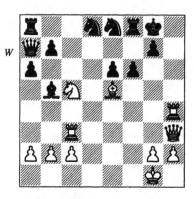

During the post-mortem both players branded this typical Andersson move the decisive mistake, but subsequent analysis with Ree showed that the mistake came later.

26...f5 is possible, because after 27 ♖h8+ ♔f7 White has nothing better than to force a draw with 28 ♕h5+ ♔e7 29 ♕g5+ ♔f7 (D).

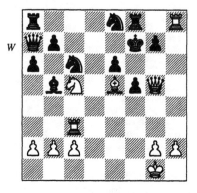

Attempts to keep the attack going demand great sacrifices, but White cannot afford to make them because his knight is still pinned; e.g., 30 ♗xg7 ♘xg7 31 ♖h7 ♖g8 32 ♔h1 ♖ad8 and now White must try to find a perpetual check. But not 32...♘e5? 33 ♘e4! with a decisive attack. Henk Jonker tried to find good play for Black with the queen sacrifice 26...♕xc5+ 27 ♖xc5 ♘xe5. The three minor pieces would certainly compensate for the queen if White did not have an immediate way to win material, also later given by Jonker: 28 ♖h8+ ♔f7 29 ♖xf8+ ♔xf8 30 ♕a3!, threatening both a crushing discovered check and 31 ♖xb5.

| 27 | ♗d4 | b6 |

The weakness that this creates is not at all obvious, but Ljubojević must have spotted it immediately.

28	♘xe6	♘xe6
29	♕xe6+	♕f7
30	♕e4 *(D)*	

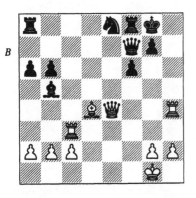

B

This tournament was played at the same time as a tournament in Orense,

Spain, where Raymond Keene and I were playing. The day before I received the Hoogoven tournament bulletin that contained this game, Keene gave me his striking opinion of Ljubojevic's play. He said he did not see Yugoslavia's top grandmaster as a deep strategist, and not even as a player with any sort of healthy ideas about chess – but this was precisely what made his play so successful and so difficult to counter; that is, it consisted of a series of tricks. Very deep tricks indeed, he added: they can be twenty moves long.

As far as this game is concerned, Keene was right on target. On the 12th move Ljubojevic started a series of unclear complications, and now, eighteen moves later, Black seems to be lost: while his rook is hanging on one side of the board, mate in one is threatened on the other. But it's still only a trick.

If Black had not been in serious time trouble, or perhaps if he had not fallen so deeply under the spell of White's play, he would undoubtedly have found the courageous path to the draw.

| 30 | ... | g5? |

Correct is 30...♕xa2!, and the black pieces seem to be co-ordinated again. A very dangerous check is threatened, and if White takes the bait he will be in big trouble. On 31 ♕xa8 Black first plays the calm 31...g5 *(D)*; White does not have a queen check on d5 and the white rook cannot leave the fourth

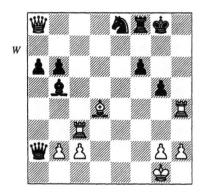

rank because of mate (32 ♖h6 ♕b1+ 33 ♔f2 ♕f1+ 34 ♔e3 ♕f4 mate).

What can White do? If 32 ♖g4 ♘d6 33 ♕f3 ♕b1+ 34 ♔f2 ♕f1+ 35 ♔g3 ♘f5+ 36 ♔h3 ♔f7 and it is all over for him.

White's best after 30...♕xa2 is to play for a draw by perpetual check with 31 ♕h7+ ♔f7 32 ♕h5+. Black cannot avoid it without exposing his king to serious danger.

31 ♖h6

A more immediate and more graceful win is 31 ♖g3 with the crushing threat 32 ♖xg5+, leaving the a8-rook hanging. White was also in time trouble, however, and this is only a small blot on the game. For that matter, in a final check of the analysis I see that it is no blot at all. White indeed wins after 31

♖g3 ♕g7, but certainly not more gracefully or more quickly than with the text-move.

31	...	♖a7
32	♖ch3 (D)	

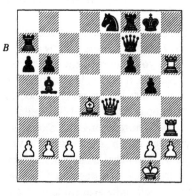

Even Ulf Andersson cannot find a decent defence here.

32	...	♕g7
33	♖g6	♖8f7
34	c4	1-0

On behalf of Raymond Keene, Ken Rogoff, and Gudmundur Sigurjonsson, who, when I showed them this game, followed it as avidly as I did when I first played it through, I want to convey the feeling that overcame us there in the Spanish town of Orense that this was the best game of the last twenty years.

Game Seventeen
Karpov – Timman
International Tournament, Skopje 1976
Sicilian Defence, Rauzer Variation

The sixth 'Sreba na Solidarnesta' international tournament, in Skopje, Yugoslavia, was the first time Karpov and I played together in a tournament since the Neimeijer youth tournament of 1967/68.

Karpov, it seems, having received the world title in 1975 without a struggle, immediately began carefully choosing tournaments to play in so as to achieve the status of an active world champion. And, unlike many of his predecessors, he succeeded. The tournament at Skopje was the first such tournament he won in a convincing fashion. There was great variety in his play: now an interesting attacking game, then a dry, technical, endgame win. Our game took place near the end of the tournament. It was a hard fight: a sharp opening developed into a middlegame where both sides seemed to have attacking chances. White's chances were more immediate, but when Karpov missed the sharpest continuation at a certain point, Black was able to save himself in a four-rook ending a pawn down.

1	e4	c5
2	♘f3	♘c6
3	d4	cxd4
4	♘xd4	♘f6
5	♘c3	d6
6	♗g5	e6
7	♕d2	a6
8	0-0-0	♗d7
9	f4	♗e7
10	♘f3	b5
11	♗xf6	gxf6
12	♔b1	♕b6
13	♗d3	b4
14	♘e2	a5
15	f5	a4
16	♘f4	♕c5 *(D)*

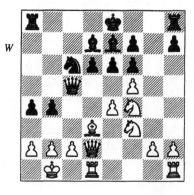

After a slight transposition of moves we have entered the 18th game of the

Fischer-Spassky match. I spent a long time thinking about whether there was an alternative to 16...♕c5, but I could see nothing else against the threatened 17 fxe6 fxe6 18 ♗c4. For instance, if 16...♘e5 then 17 ♗e2, the move White plays even after the text 16...♕c5.

17 ♗e2

A novelty in this position. Fischer, after long thought, had played 17 ♖c1 to close the queenside after 17...♖ab8 18 c3 b3 19 a3. Karpov's idea is to employ the bishop in the siege of the weak e6-point in Black's position. I was very much impressed by the idea – until ten days after the tournament, when Sosonko, Tarjan, and I found that Black can force a draw. It sounds incredible but, as we shall see, it is true.

17 ... ♖b8
18 fxe6 fxe6
19 ♘e1!

A consequence of White's 17th move. The bishop now threatens to attack the pawn from f7 or g4, and it is fortunate for Black that he can just cover both squares with his knight.

19 ... ♘e5
20 ♘ed3 ♕d4

20...♕b6 is bad because of 21 ♗h5+ ♔d8 22 ♕e2 and the bishop can no longer be kept out of g4 (if 22...♖g8 23 ♘xe5 and 24 ♗f7).

21 ♘xe5 ♕xe5? *(D)*

Now Black gets into trouble. Correct is 21...fxe5. During the game I was afraid of 22 ♘xe6, threatening mate in one, and after 22...♗xe6 23 ♕h6 ♗xa2+ 24 ♔xa2 b3+ 25 ♔a1 ♕c5 (or 25...♕b6) 26 ♖d5, White gets in first.

During my calculation of 21...fxe5 22 ♘xe6 ♗xe6 23 ♕h6 I rejected

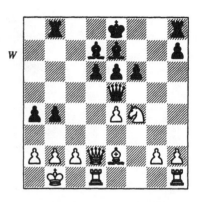

23...♕xe4 because of 24 ♕xe6 ♕xe2 25 ♖xd6, but that was an illusion; after 25...♖d8 White has no follow-up. White must therefore play 24 ♖he1 (instead of 24 ♕xe6). Black has only one answer to the triple threats (to take the bishop or to check on b5 or h5) and that is 24...♕f5. Now it is a forced draw after 25 ♖f1 ♗f8! 26 ♕h4 ♗e7 because White would be better off not to go into the endgame after 27 ♕h6 ♗f8 28 ♖xf5 ♗xh6 29 ♖f6 ♔e7 30 ♖xh6 ♖bf8.

If 22 ♕xd4 (instead of 22 ♘xe6) 22...exd4 23 ♗g4 e5 24 ♘e6 ♗f6! 25 ♖df1 ♔e7 26 ♘c7 ♗c6; or, in this line, 23 ♗h5+ ♔d8 24 ♗g4 e5 25 ♘e6+ ♔c8, with the threat 26...♖g8 27 ♗f5 ♖g6!; or, finally, if 24 ♗xd7+ (instead of 24 ♘e6) 24...♔xd7 25 ♘d5 ♗d8 and the knight only looks strong.

White's great problem is always that his king is kept in its corner by Black's far-advanced queenside pawns.

22 ♕e3! *(D)*

Very strong, and another illustration of why the player whose queen

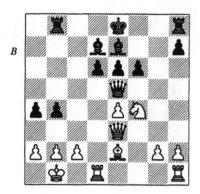

controls the most dark squares in this type of Sicilian position often stands better. Control of the g1-a7 diagonal is especially important.

22 ...   b3

I decided to sound the emergency. Black's situation is far from appetising and I did not feel like suffering martyrdom after, say, 22...0-0.

23 cxb3   axb3
24 a3   f5

On the one hand, Black's 22nd move has opened the c-file to White's advantage; on the other, Black threatens to take the e-pawn with check.

25 ♗h5+   ♔d8
26 ♖he1?

For the first time in the game, Karpov thought for a long time. And the longer he thought the more worried I became about 26 ♕a7. I originally thought that the threat of capturing on e4 with check had eliminated that possibility, and in fact this was the only reason Karpov didn't play it, as he admitted after the game. However, after the continuation 26 ♕a7 ♕xe4+ 27

♔a1 ♕b7 White's queen returns with tremendous force: 28 ♕e3! *(D)*, and Black can neither defend his e-pawn nor prevent his position from crumbling.

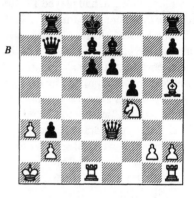

If 28...♕e4 29 ♕c3 and 30 ♕a5+, or if 28...e5 29 ♘e6+ ♗xe6 30 ♕xe5 ♔d7 31 ♖he1, etc. Yet this position is not so hopeless for Black. First of all it should be noted that Böhm's suggestion 27...♕a8 is better than 27...♕b7. The intention after 28 ♕e3 should not be to follow up with 28...♗f6, for then comes 29 ♘xe6+ ♗xe6 30 ♖xd6+, winning. However, Black has a brilliant combination to retain chances of saving the game: 28...e5 29 ♘e6+ ♗xe6 30 ♕xe5 ♔d7 31 ♖he1.

It looks like it's all over, but Black can play: 31...♕xa3+!! 32 bxa3 b2+, and now White has two possibilities:

1) 33 ♔b1 ♗a2+ 34 ♔xa2 b1♕+ 35 ♖xb1 dxe5 and Black holds the draw without any difficulty because 36 ♖xb8 ♖xb8 37 ♖xe5 can be answered by 37...♖b2+.

2) 33 ♕xb2 ♖xb2 34 ♔xb2 ♗f6+ 35 ♔c2 ♖c8+ 36 ♔d3 ♖c3+ and after capturing the a-pawn Black has excellent chances of a draw.

This fantastic escape is probably Black's best option after 26 ♕a7. Note that 26...♗f6 is inadequate on account of 27 ♕xb8+ ♔e7 28 ♕xd6+ ♕xd6 29 ♖xd6 ♔xd6 30 ♖d1+, followed by 31 exf5 with a winning advantage for White. The dour 26...♖c8 probably merits consideration, though after 27 ♘d3 ♕xe4 28 ♖he1 ♕a4 29 ♕xa4 ♗xa4 30 ♖xe6 White can reach a more favourable ending than in the game.

26 ...   ♕xe4+

Despite the worry which had dominated my mind while White was thinking about his previous move, I did not hesitate longer than ten seconds here. Better an ending, I thought, even against such an endgame artist as Karpov, than to expose my king any longer to lightning attacks.

After the game I asked my opponent how he would have answered 26...♗f6. To my surprise, he said he had planned to exchange queens after 27 ♘d3 ♕xe4 and to capture twice on e4. Naturally he would have changed his mind if I had actually played 26...♗f6, since after 27 ♘d3 ♕xe4 28 ♕h6! is crushing. The sudden danger now comes from the other side, which once again underlines the powerful position of the white queen. After either 28...♕h4 29 ♘f4 or 28...♕d4 29 ♘e5! ♕xe5 30 ♖xe5 ♗xe5 31 ♕g5+ followed by 32 ♖c1+ it is all over.

Another method of continuing, with queens on the board, is unsatisfactory: 26...fxe4 is again answered strongly by 27 ♕a7 d5 28 ♘xd5 exd5 29 ♖xd5 ♕c7 30 ♕d4 ♖g8 31 ♖d1 ♖b7 32 ♗g4! and White wins.

27 ♕xe4   fxe4
28 ♗g4 (D)

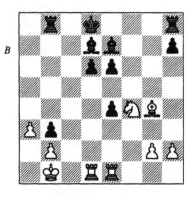

Naturally not 28 ♖xe4 e5, and 28 ♗f7 also leads to nothing after 28...♖f8 29 ♘xe6+ ♗xe6 30 ♗xe6 ♖f2 with dangerous counterplay.

28 ...   ♖g8!

The only move. Above all, Black must not allow himself to be buried alive with 28...e5 29 ♘e6+. In most cases, the e-pawn would then only get in the way because Black's counterplay is based on attacking White's b-pawn with the bishop on f6 and a rook on White's second rank.

29 ♗xe6   ♗xe6
30 ♘xe6+   ♔d7
31 ♘f4

31 ♖xe4 ♖xg2 is worse for White.

31 ...   ♗g5

32 Rxe4

White must enter this four-rook ending as after 32 Nd5 Rge8 Black keeps his strong passed pawn on e4.

32 ...   Bxf4
33 Rxf4   Rxg2 *(D)*

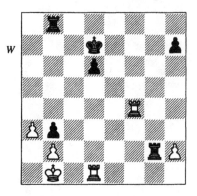

34 Rf7+   Kc6
35 Rxh7   Rb5

The draw can probably be held in more than one way. With the text-move Black plans to hold his centre pawn and exchange his b-pawn for White's a-pawn.

36 Rh3   d5 *(D)*

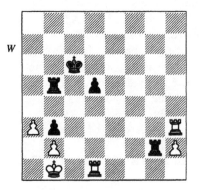

37 Rc3+   Kd6
38 h3

Typical Karpov. He has no real winning chances and is not at all in a hurry.

38 ...   Re2
39 Rcd3   Ke5
40 a4   Ra5
41 Rxb3   Rxa4
42 Rb8   Rd4

A nice finesse which makes things a little less troublesome for Black.

43 Re8+   Kd6 *(D)*

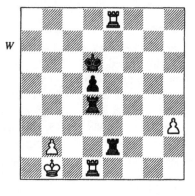

The adjourned position. I expected my opponent to seal 44 Rd8+ because the king would then have to return to e5 and thus White could reserve the choice of which rook to capture. It matters little, though, because it is still a draw.

44 Rxd4   Rxe8
45 Kc2   Re3

The most active: Black is ready to answer 46 Rd3 with 46...Re4. His king is ideally placed in the centre.

46 Rh4   Kc5

47	♖h8	♖e2+
48	♔b3	d4
49	h4	♖h2 *(D)*

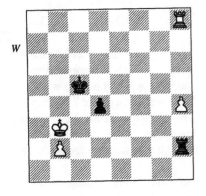

50	h5	d3
51	h6	♔b6

I had calculated long before that the king would arrive just in time.

52	♔c3	d2
53	♔c2	♔b7
54	b4	♔a7
55	b5	♔b7

White cannot win the d-pawn unless he can put Black in zugzwang. The move h6-h7 is therefore necessary sooner or later. After that, however, Black doesn't need the pawn to draw.

56	h7	♔a7
57	♔d1	♔b7

½-½

Game Eighteen
Timman – Karpov
Euwe Tournament, Amsterdam 1976
Nimzo-Indian Defence, Leningrad Variation

In May 1976 a four-player tournament in honour of Max Euwe was held for the first time. The venue was uniquely situated in the Van Gogh Museum in Amsterdam, and the demonstration room was no less unique: a tent of mirrors which for a few months stood in the Museum Square. Professor Euwe turned 75 during the tournament amid an appropriate setting. A phonograph record was even made, with text added to music found in an old barrel-organ book from the time when Euwe was World Champion: the 'Euwe March.' All together, a perfect 1930's atmosphere was created.

Karpov's participation was an extra attraction. The World Champion did not have many tournaments on his schedule for the rest of the year, and many people wondered whether he was taking too great a risk by playing in such a short tournament. After all, even a single 'accident' could seriously jeopardise his expected first place. Karpov clearly felt this himself, for he played very cautiously. In the first round he defeated Browne, who had actually achieved a drawn position but went under in terrible time pressure. Four draws followed and in the last round a win against Olafsson secured Karpov's first place.

He faced his most anxious moments in the fifth round, in the game given here. After missing a win, I finally had to be satisfied with a draw.

1	d4	♘f6	
2	c4	e6	
3	♘c3	♗b4	
4	♗g5	c5	
5	d5	d6	
6	e3	exd5	
7	cxd5	♘bd7	
8	♗d3	♕a5	
9	♘e2	♘xd5	
10	0-0	♗xc3	
11	bxc3		

This position is known with the inclusion of the moves ...h7-h6 and ♗g5-h4, which have become fairly automatic. In most variations it is very important that White's bishop cannot suddenly return to the queenside, but that is an irrelevant nuance in this game.

11 ...   c4! (D)

I saw this coming but was unable to find a satisfactory divergence from the usual continuation. The text-move is an important improvement for Black in the Leningrad Variation.

12 ♗f5

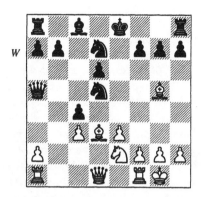

After 12 ♗c2 Black can take the time to quietly castle and maintain the inevitable threat of 13...♘xc3. A nice variation is 12...0-0 13 ♘g3 ♘xc3 14 ♕h5 g6 15 ♕h6 ♕e5 16 ♘h5 and now Black defends successfully with the Petrosian-like move 16...♕h8!.

12   ...   f6

The fact that Karpov spent forty minutes on this move shows that he had probably not hammered out the finesses of the previous move himself but had been shown them by his team of helpers. The alternatives are:

1) 12...♘xc3 13 ♘xc3! (13 ♗xd7+ ♗xd7 14 ♘xc3 ♕xg5 15 ♘e4 ♕g6 16 ♘xd6+ ♔e7 gives White no advantage) 13...♕xf5 14 ♗f4 and the threats 15 ♘d5 and 15 ♗xd6 can hardly be met.

2) 12...♘7b6 holds the pawn but leads to a rather great concentration of black pieces on the queenside: 13 ♘g3 0-0 14 e4! ♘xc3 15 ♕h5 ♗xf5 16 ♘xf5 ♘xe4 17 ♗f6! and Black must give up his queen with 17...♕xf5 18 ♕xf5 ♘xf6. This position is difficult

to judge, but it seems to me that White has the advantage.

3) 12...♘7f6 is undoubtedly the safest continuation. There can follow 13 ♗xc8 ♖xc8 14 ♗xf6 ♘xf6 15 ♕xd6 ♕c5 with equality.

13   ♘d4! *(D)*

Played after long deliberation. I had already used nearly an hour and a half. Although White does not really stand worse after 13 ♘f4 ♘xf4 14 ♗xd7+ ♗xd7 15 ♗xf4, I did not find this possibility attractive during the game. Karpov likes positions such as the one that would arise after 15...d5 16 ♕h5+ g6, with a worthless extra pawn and opposite-coloured bishops.

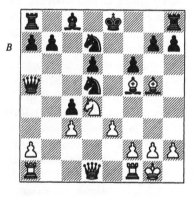

13   ...   ♘e7

I had quite overlooked this move, which Black played very quickly. Accepting the piece sacrifice is extremely risky, for example 13...fxg5 14 ♕h5+ g6 15 ♗xg6+ hxg6 16 ♕xh8+ ♘f8 17 f4, and the f-file is opened with decisive consequences (17...g4 18 f5).

The slightly more subtle 15...♔d8 (instead of 15...hxg6) is not a saving move either: 16 ♕xg5+ ♘7f6 17 ♗f7!, and the double threat 18 e4 and 18 ♗xd5 cannot be effectively parried by 18...♖f8 because of 19 ♕g7.

During the game, 13...♘e5 gave me the most headaches. Karpov said afterwards that he had feared 14 ♕h5+ g6 15 ♗xg6+ ♘xg6 16 ♗xf6 but had completely overlooked the fact that he could then castle with a winning advantage. The attempt 16 ♗h6 (instead of 16 ♗xf6) is too fantastic. The simplest answer is 16...♕c5.

White's best line after 13...♘e5 begins with 14 f4 to drive the knight from its strong central position. The resulting complications are difficult to enumerate. In the tent of mirrors, Hans Ree showed this pretty variation to the public during the demonstration: 14...♘xe3 15 ♕h5+ g6 16 ♗xg6+ ♘xg6 17 f5 ♘xf1 18 fxg6 ♕xg5 19 g7+ ♕xh5 20 gxh8♕+ and 21 ♖xf1 with a winning positional advantage for White. This variation is so beautiful mainly because it expresses the Excelsior Theme in its full glory: White's f-pawn advances undisturbed to the queening square. The opposition of the queens on a5 and h5 and the position of the minor pieces between them leads to very surprising twists and variations. Thus Black finds no salvation in the variation 17...♘xf5 (instead of 17...♘xf1) 18 ♘xf5 ♗xf5 19 ♗xf6 0-0 20 ♖xf5 and White's attack wins.

In the post-mortem, Karpov immediately replied to 14 f4 with 14...♘f7. Now direct attacking attempts have no chance of success; e.g., 15 ♕h5 ♗xf5 (not 15...g6 because of 16 ♗xg6 hxg6 17 ♕xg6 with a very precarious position for Black) 16 ♘xf5 g6 17 ♘g7+ ♔f8! 18 ♘e6+ ♔e7 and the white attack does not break through. However, with one of Black's knights out of the centre, White need not adopt overly violent methods but can continue quietly with 15 ♗h4; e.g., 15...0-0 16 ♗xc8! ♖axc8 17 ♘f5 ♖c5 18 ♕g4 g6 19 e4 with a winning game.

I am sure that Karpov saw far more of these variations than he indicated after the game. While I was thinking about my thirteenth move I noticed that he was also concentrating intensely on the position. In positions where you have to dig very deeply to decide on a continuation, variations are sometimes considered subconsciously and do not rise to the surface of conscious calculation; such variations help only in the overall evaluation of a position, which is a necessary part of judging the value of a move. It was only after the game, for example, that I recognised the variation Hans Ree had shown the public. A great deal of tension is usually released right after a game, and you may not be able to remember variations you had calculated during the game or may only vaguely recognise variations that had sprung into your subconscious mind. In any case, it seems very improbable to me that Karpov had overlooked the possibility of castling after 13...♘e5 14 ♕h5+ g6 15 ♗xg6+ ♘xg6 16 ♗xf6, since castling would have been one of his first considerations. Perhaps he then went on to look at other possibilities and, after the game, could not remember much about it.

14 ♗xd7+ ♗xd7
15 ♗f4 0-0

Karpov again keeps things as simple as possible and perhaps he is right again. He could have kept the extra pawn with 15...♕c5 (not 15...♕d5 16 e4), but he feared 16 ♕f3. Indeed, White has excellent compensation after either 16...d5 17 ♕h5+ g6 18 ♕h6 or 16...♘d5 17 ♕h5+ g6 18 ♕h6. Our World Champion, however, does not like an unsafe king. In the second variation, after 18...♘xf4 19 exf4 ♔f7 20 ♖fe1 White threatens the annoying 21 ♖e7+, and Black's king would not be at home on the queenside.

16 ♗xd6 ♖fe8
17 ♖b1 b6
18 ♗xe7 ♖xe7
19 ♘b5 (D)

This manoeuvre, begun by White's 17th move, is the only way to give Black problems. White can also continue with 19 ♕d2 followed by 20 f3 and 21 e4. He would stand well then, but the position would be too static for him to hope for much.

19 ... ♖c8
The only move.

20 ♘d6 ♖c7

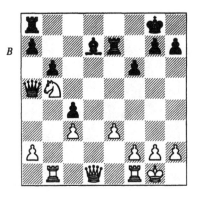

Also possible is 20...♖c6, and 21 ♕d4 is the best reply.

21 ♖b4 ♗e6

21...♕e5 is also to be considered, with the intention 22 ♘xc4 ♕xc3 23 ♕d6 ♗e8. However, White plays 22 ♕d2 followed eventually by f4.

22 ♕f3 ♕d5
23 ♕xd5 ♗xd5
24 ♖d1 ♗e6
25 ♖d4 ♖ed7
26 f3

Black has been able to defend the c-pawn sufficiently, but White's position is a little better and easier to handle.

26 ... ♔f8
27 ♘b5 (D)

The right moment, especially for psychological reasons.

27 ... ♖c5

Karpov thought about this for a long time. He showed afterwards that he probably could have played 27...♖xd4. At first sight this seems very good for White, for after 28 cxd4 and a move by Black's rook, White has 29 ♘c3 with a winning positional

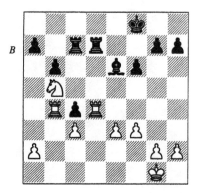

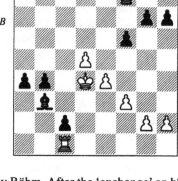

advantage. But Black's rook need not move: 28...c3! 29 ♘xc7 ♗xa2 and, amazingly, White has only one way to stop the c-pawn: 30 ♘e6+. Black must take the knight to prevent it from getting to d3 or e2 via f4: 30...♗xe6. Now comes 31 ♖b1 c2 32 ♖c1 ♗b3 33 ♔f2 b5. With his king on d2 or d3, the best White could hope for would be to return the exchange on c2; therefore, 34 e4 b4 35 ♔e3 a5 36 d5 a4 37 ♔d4 *(D)*. Black cannot prevent the white king's occupation of c5 by putting his own king on d6, for then f3-f4 and e4-e5 would follow. So it seems to be all over now, since on 37...a3 38 ♔c5 is decisive. Black, however, has a sparkling finesse which the World Champion was not able to work out completely over the board.

37...♗a2!. After 38 ♖xc2 b3 39 ♖c8+ ♔e7 40 ♖c7+ ♔d8 (but not 40...♔d6?? 41 ♖b7 followed by 42 f4 and 43 e5+ with mate!) and Black wins, so White has no better than to head for a draw with 39 ♖b2! (instead of 39 ♖c8+) 39...a3 40 ♔c3, as given

by Böhm. After the 'exchange' on b2, the white king moves back and forth between a1 and b2 so that he cannot be forced into zugzwang.

From all this it seems that White would have had to answer 27...♖xd4 with 28 exd4, which would have been more or less the same as the actual game continuation.

28 a4

Not nice, fixing the pawn on the wrong colour; but if White wants to make any progress, it's virtually unavoidable.

28	...	a6
29	♘a3	♖xd4
30	exd4	♖c6
31	♘c2	♔e7
32	♖b2	

Threatening 33 ♘b4. The push 33 a5 bxa5 34 ♖a4 ♖b6 doesn't lead to anything.

32	...	a5
33	d5! *(D)*	

The only reasonable winning attempt. 33 ♘e3 seems promising but leads to nothing after 33...♔d6; e.g.,

34 ♔f2 ♗d7! and if 35 d5 ♖c5 36 ♖xb6+ ♔c7 White loses his a-pawn. That wrongly-fixed pawn is a thorn in White's flesh, while its Black counterpart is a potential passed pawn – the knight's natural enemy.

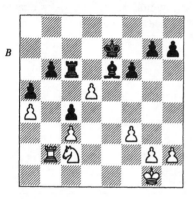

33 ... ♗xd5

The fact that Karpov thought a few minutes before making this capture indicates that he had overlooked White's last move – or that he wanted to create the impression that he had overlooked it.

34 ♘d4 ♖c5

The best square for the rook.

35 ♖xb6 h5?

Maybe a consequence of overlooking White's 33rd move. The steady reaction is 35...♔d7, to be able to defend his weak points in time.

36 ♔f2?

In slight time trouble, I reacted automatically with the answer I had planned for 35...♔d7. Things would be much more difficult for Black after 36 ♖a6. He would have to give up a

pawn due to the double threat 37 ♖a7+ and 37 ♘b5, and his compensation would be questionable.

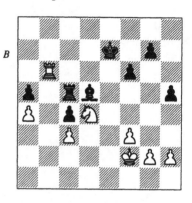

36 ... ♔d7

Now everything is in order again.

37 h4 ♔c7

38 ♖e6 (D)

A little joke at the end of an enervating game. The pawn ending is won for White after 38...♗xe6 39 ♘xe6+ ♔d6 40 ♘xc5 ♔xc5 41 ♔e3 ♔d5 42 ♔f4!, etc. Karpov, of course, will have nothing to do with it.

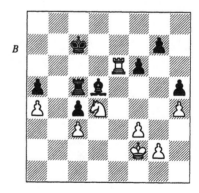

38	...	♔d7
39	♖b6	♔c7
40	♖e6	

40 ♖b1 is also nothing because of 40...♗f7 and Black is again ready to besiege White's a-pawn.

40	...	♔d7
41	♖a6	♗b7!

42	♖b6	♔c7
43	♖e6	♔d7
44	♖b6	♔c7
45	♖e6	½-½

The draw was agreed here, before adjourning. Playing for a win with 45 ♖b1 would have been risky due to 45...♗c8 46 ♘b5+ ♔d8!.

Game Nineteen
Spassky – Korchnoi
Final Candidates Match (4), Belgrade 1977
French Defence, Winawer Variation

After Korchnoi sought asylum in the West in August 1976, the Russians systematically tried to make life difficult for him. First *Pravda* and *64* published a letter signed by most Russian grandmasters condemning and criticising him. Then the Soviet Chess Federation asked FIDE to exclude Korchnoi from the matches leading to the world championship. Their motto was, perhaps, 'Even if it doesn't help, it can't hurt.'

Fortunately, it didn't help. But it meant that until further notice Korchnoi could meet Soviet opponents only in matches. The confrontation peaked in 1977, when he successively met Petrosian, Polugaevsky, and Spassky. Petrosian went down after a nerve-racking equal struggle, Polugaevsky never had a chance, and it seemed at first that Spassky would be similarly run over: after nine games Korchnoi had built up a lead of 6½-2½. At that point, Spassky began to exhibit a remarkable pattern of behaviour: he appeared at the board only to make his moves, and then he immediately sauntered backstage to muse over the course of the game – a unique method of thought which appears to be not very efficient. Instead of realising this, Korchnoi took it as a serious insult. He became extremely upset and lost four games in a row. Only then did he slowly pull himself together. With two draws and two more wins, he won the match by a comfortable margin and went on to face Karpov.

This game is from the period before the relationship between Korchnoi and Spassky was so radically disturbed.

1	e4	e6
2	d4	d5
3	♘c3	♗b4
4	e5	c5
5	a3	♗xc3+
6	bxc3	♘e7
7	a4	

In the second game of this match Spassky chose the sharpest system with 7 ♕g4, but it turned out badly for

him. He now uses the 'positional' method preferred especially by Smyslov and Fischer.

7	...	♗d7
8	♘f3	♕a5
9	♗d2	

The important alternative is 9 ♕d2.

9	...	♘bc6
10	♗e2	f6 *(D)*

Attacking the centre immediately.

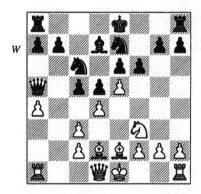

W

This was first played by Korchnoi, against me, in Leeuwarden 1976. Black provokes his opponent to open the centre at once, an idea formerly considered too dangerous because of White's bishop-pair.

In the old days Botvinnik used to close the centre with 10...c4. Planinc has had particular success against 10...c4 with 11 ♘g5, and even the great expert Uhlmann could not find a satisfactory reply; e.g., Kavalek-Uhlmann, Manila 1976: 10...c4 11 ♘g5 h6 12 ♘h3 0-0-0 13 ♘f4 ♔b8 14 0-0 ♘c8 15 ♘h5 ♖hg8 16 ♗g4 ♘b6 17 ♖e1 ♘xa4 18 ♖e3 b5 19 ♖f3 ♗e8 20 ♖g3 ♘e7 21 ♗c1 ♘g6 22 ♗a3 ♔a8 23 ♕d2 ♕c7 24 ♗h3 ♗d7 25 ♗d6 ♕c6 26 ♖f1 ♗c8 27 f4 f5 28 exf6 gxf6 29 f5! and White broke the position open.

Later, Vaganian tried 10...♕c7 and reached a good position against Klovan after 11 0-0 0-0 12 ♖e1 h6 13 ♗f4 ♘g6 14 ♗g3 ♘ce7. Kurajica, against me, later improved White's play: 13 ♕c1 f6 14 exf6 ♖xf6 15 ♕a3! c4 16 ♘e5 and White stood better.

| 11 | c4 | ♕c7 |
| 12 | exf6 | |

I play 12 cxd5 first, which amounts to a transposition of moves.

12	...	gxf6
13	cxd5	♘xd5
14	c3	

But now the game takes another route. Against Korchnoi I tried 14 c4 to aim for the endgame after 14...♘de7 15 dxc5 0-0-0 16 ♗c3 e5 17 ♕d6. The continuation was 17...♘f5 18 ♕xc7+ ♔xc7 19 0-0 ♘fd4 20 ♘xd4 ♘xd4 21 ♗d1 ♔c6 and now White should have further opened the position with 22 f4 (instead of 22 ♗xd4 as played), after which the chances would have remained balanced.

The text-move is based on a different strategy: White holds d4 so as to prevent Black from quickly freeing his game with e6-e5. The centralised position of the knight on d5 helps Black to rapidly carry out this advance anyway.

14	...	0-0-0
15	0-0	♖hg8
16	♖e1 (D)	

A very tense position. After this move the storm breaks, but 16 g3 would also have been answered by 16...e5 17 c4 ♘f4 with complications similar to those in the game.

| 16 | ... | e5! |

Very sharply judged.

| 17 | c4 | |

The standard reaction. White wants to establish a strong protected passed pawn in the centre. Spassky now had

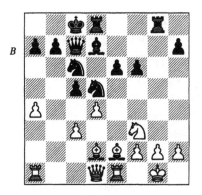

only forty minutes left on his clock, Korchnoi eighty. The tension was palpable.

17 ...   ♗h3

This blow makes the game more complicated than it would have been after 17...♘f4. But it is no worse a move, since 17...♘f4 18 ♗xf4 exf4 19 d5 ♗h3 produces the same position as the best variation after Black's next move.

17...e4 is bad because of 18 cxd5 exf3 19 ♗xf3 ♘xd4 20 ♗c3 with positional advantage for White.

18 ♗f1 *(D)*

18 g3 is bad here because after 18...♘f4 19 ♗xf4 exf4 Black already threatens a decisive double capture on g3, a good example of how quickly the black attack can develop.

A very interesting possibility is 18 ♘g5, to keep the g-file closed. Three white men are attacked, and in such cases a countersacrifice is not out of place. But which one should Black take? 18...fxg5 19 cxd5 is simply bad, and White has the advantage also after

18...♘f4 19 ♗xf4 ♖xd4 20 ♕c1; e.g., 20...♗xg2 21 ♗g4+! ♔b8 22 ♘e6, or 20...♗f5 21 ♗e3 fxg5 22 ♗xd4 ♘xd4 23 ♗d1 and Black does not have enough compensation. Much stronger is 18...♗xg2, leading to very intricate and interesting complications which do not seem unfavourable for Black. It is irrelevant, however. After 18 ♘g5 ♘c3! the white attack is refuted elegantly and convincingly. Black remains at least a pawn ahead with an overwhelming position.

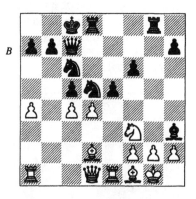

18 ...   ♘b6

The piece sacrifice Korchnoi has in mind looks overwhelming, but in the end it turns out to be not very promising. The alternatives are:

1) 18...♖xg2+. This direct try fails to 19 ♗xg2 ♕g7 20 ♘h4 ♘xd4 21 ♖a3 and the rook goes to g3.

2) 18...♘de7 19 d5 ♘d4 20 ♘xd4 cxd4. A very interesting position. Although Black seems to have a nice pawn front, it is destroyed by 21 ♕f3 ♗f5 22 ♗b4 e4 23 ♖xe4! ♗xe4 24

♕xe4, and White has all the trumps with his pair of bishops and two pawns for the exchange.

3) 18...♘f4! is undoubtedly the strongest move. After 19 ♗xf4 exf4 20 d5 ♗g4! 21 ♕b3 ♗xf3 22 ♕xf3 ♘d4 Black has a fairly large positional advantage thanks to his strong knight.

19 d5   ♘xc4

The follow-up to the previous move.

20 dxc6   ♕xc6

White's position seems very vulnerable. Strangely enough, it turns out all right. Immediate attempts to force matters fail; e.g., after 20...♗xg2 21 ♗xg2 ♕xc6, 22 ♘g5 is good enough.

21 g3 *(D)*

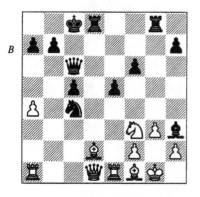

The only move. 21 ♖a2 fails to 21...♘xd2 22 ♖xd2 ♖xd2 23 ♕xd2 ♕xf3 and wins.

21 ...   ♗xf1

22 ♖xf1

Not 22 ♔xf1 because of 22...♕xf3 23 ♕xf3 ♘xd2+ and Black stays two pawns ahead.

22 ...   e4

This is the only way for Black to win his piece back, because after 22...♖d3 White can defend with 23 ♕c2 ♕d5 24 ♗e3, and 22...♖g4 is met by 23 ♕e2 ♖e4 24 ♗e3 and, at best, Black can get a third pawn for his piece.

23 ♕b3 *(D)*

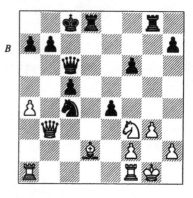

A roughly equal alternative is 23 ♕c2. After 23...♕d5 24 ♖fc1 Black has the choice of having his pawn on e4 or f3. In the first case, after 24...♘xd2 25 ♘xd2 ♕xd2 26 ♕xc5+ ♔b8 27 ♕c7+ ♔a8 28 ♖ab1 he must be prepared to defend passively with 28...♖b8. Therefore, the second choice is better because of Black's mate threats on the back rank: 24...exf3 25 ♕xc4 ♕xd2 26 ♕xc5+ ♔b8, and now 27 ♕f5 is best, to recover the pawn. The chances are equal.

Playing to win the exchange with 24 ♖fd1 (instead of 24 ♖fc1) fails after 24...exf3 25 ♗a5 ♕e6 followed by 26...♕h3 and mate.

23	...	**♕d5**
24	**♖ac1** (D)	

It is possible that Spassky had been planning 24 ♖fd1 here, since now it wouldn't fail as it did with the queen on c2 (Black's f3-pawn hangs). But 24...♘e5 would be lethal.

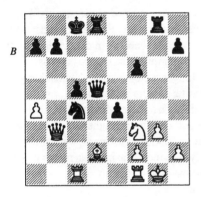

24	...	**♘xd2**

24...♘e5 seems a crushing blow, but closer analysis shows that it works out badly. White replies 25 ♖xc5+! ♕xc5 26 ♖c1, and Keene concludes that White stands clearly better after 26...♕xc1+ 27 ♗xc1 ♘xf3+ 28 ♔g2, for White's queen and bishop combine very well indeed. Stronger is 27...exf3 (instead of 27...♘xf3+) to keep the f-pawn indirectly protected after 28 ♗f4 with 28...♖gf8. Black is not badly off as far as material is concerned, but his pieces do not work well together. It is understandable why Korchnoi did not enter this variation.

25	**♘xd2**	**♕xd2**
26	**♖xc5+**	**♔b8**
27	**♖b1**	

Now it looks as though White is taking over the attack, but it has little potency.

27	...	**♖g7**
28	**♖b5**	**♖dd7**
29	**♕e6**	**e3**

The safest way to a draw.

30	**fxe3**	**♖ge7**
31	**♕g8+**	**♖d8**
32	**♕b3**	**♖8d7**

Korchnoi offered a draw here, but Spassky, with a forced draw in hand, refused.

33	**♕g8+**	**♖d8**
34	**♕b3**	½-½

Spassky offered the draw, and Korchnoi accepted. After the forced 34...♖8d7 35 ♕g8+ he could have demanded a draw by the repetition rule, but the personal tensions were not yet so great at this stage.

Game Twenty
Korchnoi – Karpov
World Championship Match (21), Baguio City 1978
Queen's Gambit Declined

After the 1977 Final Candidates Match, worse was expected of the ensuing World Championship Match, and reality confirmed those fears. Fodder for sensation-seeking journalists was plentiful in Baguio City, but what was most striking about it was how uninteresting the off-the-board complications were, compared to those in Reykjavik 1972, for example. I no longer remember whether Zukhar was sitting in one of the first four rows of the auditorium during this game or was with the rest of the Russian delegation in the rear of the hall, or whether Korchnoi or a member of his entourage was protesting about something or other, or whether the Ananda Marga members, with or without their folkloric costumes, were sitting in the hall or whether the Russians had already convinced the partisan match jury to make them leave both Korchnoi's villa and the city of Baguio.

From now on I will discuss only the game.

A very interesting opening. Karpov came up with something new, but the Russian team's preparation did not seem to be very thorough. Perhaps it was an attempt to bluff Korchnoi, but it failed miserably. Korchnoi had no problems with it and dictated matters throughout the game. Neither side seemed to have analysed carefully after adjournment. White's ultimate victory looked convincing, but analysis shows that some mistakes were made.

1 c4	♘f6
2 ♘c3	e6
3 ♘f3	d5
4 d4	♗e7
5 ♗f4	

Korchnoi earlier used to swear by the classical 5 ♗g5, but the innocent-looking text contains a fair dose of venom.

5 ...	0-0
6 e3	c5

The logical reaction now, since the development of White's queen's bishop does not exert maximum pressure on the centre.

7 dxc5	♗xc5

In Ribli-Gligorić, Bled/Portorož 1979, Black varied with 7...♘c6 8 ♕c2 ♘b4, but after 9 ♕d1 ♗xc5 10 a3 ♘c6 11 ♕c2 the play nevertheless entered the paths of this game via a different order of moves. But now Gligorić found a new set-up: instead of developing his queen on a5 he played 11...♕e7, and after 12 ♖d1 ♖d8 13

♗e2 h6 14 cxd5 exd5 15 0-0 ♗e6 16
♘a4 ♗d6 17 ♗xd6 ♖xd6 18 ♘c5
♗g4 19 ♘d4 White had a slight advantage.

8	♕c2	♘c6
9	♖d1	♕a5
10	a3	

An important position for theory,
the more so because it can arise from
the Nimzo-Indian (1 d4 ♘f6 2 c4 e6 3
♘c3 ♗b4 4 ♕c2 c5 5 dxc5 0-0 6 ♘f3
♘c6 7 ♗f4 ♗xc5 8 e3 d5 9 ♖d1 ♕a5
10 a3). In fact, the only difference is
that here Black has played ...♗f8-
e7xc5 instead of ...♗f8-b4xc5.

10 ... ♖e8 (D)

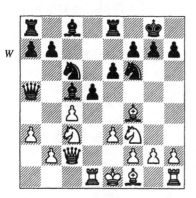

A novelty with an interesting idea
behind it but which nevertheless seems
doomed to failure. The usual move is
10...♗e7, which White answers with
11 ♘d2. Important recent examples
are:

1) 11...♗d7 12 ♗e2 ♖fc8 13 0-0
♕d8 14 cxd5 exd5 15 ♘f3 h6 16 ♘e5
♗e6 17 ♘xc6 ♖xc6 18 ♗f3 ♕b6 19
♗e5 with a lasting positional plus for

White (Karpov-Spassky, Montreal
1979).

2) 11...e5 12 ♗g5 d4 13 ♘b3 (D):

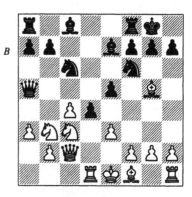

2a) 13...♕d8 14 ♗e2 h6 (in Ree-
Kuijpers, Leeuwarden 1978, Spassky's old move 14...♘g4 appeared to
be unsatisfactory after 15 ♗xe7 ♕xe7
16 exd4 ♕h4 17 g3 ♕h3 18 d5 ♘d4
19 ♘xd4 exd4 20 ♖xd4 ♖e8 21 ♖e4
♗d7 22 ♗f1 ♕h5 and now White
played the important improvement 23
h3!, instead of 23 ♗e2 ♕h3 with repetition of moves as in Portisch-Spassky,
Havana 1966) 15 ♗xf6 ♗xf6 16 0-0
♗e6 17 ♘c5 ♕e7 18 ♘xe6 ♕xe6 19
♘d5 with advantage to White (Korch-
noi-Karpov, 9th match game 1978).

2b) 13...♕b6 14 ♗xf6 ♗xf6 15
♘d5 ♕d8 16 ♗d3 g6 17 exd4 ♘xd4
18 ♘xd4 exd4 19 ♘xf6+ ♕xf6 20 0-0
♗e6 21 ♖fe1 ♖ac8 22 b3 ♖fd8 and
Black could just hold equality (Korch-
noi-Karpov, 23rd match game 1978).

11 ♘d2!

Korchnoi saw clearly that he need
not avoid the black threats. On the

contrary, he deliberately invites the following storm, which seems only to compromise the black position. The cautious 11 ♘e5 achieves nothing, and 11 b4 is simply bad due to 11...♘xb4, etc.

11 ...   e5?

Consistent but bad.

12 ♗g5   ♘d4 (D)

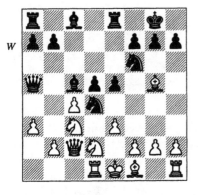

So this was the idea. Black quickly gets a decisive attack after 13 exd4 exd4+ 14 ♘e2 ♘g4. Korchnoi is unperturbed and replies without too much thought.

13 ♕b1   ♗f5
14 ♗d3   e4 (D)

'Karpov must have had this position on the board at home,' Bouwmeester remarks in his book about this match, *Het schaak der wraken* ('The Chess of Revenge').

This, I think, is a gross underestimation of Karpov's powers of judgement. A short analysis should be enough to convince any expert – Tal, Zaitsev, Balashov, or Karpov himself

– that Black is in almost insurmountable difficulties.

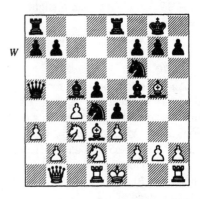

Superficially, everything seems very nice for Black: his knight move to d4 has allowed him also to develop his queen's bishop with tempo. All Black's pieces are splendidly developed and are in threatening positions. But what do they threaten? White's position offers no points of attack. Black's knight, which sprang to d4 with such force, is now hanging and in fact prevents the advance of the d-pawn. Thus, d5 is a sensitive weak point in Black's position. White threatens at any time to capture Black's king's knight with the bishop, and, after due preparation, Black's hanging queen's knight too.

It seems to me that the Russians assumed the following in their preparations: the move 10...♖e8 carried the threat of 11...e5 followed by 12...♘d4; White's reply would obviously be 11 ♘e5. That move was undoubtedly analysed thoroughly, and the probable conclusion was that Black would have little to fear. Perhaps 11 ♘d2 was discussed briefly and dismissed on the grounds that Korchnoi would quickly get into time trouble due to the inevitable complications, and in that case the correctness of the black moves would not play too great a role.

Korchnoi, however, showed his best side: no time trouble, but a clear-headed, strong reaction.

15 ♗c2

Good enough to keep a clear advantage, but the Steinitzian retreat 15 ♗f1! would have led to a winning position after some complications. For instance:

1) 15...♘g4. In my original annotation I stated: 'Given by Kholmov in *Shakhmaty v SSSR*. He continues 16 ♘xd5 ♘e5?! 17 exd4? e3! 18 ♕xf5 ♘f3+!! 19 ♕xf3 exd2 mate (exclamation and question marks by Kholmov). Despite the three successive piece sacrifices, the variation is rather clumsy and pedestrian, and is scarcely relevant since the black knight's move to e5 is intended merely to tempt White to capture on d4. Moreover, 15...♘g4 is just a blow in the air after the simple 16 cxd5. Then the c4-square becomes available to both the knight and the king's bishop while the knight on d4 stays in the trap.' I was not the only one to think this. In his *Het matchboek Karpov-Kortchnoi* Hans Ree observes with regard to Kholmov's variation: 'Really very nice, but the distribution of punctuation marks leads one to

suppose that he himself (Kholmov that is) doesn't take it very seriously.'

But not everyone was of this opinion. Dvoretsky emphatically recommends the line given by Dolmatov: 15...♘g4 16 cxd5 ♘e5. He then considers 17 ♗f4 ♘d3+ 18 ♗xd3 exd3 19 0-0 ♘e2+ 20 ♘xe2 dxe2 21 ♕xf5 to be the best line for White.

Chances are then roughly equal. The question remains whether Black's attack after 17 exd4 ♗xd4 18 ♗e3 ♗xe3 19 fxe3 ♕c5 is really so strong as Dvoretsky wishes it to appear.

After 20 ♘dxe4 ♕xe3+ 21 ♗e2 in my opinion Black has insufficient compensation for the piece. In order to substantiate this assessment I give the following variations:

1a) 21...♗g4 22 ♘g3 (above all, not 22 ♕c1?? ♘d3+) 22...♖ac8 23 ♕c2 ♖c4 24 ♕d2 ♕b6 25 d6 and Black's attack no longer amounts to much.

1b) 21...♘g4 (the best chance) 22 ♖d3! ♕b6 (not 22...♗xe4 because of 23 ♖xe3, winning; 22...♕f4 23 ♖f3 ♕e5 24 ♖xf5! ♕xf5 25 ♗xg4 ♕xg4 26 0-0 also offers no chance) 23 ♖f3 (not 23 ♖g3 ♘f2!) 23...♗g6 (or 23...♘e3 24 ♖xe3 ♕xe3 25 ♘f6+ gxf6 26 ♕xf5 ♕c1+ 27 ♘d1, followed by 28 0-0 with a winning advantage for White) 24 ♖g3! and White keeps the upper hand in all cases; e.g.: 24...♘f2 25 ♖xg6, or 24...f5 25 ♕c1!.

2) 15...♗xa3. The most important move. White has the following possibilities after the forced 16 ♗xf6 gxf6 *(D)*:

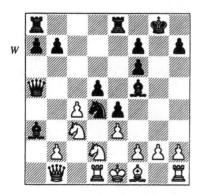

2a) 17 ♘xd5? ♗b4! 18 ♘xf6+ ♔g7 19 ♘xe8+ ♖xe8 and Black has a continuing crushing initiative despite his material deficit. If White parries the main threat 20...♘b3 with 20 b3, then 20...♗g4 is very strong.

2b) 17 exd4 e3 18 ♕xf5 exd2+ 19 ♔xd2 ♗xb2 20 ♕c2 ♕b4! and Black has his opponent in a vice; e.g., 21 ♗d3 dxc4 22 ♗xh7+ ♔g7 and Black wins the sacrificed material back with interest, or 21 h4 ♖e4! with a strong attack.

2c) 17 cxd5!, as was the case after 15...♘g4, is the correct way to take the d-pawn. The best for Black is again 17...♗b4, but now comes 18 exd4. After 18...e3 19 ♕xf5 ♗xc3 20 bxc3 ♕xc3 21 ♕g4+! ♔h8 22 fxe3 ♖xe3+ 23 ♗e2 ♖ae8 24 0-0 Black's attack has burned itself out. In other cases, too, White keeps a material advantage.

15 ...   ♘xc2+

Black exchanges his awkwardly placed knight, but his problems remain because his other pieces are not well co-ordinated.

16   ♕xc2 (D)

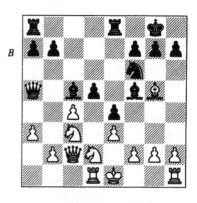

16 ...   ♕a6

It is always difficult to choose between two evils. Kholmov gives the text-move a question mark and claims that 16...dxc4 offers equal play. He gives two lines after 17 ♗xf6 gxf6:

1) 18 b4 cxb3 19 ♘xb3 ♕xa3 20 ♖a1 ♕b4 21 ♖a4 ♕b6 22 ♘d5 ♕c6! and Black is saved. This may be the continuation Karpov feared, but White has no way to undertake really dangerous action against the black king, as can be seen from 23 ♕xc5 ♕xa4 24 ♘xf6+ ♔g7 25 ♕xf5 ♕xb3 26 ♕g5+ ♔h8 (not 26...♔f8?? 27 ♘d7 mate) 27 0-0 ♖e6 possibly followed by 28...♖xf6, after which White has no more than a draw by perpetual check.

2) 18 ♘xc4 ♕a6 19 ♘d5 ♖ac8 20 ♕c3 ♗e7 and White loses material. This is mainly because of his 19th move, but other moves also offer him no advantage.

But why should White take the c-pawn right away? Much stronger is 18

0-0, to attack the e-pawn. After all, Black's weakened king position invites attack. Black has no satisfactory solution to his problems; for example, 18...♔g7 19 ♘xc4 (now this is correct; less clear is 19 ♘dxe4 ♖e5) 19...♕a6 20 ♖d5 and White's advantage is undeniable.

It should also be pointed out that 16...d4 (instead of the text-move) only leads Black into a dead end after 17 ♘b3 d3 18 ♘xa5 dxc2 19 ♖c1 and Black loses a pawn without any compensation.

17 ♗xf6

Korchnoi gives up his other bishop for a knight so that he can safely win a pawn. 17 cxd5 would have made it unnecessarily difficult to castle.

17 ... ♕xf6

18 ♘b3

As in the variations after White's 15th move, capturing on d5 with the knight deserves no recommendation. After 18 ♘xd5 ♕g5 19 0-0 Black gets very good attacking chances with 19...♗d6 (threatening 20...♗h3 without having to worry about 21 ♘f4) 20 ♔h1 ♖e6. But not 19...♗g4?, as given by Kholmov, because of 20 ♘xe4! ♗xd1 21 ♖xd1 ♕g6 22 f3 with superior play for White.

Korchnoi intends to capture the black d-pawn with a rook.

18 ... ♗d6

19 ♖xd5 ♖e5 *(D)*

After this almost pointless move Black might have quickly gone downhill. 19...♗e5 is required. After the

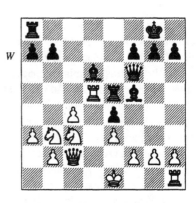

virtually forced 20 ♘d4 ♗xd4 21 ♖xd4 ♕g5 Tal gives 22 ♔f1 an exclamation mark in *64*, and almost the entire international chess press accepted this without question. It is far from convincing, however. White's king's rook will be excluded from the game for a long time, and Black can take advantage of this with 22...♖ad8 *(D)*. For example:

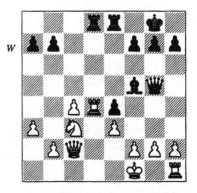

23 ♘d5 ♗e6 or 23 ♘e2 ♗g4 24 ♖xd8 ♗xe2+! 25 ♕xe2 (25 ♔xe2 ♕h5+!) 25...♖xd8 26 g3 ♖d3 27 ♔g2 ♕f5 with sufficient compensation for

the pawn, considering that 28 ♖d1? fails to 28...♕f3+. Perhaps better is first 23 ♖xd8 ♖xd8 and only then 24 ♘e2. Black's most promising continuation then is probably 24...♖d3 25 ♘d4 h5 with compensation for the pawn.

22 g3!, given by Andersson, is much stronger than 22 ♔f1. It seems at first sight to create a serious weakness, but a closer look shows that White's king does not face any serious danger. White will 'castle' artificially on the queenside via d1 or d2, and Black's compensation seems insufficient; e.g., 22...♖ad8 23 ♘e2 ♗g4 24 ♖xd8 ♖xd8 (now the capture on e2 is not with check) 25 ♘d4. Incidentally, the question as to whether White can do better with 22 ♔f1 or 22 g3 is not really relevant, for Dvoretsky shows that 22 0-0! is possible. Viewed superficially, Black then gets excellent play with 22...♗h3 23 f4 exf3 24 ♖xf3 ♖xe3. However, White takes advantage of Black's 'back-rank problem' with 25 ♕d2! ♖e1+ 26 ♔f2 ♕xg2+ 27 ♔xe1 ♖e8+ 28 ♖e4 and wins.

No more satisfactory for Black is 19...♕g6.

Kholmov shows that White beats off the enemy attack with 20 0-0 ♕h6 (or 20...♗h3 21 f4) 21 g3 ♗g4 22 ♘xe4 ♗f3 23 ♘bd2 ♖xe4 24 ♘xf3! and Black is two pawns behind without the slightest compensation.

20 ♘d4   ♖c8

This makes possible a very strong tactical manoeuvre, but there is no reasonable alternative.

21 ♖xe5 (D)

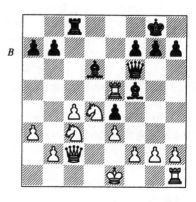

B

Korchnoi exchanges some pieces with the clear intention of castling as soon as possible. Objectively, this does not throw away the win, but it does give Black the chance to fight back and reach an ending which is not altogether hopeless.

White can make short work of his opponent with 21 f4!. If Black captures en passant he loses a piece without compensation: 21...exf3 22 ♘xf5 fxg2 23 ♖g1. If he takes on d5, his pair of bishops will have no future and White will be a pawn ahead with the better position.

21 ...   ♕xe5
22 ♘xf5   ♕xf5
23 0-0

The best. White returns the pawn temporarily but keeps the initiative. 23 ♘xe4 is less convincing due to 23...b5. After 24 0-0 ♖xc4 25 ♕d2 ♗c7 26 ♘g3 ♕e6 27 ♕d3 g6 followed by 28...♗e5, Black is very active and faces little genuine danger of losing.

23	...	♖xc4
24	♖d1	♕e5 *(D)*

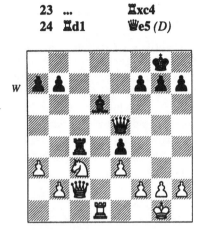

Tal rejects this move and gives 24...♗e7. He considers Black's prospects to be not bad, having in mind the variation 25 ♖d4 ♖xd4 26 exd4 ♕g5 27 ♘xe4 ♕d5 28 ♕d3 ♕a2. Except for Kholmov, the commentators once again accepted this uncritically. Kholmov's analysis of the match in *Shakhmaty v SSSR* is generally deep and good, but he treats certain parts of this game somewhat superficially, probably because of lack of time or space. In the same issue (December 1978) of that Russian magazine, he provides excellent extensive analysis of the twentieth match game.

At this point he shows that he was very alert. He completely refutes Tal's analysis with the powerful move 27 g3! (instead of 27 ♘xe4). White not only makes room for his king but is also ready to answer 27...e3 with 28 f4. White has a won position after 27...♕g4 28 ♕xe4, and after 27...f5

28 ♘d5 White has a winning attack. Finally, Kholmov points out that Larsen's 26...♗f6 (instead of 26...♕g5) fails to 27 ♘xe4 ♗xd4 28 ♘f6+! with mate or win of the queen.

We may conclude that the move chosen by Karpov is the most stubborn continuation.

25	g3	a6
26	♕b3	b5

Black's pieces seem to be working together well again. With his next move Korchnoi proves that the opposite is true.

27	a4!	♖b4

This leads to a hopeless ending, but there is nothing better.

28	♕d5	♕xd5
29	♖xd5	♗f8
30	axb5	a5 *(D)*

The only fighting chance. The winning process would run smoothly after 30...axb5 31 ♖xb5.

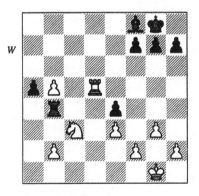

31 ♖d8

A remarkable decision. The alternative 31 b6 ♖xb6 32 ♖xa5 ♖xb2 33

♘xe4 leads to an ending that would be drawn without the minor pieces but which must be a win with the bishop and knight on the board. This is because the play takes place only on one side of the board, a situation in which the knight is clearly stronger than the bishop-long diagonals play no role.

A recent example is Portisch-Pritchett, Buenos Aires Olympiad 1978 (played shortly after this match).

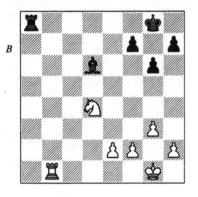

B

26...h5 27 ♖b7 ♗e5 28 ♘f3 ♗f6 29 ♔g2 ♖e8 30 e3 ♖e7 31 ♖b5 ♔g7 32 ♘d2 ♖e5 33 ♖b4 ♗e7 34 ♖b7 ♗f6 35 ♔f3 ♖e7 36 ♖b3 ♖e6 37 ♘e4 ♗e7 38 ♖b7 ♖e5 39 ♖d7 ♖e6 40 ♘c3 ♗f8 41 ♘e2 ♖e7 42 ♖d3 ♖e5 43 ♘f4 ♖e7 44 ♖d5 ♖c7 45 ♘d3 ♖c6 46 e4 ♖a6 47 ♔e3 ♔g8 48 h3 ♗h6+ 49 f4 ♖a3 50 g4 hxg4 51 hxg4 ♗g7 52 ♖d8+ ♔h7 53 g5 ♖a1 54 e5 ♖g1 55 ♘c5 ♖g3+ 56 ♔f2 ♖a3 57 ♘e4 ♖a2+ 58 ♔f3 ♖a3+ 59 ♔g4 ♖a4 60 ♘f6+ ♗xf6 61 gxf6 ♖a6 62 ♖f8 ♖a7 63 e6 fxe6 64 ♖e8 ♔h6 65 ♖h8+ ♖h7 66 ♖xh7+ ♔xh7 67 ♔g5 ♔h8 68 ♔xg6 ♔g8 69 f7+

♔f8 70 ♔f6 e5 71 ♔xe5 ♔xf7 72 ♔f5, 1-0.

Pritchett defended himself not at all badly in this game but finally could not avoid going under. The execution of the victory took forty-six moves, which provides food for thought: Korchnoi was undoubtedly hoping for a quicker win and correctly saw that keeping the advanced passed b-pawn would guarantee it.

    31 ...   **♖xb2**
    32 ♖a8   **f5**

Black has two ways of trying to reach an ending of four pawns to three on one wing, but both fail:

1) 32...♖b3 33 ♘d5 g6 34 ♖xa5 ♗c5 35 b6! ♗xb6 36 ♖a8+ ♔g7 39 ♖b8 winning a piece.

2) 32...a4 33 ♖xa4 ♖b3 34 ♖c4 g6 35 ♖c6 (threatening 36 b6) 35...♗g7 36 ♖c8+ ♗f8 and now after 37 g4, the strongest move, Black has no chances whatsoever; e.g., 37...♔g7 38 ♖c6 or 37...f5 38 gxf5 gxf5 39 ♔g2 ♔f7 40 ♖c7+ and now 40...♔e6 is met by 41 ♘e2, and after 40...♔g6 41 ♖c6+ followed by 42 b6 White also has matters all his own way.

The text gives White the greatest technical problems as the knight will later have to move to the edge of the board to defend the b-pawn.

    33 ♖xa5   **♗b4**
    34 ♖a8+   **♔f7**
    35 ♘a4 *(D)*

The attack on the rook is necessary because after 35 ♘d5 ♗e1 Black gets counterplay.

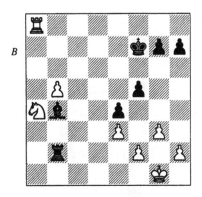

35	...	♖b1+
36	♔g2	♗d6
37	♖a7+	♔f6
38	b6	♗b8

Kholmov looks at 38...h5, but then White wins easily after 39 ♘c3 ♖b3 40 ♘d5+ ♔e6 41 ♘f4+! ♗xf4 42 gxf4 g6 43 b7 and the white king penetrates via g5.

39 ♖a8 (D)

An idea of Panno's is 39 ♖c7, which is quite justified tactically, as we see in 39...♗xc7 40 bxc7 ♖c1 41 ♘b6 ♖xc7 42 ♘d5+ or 39...♖b4 40 ♘c5 ♖xb6 41 ♘d7+ ♔g6 42 ♖c8. But the move achieves little after 39...h5 for instance. The winning variation given in the notes to the previous move is no longer possible.

39 ... ♗e5

Various commentators have incorrectly called this the decisive mistake. 39...♗d6, given as better, loses much more quickly because the white knight then plays a decisive role in the struggle: 40 ♘c3 ♖b3 41 ♘d5+ ♔e5 42 ♘c7!. The main threat is 43 ♖e8+, and

42...♖xb6 fails to 43 ♖a5+ ♔f6 44 ♘d5+. Relatively better is 41...♔e6 (instead of 41...♔e5), but White plays 42 ♘c7+ ♔d7 43 ♘e8! and simplifies to a winning ending; e.g., 43...g6 44 ♘xd6 ♔xd6 45 ♖b8 ♔c6 46 h4! and Black has no defence. The pawn ending after 46...♖xb6 47 ♖xb6+ ♔xb6 48 g4! is lost, and 46...♖b1 47 ♖h8 ♖xb6 48 ♖xh7 ♔d5 49 ♖h6 followed by 50 h5 is equally hopeless. After the text-move White can indeed advance his passed pawn, but his knight does not give it strong support from c5, and it is this factor which makes the win difficult.

40	♘c5	♗d6
41	b7	♔e7
42	♖g8	♗e5
43	f4	

The sealed move, and clearly the strongest. Black must capture en passant because his bishop is tied to the defence of g7 and b8. White's king will now have more room to manoeuvre.

43 ... exf3+

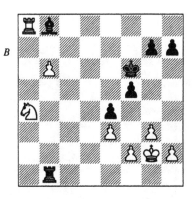

44 ♔xf3   ♔f7 (D)

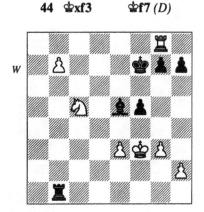

45 ♖c8

Keene, in his book on the match, writes that Korchnoi's team analysed the adjourned position until the last possible moment and wasted a lot of time on the unnecessary piece sacrifice 45 ♖d8 ♔e7 46 ♖d7+ ♔e8 47 e4 ♖b5 48 exf5 ♖xc5 49 ♖xg7. They could not find a clear winning line after 49...h6!. Korchnoi chose the text-move at the last moment; since no concrete winning variation had been found, he decided to hold the position as it was.

However, Keene and Stean were on the right track. The introductory moves of the variation, 45 ♖d8 ♔e7 46 ♖d7+ ♔e8 47 e4 ♖b5 are completely logical. Maybe they underestimated White's chances. After a brief look, Andersson and I came to the conclusion that White must be winning and that a forced winning variation, hidden or not, existed. After nearly an hour's search, our analysis continued with 48

♖d5! *(D)*, the most obvious move and the strongest. Black has two reasonable replies:

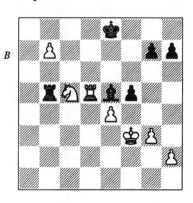

1) 48...♗b8 (to keep White's king out of the centre for the moment) 49 exf5 ♗a7 (threatening to simplify to a drawn rook ending) 50 f6! (a characteristic tactical twist) 50...gxf6 51 ♘e4 with an easy win.

2) 48...fxe4+ 49 ♔xe4 ♗b8 50 ♔d4 (or 50 ♔d3) 50...♗a7 51 ♔c4 ♖b6 (on 51...♖b1 or 51...♖b2, 52 ♘b3 is immediately decisive) 52 ♘e4! *(D)*.

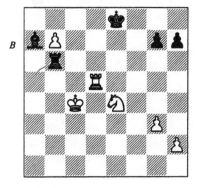

Another characteristic idea. White threatens 53 ♖b5 to swap rooks and to make it difficult for Black even to give up his bishop for the b-pawn. The last stand now is 52...♗b8 53 ♖b5 ♖e6 54 ♘c5 ♖e2, but White still wins after 55 ♘a6 ♗a7 56 b8♕+ ♗xb8 57 ♖xb8+ ♔f7 58 h3! ♖h2 59 h4. But definitely not 58 h4? ♖e3 59 ♖b3 ♖xb3 60 ♔xb3 ♔g6 and the black king penetrates, ensuring a draw.

All in all, a not too difficult and fairly forced variation. Note that White keeps the pawn formation h2-g3 intact; to limit the diagonal of Black's bishop.

To give a balanced view of the circumstances, it is not inappropriate to point out that Andersson and I did this analysis far from the pressure and the heat of battle whereas Korchnoi's seconds had to try to find something in a few short hours. This was not the first time that the requisite sharp, objective vision was clouded by such factors.

45 ...   ♔e7
46 h3 *(D)*

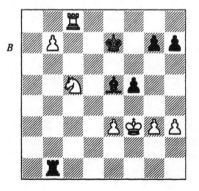

Keene gives this an exclamation mark and even describes it as a subtle trap. And it is, too. Objectively, the best move is 46 ♖g8, to answer 46...♔f7 with 47 ♖d8 (see the notes to the previous move). The text-move lengthens the diagonal of Black's bishop and puts the win in doubt. Karpov, however, is not able to take full advantage of it.

46 e4 is another interesting winning try. The difference from the winning variation in the notes to White's 45th move is that with 46...fxe4+ 47 ♔xe4 ♗d6 48 ♔d5 ♗xc5 49 b8♕ ♖xb8 50 ♖xb8 Black reaches an ending that is a theoretical draw with the bishop on the a1-h8 diagonal – but it's hard to see how to get it there. Best seems 50...♗g1 51 h3 ♔f7, and I think Black need not despair.

46 ...   h5?

A baffling inaccuracy. Black wants to prevent the advance of White's g-pawn, but in so doing he makes possible a smooth winning method that was not in the position before. 46...g6, given by Larsen, is equally unsatisfactory because of 47 ♘d3 ♗d6 48 ♖h8 h5 49 ♘f4 ♔f6 50 ♖h7 and sooner or later Black will have to permit a rook ending that he will slowly but surely lose.

The move 46...♖b5!, however, puts some spokes in the wheel and gives White serious problems; e.g., 47 g4 fxg4+ 48 hxg4 ♗d6 49 ♔e4 h6 (not 49...g6 50 g5! and Black does not get a passed pawn) 50 ♔d3 (if 50 ♔f5 then not 50...♗xc5 51 b8♕ ♖xb8 52 ♖xb8 ♗xe3 53 ♔g6 ♗d4 54 ♖g8 and White wins, but 50...♔f7 and if 51 e4?? then White is suddenly mated with 51...g6) 50...♖b4! 51 e4 (if 51 ♔c3, now 51...♗xc5) 51...♗e5! *(D)*.

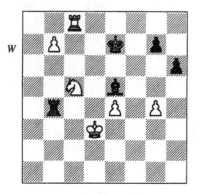

This last variation was given by Andersson. It is difficult to see how White can make progress after 46...♖b5.

47 ♖g8   ♔f7
48 ♖d8 *(D)*

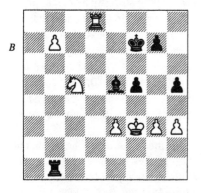

With White's pawn on h3 and Black's on h5 this leads to a fairly easy

win. The main variation runs 48...♔e7 49 ♖d7+ ♔e8 (otherwise he loses material: 49...♔f6 50 ♖d5 ♗b8 51 ♖d8 ♗c7 52 b8♕ or 50...♗c7 51 ♘a6! ♖xb7 52 ♖d7 winning a piece) 50 ♖d5 ♗b8 51 ♖xf5 and White wins the black h-pawn also after 51...♗d6 52 ♘e4. If his pawn were still on h7, Black would have good drawing chances after 52...♗e7 followed by 53...♖xb7.

48 ...   g5
Desperation.

49 g4
The surest way. White is not misled by 49 ♘d3, which leads to a draw after 49...g4+ 50 hxg4+ hxg4 51 ♔f2 ♔e7! 52 ♘xe5 ♔xd8 53 b8♕+ ♖xb8 54 ♘c6+ ♔c7 55 ♘xb8 ♔xb8 56 e4 ♔c7 57 ♔e3 ♔d6 (Tal).

A good move is 49 ♘d7, given by Kholmov. After 49...g4+ 50 hxg4 Black has two ways of recapturing:

1) 50...fxg4+ 51 ♔e4 ♗xg3 52 b8♕ ♗xb8 53 ♖xb8. Kholmov stops here. If Black does not exchange rooks, 54 ♘e5+ will be decisive, and 53...♖xb8 54 ♘xb8 h4 55 ♘c6 ♔f6 56 ♔f4 h3 57 ♘e5 g3 58 ♘g4+ followed by 59 ♔xg3 also leads to an easy win for White.

2) 50...hxg4+ 51 ♔e2 ♖b2+ 52 ♔d3 ♗xg3 53 b8♕ ♗xb8 54 ♖xb8. Kholmov again gives no further analysis. This time, avoiding the exchange of rooks is bad because of 55 ♖b6 followed by 56 ♘e5, and 54...♖xb8 55 ♘xb8 ♔f6 56 ♘c6 g5 57 ♘d4 g3 58 ♔e2 ♔g4 59 ♔f1 is also hopeless for

Black because 59...f4 60 e4 f3 fails to 61 ♘xf3.

49 ... hxg4+

There is no time for 49...fxg4+ 50 hxg4 h4 on account of 51 ♘d7 and Black doesn't even get a pawn for the piece.

50 hxg4 ♔e7
51 ♖g8 fxg4+

If 51...♔f7 then again 52 ♖c8!. Kholmov then gives 52...fxg4+ 53 ♔xg4 ♗d6 54 e4 ♗f4 55 ♔f5 ♖f1 56 ♘d7 ♔e7 57 e5 and wins.

52 ♔xg4 ♔f7
53 ♖c8 ♗d6
54 e4

Certainly not 54 ♔f5?? because of 54...♗xc5 drawing. White must keep his e-pawn safe.

54 ... ♖g1+
55 ♔f5 g4
56 e5

Korchnoi has plotted a very elegant course to victory. 56 b8♕ is good enough too, of course.

56 ... ♖f1+
57 ♔e4 ♖e1+
58 ♔d5 ♖d1+
59 ♘d3!

This is the point.

59 ... ♖xd3+
60 ♔c4 1-0

Game Twenty-one
Kasparov – Polugaevsky
46th USSR Championship, Tbilisi 1978
Sicilian Defence, Modern Paulsen Variation

Karpov is the only member of the generation of Russian players born around 1950 to have really reached the top. For a while it seemed that Romanishin would succeed too, but after a few tournament victories his results fluctuated again. The older generation of Petrosian, Polugaevsky, and Tal will not be easily surpassed, it seems. But Garry Kasparov might well be the one to do it: he won the tournament at Banja Luka 1979 two full points ahead of second place, and during the tournament he celebrated his sixteenth birthday.

Kasparov had made his debut the previous year in the Soviet Championship, where he scored fifty percent. His win against Polugaevsky was undoubtedly the most striking. After his very opportunistic pawn sacrifice in a well-known theoretical position the play became extremely sharp, but it was soon apparent that Black was not in great danger despite all the complications. Polugaevsky went wrong only in the endgame, after refusing a draw offer.

Polugaevsky is a generally solid player who seldom loses despite his fairly enterprising style. This was his only loss in the Championship. In fact, it was not until the Spartakiade, half a year later, that he lost another game – to Kasparov.

1	e4	c5
2	♘f3	e6
3	d4	cxd4
4	♘xd4	a6

Polugaevsky does not play this system often. He prefers the Najdorf and sometimes the Scheveningen.

5	♘c3	♕c7

5...b5 is known to be somewhat premature because of 6 ♗d3. A recent example is Tal-Ljubojević, Montreal 1979: 6...♗b7 7 0-0 ♘c6 8 ♘xc6 ♗xc6 9 ♕e2 ♘f6 10 e5 ♘d5 11 ♘xd5 ♗xd5 12 a4 ♕a5 13 ♖d1 with advantage to White.

6	♗e2	b5

This advance is completely sound now that White has developed his king's bishop.

7	♗f3	♗b7
8	0-0	♘c6
9	♘xc6	dxc6 *(D)*

A known theoretical position. Most of the examples now continue 10 a4; for example, 10...♗d6 11 axb5 cxb5 12 e5 ♗xe5 13 ♘xb5 axb5 14 ♖xa8+ ♗xa8 15 ♗xa8 ♗xh2+ 16 ♔h1 ♗d6 with roughly equal play (Estrin-Polugaevsky, USSR 1964). A more cautious approach is 11 g3. White won quickly with this in Liberzon-Torre, Bad Lauterberg 1977: 11...♗e5 12 ♗g2 ♘f6 13 f4 ♖d8 14 ♕f3 ♗d4+ 15 ♔h1 e5? 16 g4! exf4 17 ♗xf4 ♕e7 18 e5 ♘d5 19 ♗g5 f6 20 exf6 gxf6 21 ♖ae1 ♗e5 22 ♘xd5 and Black resigned. Better is 15...0-0 and not much is going on.

Kasparov decides to sacrifice.

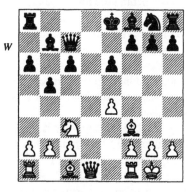

10 e5!?

Good or bad? Kasparov and Sakharov put a '?!' (dubious) after the move in their notes in the *Informant*. My analysis indicates that it is neither better nor worse than the normal theoretical paths. Nearly all the variations lead finally to equal positions.

10 ... ♕xe5

Naturally, he accepts the offer.

11 ♖e1 ♕c7

Black can force an ending with 11...♕d6, since after 12 ♕e2 ♘f6 he would simply be a pawn ahead. Barle-Miles, Bled/Portoroz 1979, continued 12 ♗g5 ♕xd1 13 ♖axd1 ♗e7 14 ♘e4 ♘f6 15 ♗xf6 gxf6 16 ♗h5 ♖a7! 17

♘d6+ ♗xd6 18 ♖xd6 ♔e7 19 ♖ed1 ♗a8 and Black consolidated his extra pawn. White's 12 ♗g5 hardly seems the right way to get compensation for the pawn. More purposeful and better is 12 ♕xd6 ♗xd6 13 ♘e4 ♗e7 14 ♗e3 followed by 15 ♘c5, after which White has reasonable pressure for the pawn. Understandably, Polugaevsky chooses the text-move, having correctly calculated that he will face little danger despite the presence of queens on the board.

12 ♗h5

There is no other way to try to prove the correctness of the pawn sacrifice.

12 ... ♗e7 (D)

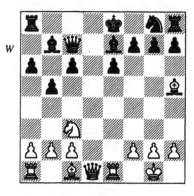

This move ought to do in any case. 12...g6 is bad, of course, because of 13 ♕d4.

13 ♖xe6 g6

The sharpest: Black aims to win material. 13...♘f6 is quieter. Kasparov and Sakharov reject that move because of 14 ♘e4, with the point that 14...♘xh5 15 ♕xh5 0-0 16 ♗f4 leads to 'slightly better play for White.' This judgement is undoubtedly correct if Black now takes on f4, but he has better: 16...♕d7!, and White's rook is suddenly in serious trouble. It has only one square, as the combinational try 17 ♘g5 would work only after 17...♗xg5 18 ♖d6 ♕f5 19 ♕xg5 ♕xc2? 20 ♗e5, but not after 17...h6 18 ♖xh6 gxh6 19 ♕xh6 ♕f5 and White has run out of steam. Therefore, 17 ♖e5. But now comes 17...f6 *(D)*.

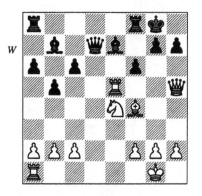

Things look precarious for White because after 18 ♘c5 ♗xc5 19 ♖xc5 ♕d4 he loses material on the queenside. However, he can just save himself with 18 ♖d1 ♕e8 19 ♘d6! ♕xh5 20 ♖xh5 ♖ad8 21 ♖h3 followed by 22 ♖hd3 – a narrow escape.

The question arises whether 14 ♘e4, given an exclamation mark by Kasparov and Sakharov in their notes, is really that strong. More solid is 14 ♗g5 0-0 15 ♖e1. After 15...♖fe8 16 ♗f3 ♖ad8 17 ♕c1 the position is about balanced.

14 ♖e1

A forced piece sacrifice. 14 ♕d4 is bad because 14...fxe6 15 ♕xh8 0-0-0 16 ♗g4 ♗f6 is in Black's favour. Bellin notes in *International Chess* that 15 ♗f4 (instead of 15 ♕xh8) is refuted by 15...e5 16 ♗xe5 ♕d8. Simpler, however, is 15...♗f6 (as in Shamkovich-Arnason, Lone Pine 1980), and White is behind too much material.

14 ...   ♖d8

Polugaevsky does not want to accept the sacrifice immediately, but 14...gxh5 is not so very risky. Kasparov and Sakharov give two continuations and conclude that Black gets a clear advantage in both.

1) 15 ♗g5 c5. Thus far Kasparov and Sakharov. Black indeed has the better prospects, as we see in 16 ♘d5 ♗xd5 17 ♕xd5 ♖d8 18 ♕f3 ♔f8! and White's grip on the position weakens, allowing Black to bring his material advantage to bear.

2) 15 ♕d4. Without doubt the strongest move. White forces 15...f6, after which he has the following possibilities:

2a) 16 ♕d1. This is given by Kasparov and Sakharov. By playing his queen back, White ensures that the enemy king is kept in the centre. Initially I thought that this was White's best attacking continuation, but closer examination showed me that White's game runs out of steam, as a result of which Black is able to consolidate his material advantage. The best continuation is the enterprising thrust 16...b4.

After 17 ♕xh5+ ♔f8 18 ♘e4 ♕e5 19 ♗h6+ ♘xh6 20 ♕xh6+ ♔f7 White's attack is beaten off. So he has to play 18 ♗h6+ at once, but also in this case Black can escape perpetual check: 18...♘xh6 19 ♕xh6+ ♔f7 20 ♕h5+ ♔g8. In my original note I said that White would now get dangerous threats with 21 ♖ad1 ♖d8 22 ♖xd8+ ♕xd8 23 ♘e4. However, this comes up against 23...♗c8 24 ♖e3 ♗f5!, when the black king is conclusively protected.

2b) 16 ♗f4. This is given by Bellin, who has investigated this game in some depth. Initially I thought that this move was less good, but I later reconsidered this assessment. It is entirely logical to develop the bishop. Black has a tough time, because on 16...♕d7 White continues with the strong 17 ♕c5. If he now castles long it all ends in disaster: 17...0-0-0 18 ♕a7 ♗d6 19 ♖ad1 ♕c7 20 ♖xd6 ♖xd6 21 ♘e4 ♖d1 22 ♖xd1 ♕xf4 23 ♘d6+ and wins. So the black king again has to move to f8, but then White, with his beautifully developed queen's bishop, has better chances than in variation 2a. Black's best reply to 16 ♗f4 is 16...c5, in order to get counterplay that is as active as possible. In my original notes I gave the continuation 17 ♕e3 ♕c6 18 ♕h3 f5 (prevents 19 ♖e6 and frees the path to g6 for the queen) 19 ♖ad1 ♕g6 20 ♘d5 ♖d8 with, by way of conclusion: 'and White's attack is over'. Perhaps that is so, but instead of 20 ♘d5 the

move 20 ♖e3! is much stronger. White then retains all kinds of attacking chances. Whether this is sufficient is another question. In any case it is clear that White has to look in this direction, which does not alter the fact that Polugayevsky could have accepted the sacrifice without hesitation.

Young geniuses are usually incorrigibly optimistic. It is remarkable that Kasparov, after the game, should have had so little faith in his own conception, as shown by his notes.

15 ♕f3   c5 (D)

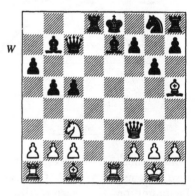

Still postponing the capture on h5, and rightly so. 15...gxh5 would now be very strongly answered by 16 ♗f4.

16 ♗f4   ♕b6

The simplification 16...♗xf3 17 ♗xc7 ♗xh5 18 ♗xd8 ♔xd8 is bad for Black because his game is completely disorganised after 19 f3; e.g., 19...g5 20 ♖ad1+ ♔e8 21 ♖d6! and the time is ripe for White to reap the fruits of his labour.

17 ♕g3   gxh5

18 ♗c7

The primitive 18 ♕g7 fails to 18...♕g6 19 ♖xe7+ ♘xe7 20 ♕xh8+ ♔d7 21 ♖d1+ ♗d5! and Black wins.

The text-move speaks for itself, yet there is an alternative: 18 ♗e5. The idea is to continue with 19 ♗c7 only after 18...f6, which cuts off the black queen's route to g6. Black has a pretty refutation in hand, however: 18...♘f6 19 ♗c7 ♕c6 20 ♗xd8 ♖g8!! *(D)*.

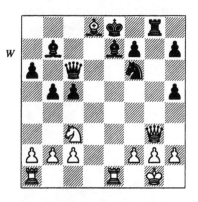

Oddly enough, after this powerful move it seems that White has run out of ammunition. The queen sacrifice 21 ♗xe7 ♖xg3 22 ♗xf6+ ♔f8 23 ♘e4 ♖g6 is insufficient, and after 21 ♖xe7+ ♔xd8 22 ♕b8+ ♔xe7 White can't even force a draw because the black king escapes via f5.

Andersson's attempt to improve the white play with 19 ♕f4 (instead of 19 ♗c7) also fails, because of the laconic reply 19...♔d7.

18	...	♕g6
19	♗xd8	♕xg3
20	hxg3	♔xd8

Although most of the tension has been resolved by the forced simplification, the position has not become any less interesting. Black can be satisfied with his material advantage, but his problem is how to complete his development while also ensuring good co-ordination among his pieces.

21 ♖ad1+ *(D)*

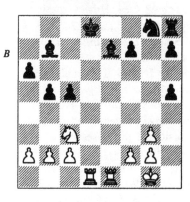

21 ...   ♔c7

The most obvious, although there is also an idea behind the alternative 21...♔c8. He must meet 22 ♘d5 by 22...♗xd5, as in the game (22...♗d6 is refuted by 23 ♘b6+ ♔c7 24 ♖e8), and after 23 ♖xd5, ♘f6 is possible. If now White thoughtlessly plays 24 ♖f5, Black achieves the desired co-ordination with 24...♔d7. Much stronger, however, is 24 ♖de5 and after 24...♗d6 only now 25 ♖f5. The important black f-pawn falls, and Black does not get a dangerous enough initiative; for example, 25...♘g4 26 ♖xf7 c4 27 ♖f5 with a winning position. Black must therefore play more modestly.

22	♘d5+	♗xd5
23	♖xd5	h6!

Black finds a subtle way to complete his development: he brings his rook into the game first. He thus unavoidably loses his foremost h-pawn.

24	♖xh5	♖h7
25	♖he5	♔d7
26	♖5e3! *(D)*	

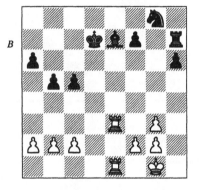

Kasparov manoeuvres very efficiently. Black has hardly any weaknesses, and if he manages to bring his rook into play undisturbed, White will be in serious trouble. However, the white rook operating along the third rank harasses the most vulnerable points in the black position, a6 and f7. Thus White can just maintain the balance.

26	...	♖g7

Black can play 26...c4 to keep the white rook out of a3, but it has the disadvantage that White can force the c-pawn's exchange with 27 b3. The opening of the c-file would be very favourable for White.

27	♖d3+	♔c7
28	♖a3	♖g6
29	♖f3	♗f6!?

After the simpler 29...♖g7 White has nothing better than to attack the a-pawn again with 30 ♖a3. Polugaevsky's winning attempt is not unjustified. but it's rather naive.

30	c3	♔d7
31	♖d3+	♔c7

And now we see how naive Black's winning attempt was. The combatants could shake hands after 32 ♖f3.

32	♖e8 *(D)*

White, in turn, dares a winning attempt; this one, however, is much riskier than Black's was.

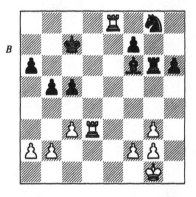

32	...	♘e7?

Polugaevsky, in time trouble, suddenly loses the thread completely. After 32...♗e7 it is not clear whether White's rook has penetrated or fallen into a trap. White no longer has perpetual check or repetition of moves, so Black can slowly but surely direct his pieces to strong posts; e.g., 33 ♖f3

♖g7 34 ♖f5 a5 followed by 35...a4 or 35...b4. The white rooks are actively placed, but Black's pieces are very elastic. White would have to fight for a draw.

After the text-move Black loses an important supporting pillar of his position, the f-pawn. In return, he gets his knight to c6, which is not even the best place for it.

33   ♖ed8

More convincing than 33 ♖f8 ♖g7 34 ♖f3 ♘g6 and Black has some fight left.

33	...	♘c6
34	♖8d7+	♔b6
35	♖xf7	♗e7

Too late, but there was little else to do against the threat of ♖d6.

36	♖e3	♗d6
37	f4 *(D)*	

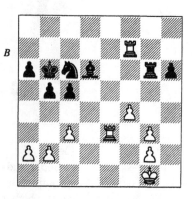

Takes the e5-square from the knight. Black is helpless, all the more so because his minor pieces are not working together effectively.

37	...	c4

38	♔h2	♗c5
39	♖e2	b4 *(D)*

A last try. The idea is to create some counterplay with 40...b3.

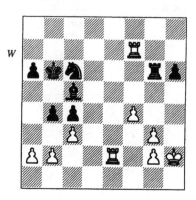

40   ♖e4

White exchanges his g-pawn for the black c-pawn.

40	...	bxc3
41	bxc3	♗f2
42	♖xc4	♗xg3+
43	♔h3	♗e1 *(D)*

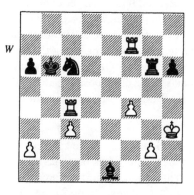

At first sight it seems that Black has obtained some counterplay, but the following strong move ends all illusions.

44 a4!

This move is based on the fact that the exchange of rooks brings Black no relief: 44...♖g3+ 45 ♔h2 ♖xc3 46 ♖xc3 ♗xc3 47 ♖h7 ♔a5 48 ♖xh6 ♘b4 49 g4 ♔xa4 50 f5 a5 51 f6 and White's connected passed pawns are faster than Black's wing pawn.

44 ... ♘a5

But this only makes it worse.

45 ♖b4+ ♔c5

A blunder in a totally lost position. If 45...♔c6, 46 ♖f5 follows anyway, since after 46...♗xc3 he calmly takes the knight: 47 ♖xa5.

46 ♖f5+ 1-0

A quite abrupt end to an exhilarating fight.

Game Twenty-two
Spassky – Timman
Montreal 1979
Grünfeld Defence, Exchange Variation

The ten-player supergrandmaster tournament in Montreal was immodestly described on the cover of the French-language tournament book as the most important in the history of chess. With an average Elo rating of 2622 and a prize fund of $110,000, it sounded tremendous; yet for such an important tournament there were serious organisational faults. It was played on the island of St. Helena at the mouth of the St. Lawrence River, the site of Expo 1967. The tournament hall was a fairly large theatre in a somewhat decaying building. The drafts were so strong that a few players sometimes put on their coats during the game. Often the boards and pieces were not set up until five minutes before the beginning of the round. Apparently, the tasks had not been very efficiently divided among the local organisers. Or did they find it beneath their dignity to perform such chores? The arbiter, Svetozar Gligorić, usually had to do most of the work, but once I saw Spassky carrying the boards into the hall while Hort was setting out the name cards.

But let's forget all that. The attractive prize fund in any case ensured that the games would be extremely hard fought. Witness the following game.

1	d4	♘f6
2	c4	g6
3	♘c3	d5
4	cxd5	♘xd5
5	e4	♘xc3
6	bxc3	♗g7
7	♗c4	

The Exchange Variation is still one of the most dangerous weapons against the Grünfeld Defence, but nowadays 7 ♘f3 is also played regularly; e.g., Karpov-Ljubojević, Montreal 1979: 7 ♘f3 c5 8 ♗e2 0-0 9 0-0 ♗g4 10 ♗e3 ♕a5 11 ♕b3 cxd4 12 cxd4 ♘c6 13 ♖ad1 ♕b4 14 h3 ♗xf3 15 ♗xf3 ♖fc8 16 ♕xb4 ♘xb4 17 e5 ♖c7 18 ♖c1 ♖ac8 19 ♖xc7 ♖xc7 20 ♖b1 ♘xa2 21 ♖a1!.

7	...	c5
8	♘e2	0-0
9	0-0	♘c6
10	♗e3	♗g4
11	f3	♘a5

Delaying the exchange on d4 has a dual purpose: first, White cannot protect his bishop on c4 with ♖a1-c1; second, the variation with ♗c4-d5 is not so attractive for White with the c-file closed. Thus White is more or less forced to play the classical exchange sacrifice after 12 ♗d3 cxd4 13 cxd4 ♗e6 14 d5. But Spassky, who has been playing the Exchange Variation against the Grünfeld ever since his youth, has never shown any interest in the exchange sacrifice. He chooses another continuation, which is associated with great risk.

12 ♗d5   ♗d7 (D)

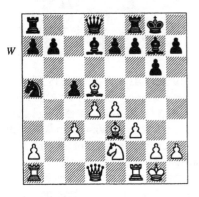

13 ♗g5

The usual move is 13 ♖b1, as in Hort-Timman, Nikšić 1978. After 13 ♖b1 ♕c8 14 dxc5, Black could have had a good game with 14...♖d8, as Hort suggested after the game. Needless to say, taking on c5 meant that White's strategy was a failure. There were no good alternatives, however, because Black threatened to get the better position with 14...e6 15 ♗b3 ♘xb3.

Spassky therefore chooses a continuation that lets him keep his bishop on d5 for a while. It is a remarkable idea because the move ♗g5 in connection with the pawn exchange on d4 (and therefore played on move 14) is never mentioned as an alternative to

the usual 14 ♖b1 (after the pawn exchange). Even now, after 13...cxd4 14 cxd4 White's position remains very good and he can sacrifice his d-pawn with little to worry about. You can see that after 14...♗b5 15 ♖b1 ♗xe2 16 ♕xe2 ♗xd4+ 17 ♔h1 Black has serious problems.

13 ...   ♗b5
14 ♖b1   ♗a6

Not so good is 14...♕d7, because after 15 ♖xb5 ♕xb5 16 ♗xe7 White clearly has the better chances. But now Black is ready for 15...♕d7 followed by 16...e6, after which White's position would collapse. Therefore, the following supersharp attacking attempt is born of necessity.

15 f4   ♕d7

Black can insert 15...h6 here, at a moment when White is forced to move his bishop to h4. But my intuition warned me that it was too risky, and a closer look shows that this was the correct evaluation; after 15...h6 16 ♗h4 ♕d7 17 f5 gxf5 White launches an offensive full of bold sacrifices: 18 ♘g3! e6 19 ♘h5!! *(D)* and now:

1) 19...♗xf1 20 ♗f6! exd5 21 ♗xg7 and White's attack quickly becomes decisive. The imperturbable manner in which White's attack is conducted in this variation is rather typical of this position; Black's pieces are active and well co-ordinated, but they are not well placed for defence.

2) 19...f6 20 ♖xf5! exd5 21 ♗xf6 ♗xf6 22 ♘xf6+ ♖xf6 23 ♖xf6 ♕g7 24 e5. Although the attack has been

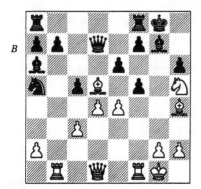

temporarily halted and the material situation has not turned out too badly for Black, White has the better chances because Black's minor pieces cannot be brought onto the battlefield very easily.

**16 f5   gxf5
17 ♖f3 (D)**

It took Spassky quite a while to find this unsophisticated continuation of the attack. Now 17 ♘g3 e6 18 ♘h5 is not sufficient because of 18...f6. Although 19 ♖xf5 is still possible (as in variation 2 above), under these circumstances it is just too fantastic: Black reacts cold-bloodedly with 19...exd5 20 ♗xf6 ♗xf6 21 ♘xf6+ ♖xf6 22 ♖xf6, and with the pawn on h7 instead of h6, Black's king position is adequately defended and he has time for 22...dxe4 with a winning advantage.

17 ...   fxe4

It took me almost an hour to find a fully satisfactory defensive scheme. I initially considered 17...e6, but after I found the complicated refutation 18 ♖g3 ♔h8 (18...f6 is insufficient due

to 19 ♗h6 ♖f7 20 ♘f4! exd5 21 ♘h5 with a winning attack) 19 ♘f4 exd5 20 ♕h5 fxe4 21 ♖h3 ♕f5 22 g4 ♗e2 23 ♘xe2 ♕g6 24 ♕h4 e3 25 ♖f1, with the unavoidable threat of 26 ♘f4, I realised that 19 exf5 ♕xd5 20 f6 produces a much more plausible win. Remember this long variation, however, for it will come up again.

Choosing between the text and the insertion of 17...h6 gave me the biggest headache. After the subtle reply 18 ♗c1! Black's position is critical. Taking on e4 is now forced, and after 18...fxe4 19 ♖g3 (D) I investigated:

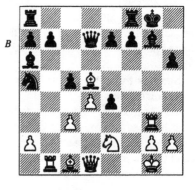

1) 19...♕xd5 20 ♗xh6 ♕h5 21 ♗xg7 ♕xe2 22 ♕c1! with the devastating threat of 23 ♕h6.

2) 19...♔h7 20 ♘f4 ♗d3 21 ♕h5 ♗xb1 22 ♖xg7+ ♔xg7 23 ♘e6+ and White has a mating attack.

18 ♖g3 *(D)*

18 ...   ♗xe2!

A necessary exchange, because the white knight threatened to enter the thick of the fight by going to f4. Nevertheless, after 18...♔h8 19 ♘f4 Black is not lost because he still has the finesse 19...♗d3. White's attack is not yet strong enough for him to sacrifice a rook: 20 ♕h5 ♗xb1 and if now 21 ♗xf7 ♖xf7 22 ♕xf7 ♖f8 or 21 ♗h6 ♗xh6 22 ♕xh6 ♖g8 23 ♗xf7 e3 or 21 ♗e6 ♗xd4+! 22 cxd4 ♕xd4+ 23 ♔h1 ♗xa2, White's attack is repulsed and Black's material plus will be decisive.

But the rook sacrifice is unnecessary. White's pieces occupy ideal attacking positions and he can take the time to play 20 ♖c1. The most important strength of Black's defensive

set-up is the fact that his e- and f-pawns are not yet advanced, but aside from that it is surprising how few defensive possibilities Black has. The main variation is 20 ♖c1 ♕f5 21 ♕h5 (threatening 22 ♗h6) 21...e6 22 ♖h3 exd5 23 g4 ♗e2 24 ♘xe2 ♕g6 25 ♕h4 and we get almost the same position as in the note after Black's 17th move. After 25...h6 26 ♘f4 ♕h7 27 ♗xh6 ♗xh6 28 ♕f6+ ♔g8 29 ♖xh6 White's attack has reached storm proportions.

19 ♕xe2   ♔h8
20 ♗xe4

One of the ideas of Black's defence becomes clear after 20 ♕xe4 f5 21 ♕h4 ♕xd5 22 ♖h3 ♕g8 and Black wins.

20 ...   f5
21 ♗f3

Quite rightly refraining from further attacking tries and placing the bishop on the long diagonal where it can exert the most pressure.

21 ...   cxd4 *(D)*

There is no time to protect the e-pawn; after 21...e6 22 dxc5 White's bishop-pair comes to life and after 22...♗xc3 he would have more than sufficient compensation for the pawn.

22 ♗xe7!

The only way to stay in the game. The endgame after 22 ♕xe7 ♕xe7 23 ♗xe7 ♖fe8 24 ♗b4 ♘c6 offers White little chance of survival.

22 ...   d3

The beginning of a forced simplification leading to a roughly equal

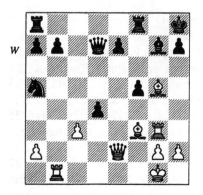

endgame. The point of White's play becomes clear after 22...♖f7 23 ♖xg7! ♖xg7 24 ♗f6 dxc3 25 ♗xc3. White does not hurry to regain the exchange, while Black's task of defending himself becomes extremely difficult and unpleasant.

A good alternative is to sacrifice the exchange by 22...dxc3 (D):

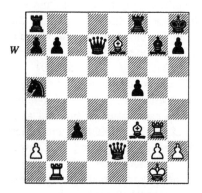

If White accepts, then after 23 ♗xf8 ♖xf8 Black has excellent prospects: his king is safe, and White's rook on g3 is therefore out of play. The advanced passed pawn on c3 is extremely unpleasant for White. The attempt to improve White's play with 23 ♖d1 fails: 23...♗d4+ 24 ♔f1 ♖ae8! 25 ♗xf8 ♖xe2 26 ♗xe2 c2 27 ♖c1 ♕c7 and Black is winning. White's best bet is to sacrifice the exchange with 23 ♖xg7. After 23...♕d4+ 24 ♔f1 ♕xg7 25 ♗b4! ♘c6 (25...c2 26 ♖c1 ♕b2? 27 ♕d2 is senseless, and White wins) 26 ♗xc6 bxc6 27 ♖b3! Black has nothing better than 27...♖ae8, which gives White the opportunity to simplify to a drawish endgame with 28 ♗xc3 ♖xe2 29 ♔xe2 (29...♖f6? fails to 30 ♖b8+), and with nothing but isolated pawns, Black has no realistic winning chances.

23 ♗xf8　　　dxe2

Sacrificing the exchange now is out of the question as White immediately sacrifices back: 23...♖xf8 24 ♖xg7 (24...♔xg7? 25 ♕e5+ or 24...♕xg7 25 ♕xd3 with a positional advantage for White).

24 ♗xg7+　　　♕xg7
25 ♖xg7　　　♔xg7 (D)

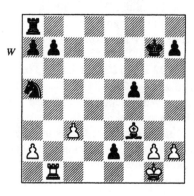

Attack and defence have balanced each other, and if White had now chosen 26 ♗xe2 a cease-fire would probably have been signed in short order. One possibility is 26...♖c8 27 ♖b5 b6 28 ♖xf5 ♖xc3 29 ♗f3; if Black now risks winning the a-pawn with 29...♖c1+ 30 ♔f2 ♖c2+, White becomes too active with 31 ♔e3 ♖xa2 32 ♗d5. The safest plan is to bring the knight into play immediately with 29...♘c4.

Instead, Spassky begins to play carelessly.

26 ♔f2   ♖c8

Based on a neat trap: 27 ♗xb7? fails to 27...♖b8 28 ♗e4 e1♕+! 29 ♔xe1 ♖e8 winning a piece.

27 ♔xe2   b6
28 ♖d1

White gives up a pawn to activate his rook. He is in no danger of losing because of this move, but neither is there any clear reason to play it. After 28 ♖c1 ♔f6 Black has a somewhat better position due to his well-co-ordinated pieces, but it would not be enough for White to worry about.

28 ...   ♖xc3
29 ♖d7+   ♔g6
30 ♖xa7   ♖c2+
31 ♔d3   ♖xa2
32 ♖d7

White's rook is again in the most active position. The direct attack 32 ♖a6 is bad due to 32...♖a3+ 33 ♔c2 ♘c4 with excellent winning chances for Black.

32 ...   b5

33 ♖d6+   ♔g5 (D)

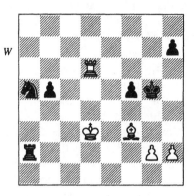

34 ♖b6?

This is not the best way to exploit the active position of White's pieces. With 34 ♖d5 b4 35 ♗e4 he can win the f-pawn and simultaneously bring his bishop to the b1-h7 diagonal, neutralising Black's passed b-pawn.

34 ...   ♖b2
35 g3

White's best chance under the circumstances. The mating threat 36 h4 forces Black to exchange a pair of pawns on the kingside. Black, it is true, gets rid of one of his isolated pawns, but it is more important that the total number of pawns is reduced and that, except for the passed b-pawn, Black is left only with the insignificant h-pawn.

35 ...   ♖b3+
36 ♔e2   f4
37 ♖d6

Forcing the capture on g3. Too ambitious is 37 h4+ ♔f5 38 g4+ ♔e5 39 ♖h6 as after 39...♘c4 40 ♖xh7 ♖e3+

41 ♔f2 ♘d2 White will be pushed even farther back, and he cannot exchange rooks (42 ♖e7+ ♔d4 43 ♖xe3 fxe3+ 44 ♔e2 ♘xf3 45 ♔xf3 ♔d3 and Black wins).

37	...	fxg3
38	hxg3	♘c4
39	♖d5+	♔f6
40	♔f2! *(D)*	

Now that he is in danger, Spassky defends himself very well. This move protects the g-pawn and frees his bishop to go either to e2 or to e4, depending on Black's moves.

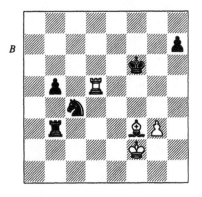

| 40 | ... | ♖b2+? |

It happens quite often that a player makes a mistake on his 40th move. The text-move helps only White, and Black's winning chances melt like snow in the sun.

40...♘e5 is no more effective, because of 41 ♗e2. Black should have realised that f5, not e5, is the ideal place for the knight and that 40...♘e3! is the correct move. After 41 ♖d7 h6 Black maintains winning chances; for

example, 42 ♖h7 ♔g6! 43 ♗e4+ ♔g5 44 ♖g7+ ♔f6 45 ♖g6+ ♔e5 and a draw is nowhere in sight for White: Black consolidates a solid extra pawn.

The exchange sacrifice 41 ♖xb5 ♖xb5 42 ♔xe3 ♖b2 43 ♗e2 ♔e5 is also not a watertight method of drawing. White's best chance is 41 ♖c5!, as Spassky suggested later, in order to keep as many checking options as possible. Black still has practical chances after, say, 41...b4 42 ♖c7 h6 43 ♖c6+ ♔e5 44 ♖xh6 ♘f5 followed by 45...♖b2+, but it is doubtful whether they are very real.

This ending bears a striking resemblance to an ending from the first game of the Spassky-Petrosian World Championship Match in 1969. After Black's 51st move the following position arose:

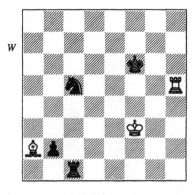

After putting up a heroic resistance, Spassky went wrong with 52 ♖h6+ and had to resign after 52...♔e5 53 ♖b6 ♘a4 54 ♖e6+ ♔d4 55 ♖e4+ ♔c5 56 ♖xa4 ♖a1. Later analysis showed that White could have drawn with 52 ♔e3; e.g., 52...♘a4 53 ♖h4! ♘c3 54 ♖b4 ♘d5+ 55 ♗xd5, etc.

Although I knew during the game that my practical chances were not as good as Petrosian's were, I still had to play the game and hope that it would turn out just as well for me.

41 ♗e2 b4
42 ♔f3

The sealed move. Home analysis revealed that Black has no winning chances.

42 ... ♘e5+

42...♘a3 43 ♗d3 achieves even less.

43 ♔e3

White's pieces are again working in harmony, and Black has no objective winning chances at all. But I had one more trap up my sleeve.

43 ... ♖c2
44 ♖b5 ♘c4+
45 ♔d3

Exactly what I was hoping for! After 45 ♔f3 Black has no possibility of making progress.

45 ... ♖d2+
46 ♔xc4 ♖xe2 *(D)*

The outlines of the trap are becoming visible. No matter how White captures Black's b-pawn, the resulting pawn endgame is a win for Black, as can easily be seen. Unfortunately for Black, the rook ending is still a draw.

47 ♖h5

The most convincing method. It would have been more difficult after 47 ♔d3 ♖b2.

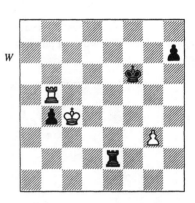

47 ... ♔g6

Unfortunately, 47...♖e4+ 48 ♔d3 ♔g6 is not playable because in the pawn endgame after 49 ♖xh7, etc., White's king is within reach of the b-pawn's queening square.

48 ♖h4 *(D)*

Spassky needed a good half hour to convince himself that this move guaranteed the draw. After the game he said he feared that 48 ♖h3 might give Black winning chances after 48...♖e4+ 49 ♔b3, but in the post-mortem we couldn't find any. The main variation we examined was 49...h5 50 ♔a4 ♔g5 51 ♖h1 ♖e5 (threatening 52...♔g4) 52 ♖h4 b3 53 ♔a3! ♖e3 54 ♖h3 and Black has made no progress. It is remarkable how the seemingly weak position of the white rook on h3 still manages to spoil whatever winning chances Black might have.

But a closer analysis shows that Spassky's intuition did not fail him. Black must not play the routine 49...h5? but must reserve that square for the rook; so 49...♖g4 50 ♔a4 ♖g5!

51 ♔xb4 ♖h5. In this position Black is again headed for a winning pawn endgame.

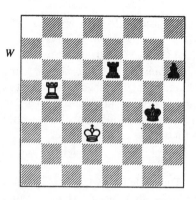

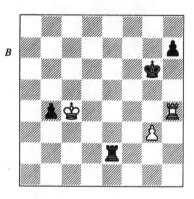

48	...		♖g2

48...♖e3 is stronger, but even then the draw is inevitable if White plays accurately. The next few moves are forced: 49 ♖g4+ ♔f5 50 ♖g7 (not 50 ♖h4 ♖e4+) 50...♖e4+ 51 ♔d3 h6 (51...h5 52 ♖h7 ♔g6 53 ♖xh5 draws immediately) 52 ♖h7 ♖e6 53 ♖b7 ♔g4 54 ♖xb4+ ♔xg3 55 ♖b5! ♔g4 *(D)* and now it all depends on this position:

During the post-mortem analysis Spassky suggested 56 ♔d2 h5 57 ♖b1,

but now after 57...♔f3 Black cannot exchange rooks with 58 ♖e1. The correct method is 56 ♖b4+, and now after 56...♔f3 White can let his king be cut off because 57 ♖h4 ♖d6+ 58 ♔c3 ♔g3 59 ♖h1 leads to a theoretical draw.

49	♖g4+	♔f5
50	♖h4	

With the black rook on e3 this would not have been possible (50...♖e4+); with the rook on g2 it leads directly to a draw. Only after 50 ♖g7 h5 followed by 51...h4 could Black have won.

50	...	b3
51	♖xh7	b2
52	♖b7	½-½

Game Twenty-three
Timman – Tseshkovsky
Bled/Portorož 1979
English Opening

The Vidmar Memorial Tournament is held every two years. For some reason or other, the fifth of the series, in 1979, attracted me immediately. Not that I have ever played through a game of Vidmar's – at least, never a game he won; but probably I have seen a number of his losses printed among the collected games of Alekhine, Capablanca, and Euwe. Frankly, this splendid tournament is a rather exaggerated mark of honour for a not very brilliant chess player.

The first six rounds were played in Bled, Yugoslavia, beside a lake of serene, almost sterile beauty. The last nine were played in Portorož, a rather mundane bathing resort with a casino which accepts only Italian lire. Venice is two hours away in a fast boat. Yet it was not even these attractive locations that made the tournament so tempting from the first moment. It was something else: a tournament that seemed cut out for me to win. Though not as strong as Montreal, it was strong enough to make a first place honourable. Larsen, at the opening ceremony, seemed to be thinking the same thing. He had just arrived by train, and the refreshing white wine being passed around was obviously doing him some good – and me too, for that matter. 'Who is going to win the tournament?' one of the organisers asked us. Politely, I made a noncommittal reply, whereupon Larsen, bursting with self-confidence, swallowed a good mouthful of wine and declared, 'I am going to win the tournament!' I must admit that I was at first taken aback by this display of naked optimism, and I often recalled it during the tournament.

The struggle for first place did indeed take place between Larsen and me, after Ribli dropped out of the running by losing spectacularly to Marjanović in the eleventh round. Larsen was still half a point ahead of me after that round, but the situation was reversed when he lost to Chi and I beat Tseshkovsky.

That victory meant a great deal to me. Not only was I clearly at the top of the crosstable for the first time in the tournament, but also it had been a long time since I last beat a Russian grandmaster. A psychological factor entered into the game, too: although Tseshkovsky did most of the playing, so to speak, I went into the complications with a healthy measure of optimism and confidence.

| 1 | ♘f3 | ♘f6 | 3 | ♘c3 | d5 |
| 2 | c4 | g6 | 4 | cxd5 | ♘xd5 |

5 ♕a4+   ♘c6

Tseshkovsky is an enormous deep-sea diver, as Langeweg once expressed it. He can sometimes sink into thought for an hour or more, even in the opening. He began very early in this game; he thought about the text-move for more than forty-five minutes. It is undoubtedly a better attempt to get counterplay than the usual 5...♗d7, but, as we will see, he was not completely familiar with all the position's subtleties.

6 ♘e5   ♘b4
7 a3 *(D)*

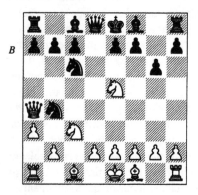

7 ...   ♗g7

The only reasonable move. He had already written 7...♘c2+ on his score-sheet, but White would emerge with a great advantage after 8 ♕xc2 ♘xe5 9 d4!. Note the importance of White's seventh move: now 9...♕xd4 would fail to 10 ♘b5 because Black has no check on b4.

8 axb4

The obvious 8 ♘xf7 would be to Black's advantage after 8...♘d3+! 9

exd3 ♔xf7. But White has the possibility 8 d4, with the tactical justification 8...♕xd4? 9 ♘f3 with win of material. Things are less clear, however, after 8...♗xe5 9 dxe5 ♘d5, when Black's centralised position compensates for the lack of his king's bishop. In *Informant 27,* Tseshkovsky gives 10 ♗d2 ♘b6 11 ♕f4 ♕d4 12 0-0-0 with unclear play. Black can try 11...♗e6, but after 12 0-0-0 ♕d4 the situation is still difficult to judge (13 ♘b5 ♕c5+).

8 ...   ♗xe5
9 b5   ♘b8
10 g3

The fianchetto of the bishop looks good, but it does not achieve much for White. To be considered is 10 e3 followed by 11 d4 in order to build up a solid centre immediately.

Timman-Sax, Rio de Janeiro 1979, showed that this plan is indeed correct – it is good enough, in fact, to refute the black set-up: 10 e3 ♗g7 11 d4 0-0 12 ♗e2 c6 13 0-0 cxb5 14 ♕xb5 ♘c6 15 ♗f3 a6 16 ♕b3 ♕d7 and now White could have placed his opponent in a paralysing grip with 17 ♗d2 (instead of 17 ♖d1 as played) followed by 18 ♖fc1.

10 ...   0-0
11 ♗g2   ♗g7
12 0-0

The *Informant* considers postponing castling and gives the variation 12 d3 c6 13 ♗f4 e5 14 ♗e3 a6 15 ♕a3 with a clear advantage for White. But Black has a much better move than the weakening 13...e5; namely, 13...cxb5

14 ♕xb5 ♘c6. Black has quite enough compensation for the pawn after 15 ♗xc6 bxc6 16 ♕xc6 ♗h3.

12 ... **c6**

Naturally. Without this pawn sacrifice, White would get a clear positional advantage.

13 d3 **a6!** *(D)*

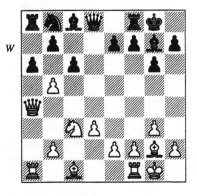

Again a move that strikes at the heart of the position. He forces his opponent to capture on c6.

14 bxc6 **♘xc6**

15 ♗xc6

Tseshkovsky was already running into time trouble. Although I saw that the text-move was risky, it seemed to be the only way to keep the game complicated. Other moves would allow Black to complete his development soundly and with easy equality.

15 ... **bxc6**

16 ♕h4

Black's bishop pair would provide excellent compensation for the pawn after 16 ♕xc6 ♖b8. After the text White threatens to get the advantage

with 18 ♗h6. Black's reaction is adequate, however.

16 ... **♖b8**

17 ♘a4

Again threatening 18 ♗h6, but Black has a strong reply which takes all the sting out of the white strategy. Perhaps the pawn sacrifice 17 ♗h6 is White's best chance. After 17...♗xh6 18 ♕xh6 ♖xb2 he has sufficient compensation for the pawn. White's best would then be to force the exchange of Black's rook with 19 ♖fb1.

17 ... **h5!** *(D)*

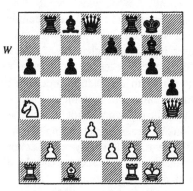

Not only preventing ♗c1-h6 but also making the g4-square accessible to Black's queen's bishop.

18 ♗d2

Intending 19 ♗c3. 18 ♗g5 would be simply answered by 19...♖e8.

18 ... **♗g4**

19 f3

I saw that Black would have tactical possibilities after this, but I chose it very quickly because there was very little choice.

19 ...   ♗xb2

The introduction to a deep combination. I was more concerned, however, about 19...♗f6. The exchange of dark-squared bishops is in itself favourable for White, but after 20 ♗g5 ♗xg5 21 ♕xg5 ♗h3 he faces an unpleasant choice: either to seriously weaken his pawn structure after 22 ♖fd1 ♕d4+ 23 e3, or to position his rook passively with 22 ♖f2. The latter is probably the lesser evil. In his annotations to the game, Tseshkovsky gives 22 ♖f2 ♖b4 (probably to prevent 23 ♕h4, which would force the bishop back), and he concludes that Black stands clearly better. However, it is not at all clear after 23 ♕c5!. Black must permit the exchange of queens with 23...♕d6 in order not to lose a pawn, but then the advance of the white e-pawn will not be such a serious weakness in the ending because Black will not have any real attacking chances: thus 24 ♕xd6 exd6 25 e3 with a tenable position.

20 ♘xb2   ♕d4+
21 ♔h1   ♖xb2
22 ♖ad1

The only move. After 22 ♗h6 ♖xe2 White cannot capture on g4 because of mate.

22 ...   ♖xd2 (D)

This was the idea. 22...♕e5 is pointless because of 23 fxg4 ♕xe2 24 ♕g5 hxg4 25 ♕e3 and White simplifies to an ending that must be a win for him.

23 ♖xd2   ♕e3

The real point of Black's combination now surfaces. White must return the exchange due to the threat 24...g5.

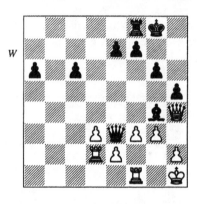

24 fxg4   ♕xd2

Black played this immediately – which is understandable, as he had little time left on his clock. But 24...g5! is safer, and only after 25 ♕xh5 to take the rook with 25...♕xd2. Then White's queen would be out of play and threatened with capture via 26...♔g7 followed by 27...f6 and 28...♖h8. It would make sense for White, therefore, to force a perpetual check with 26 ♖f5 ♕e1+ 27 ♔g2 ♕xe2+ 28 ♔h3 f6 29 ♕g6+ ♔h8 30 ♕h6+ draw. Tseshkovsky may have seen 24...g5 without quite realising that this was the time to think of a draw. Naturally one does not make such a long combination merely to force a draw. But after the text White gets the advantage.

25 ♕xe7

The white queen is dominantly placed here.

25 ...   hxg4

26 ♜f4 *(D)*

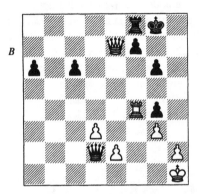

The smoke has cleared and Black is a pawn ahead. White will win it back by force, however, and a close study of the position shows that White's king is safer than Black's. White's e-pawn in particular provides strong protection, and besides, the white pawn structure is more compact than Black's.

26 ... ♛a2

The continuation shows that 26...♛a5 followed by 27...♛d8 would have saved a tempo. The most sensible move, however, is 26...f5. After 27 ♜d4 ♛a2 Black stands better. Correct is 27 ♛e6+ ♚g7 28 ♜d4, which offers good winning chances if Black posts his queen passively with 28...♛g5, but only a draw if he decides on 28...♜f6!. After 29 ♜d7+ ♚h6 White has no better than to take on f6, which allows Black a perpetual check.

27 ♜xg4 ♛d5+
28 ♚g1 ♛d8

See the note to Black's 26th move. Black decides against 28...♜b8 since

White would be the only player with attacking chances after 29 ♚f2.

29 ♛xd8 ♜xd8
30 ♚f2 *(D)*

The ending is not an easy one for Black; he has two isolated pawns and the white pieces are slightly more active.

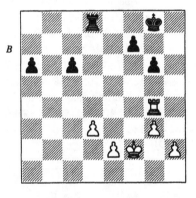

30 ... ♚f8

The Hungarian magazine *Magyar Sakkelet* gives 30...a5 with the variation 31 ♚e3 ♜a8 32 ♜a4 ♚f8 33 ♚d4 ♚e7 34 ♚c5 ♚d7 35 ♚b6 ♜b8+ 36 ♚xa5 ♜b2 with a draw. But it isn't that simple. Much stronger is 31 ♜c4!, when Black must give up his c-pawn (31...♜c8 32 ♜c5). After 31...♜a8 32 ♜xc6 a4 33 ♜c2 a3 34 ♜a2 White is not yet winning, but he has very real chances. The white king can walk unhindered to the centre and later to the queenside. White's only weakness is the h-pawn, but in an emergency it can be covered by advancing the e-pawn.

31 ♚e3 ♚e7
32 ♜e4+

I played this quickly, uncertain whether or not the pawn ending after 32...♔d6 33 ♖d4+ ♔c7 34 ♖xd8 ♔xd8 was a win. Black, in time trouble, understandably did not want to chance it.

Closer analysis, however, showed that it is a draw. The main variation runs: 35 ♔d4 ♔e7 (or 35...♔d7, but not 35...♔c7 because of 36 h4 f5 37 e4 and White gets two passed pawns. After either 35...♔d7 or 35...♔e7, then 36 h4 f5 37 e4 would be satisfactorily answered by 37...♔e6.) 36 ♔c5 a5 37 ♔c4 ♔d6 38 ♔b3 ♔d5 39 ♔a4 (Black would have winning chances after 39 e3 c5) 39...♔d4 40 ♔xa5 ♔e3 41 ♔b6 ♔xe2 42 ♔xc6 ♔xd3 43 ♔d5 ♔e3 44 ♔e5 (D).

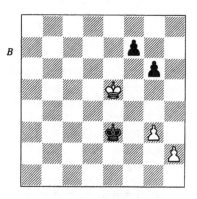

Now Black loses after the automatic 44...♔f3? 45 ♔f6 ♔g2 46 ♔xf7 ♔xh2 47 g4, but the game is drawn after 44...f5! 45 ♔f6 f4 46 gxf4 ♔xf4 and the white h-pawn is rendered harmless.

32	...	♔f6
33	♔d2	

Black's king is now cut off from the queenside and White's can approach the weak pawns unhindered. 33 ♖a4 is less accurate because of 33...♖e8+ 34 ♔d2 ♖a8 35 ♔c3 ♔e5 36 ♔c4 ♔d6 and the black king is in time to prevent his colleague from penetrating.

33	...	♖b8
34	♔c3	♖b5
35	♖c4 (D)	

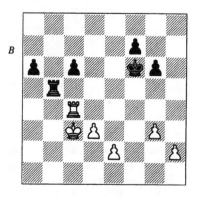

Playing on the opponent's time trouble. If now 35...♖b6 White can simplify to a pawn ending with 36 ♖b4, but after 36...♖xb4 37 ♔xb4 ♔e5 Black can enter the main variation in the note to White's 32nd move, since 38 e3 ♔d5 39 ♔a5 c5 40 ♔xa6 c4 offers White nothing positive. Perhaps I would have tried it another way; e.g., 36 h4 followed by 37 g4. Black would still have faced many problems and the draw would not yet have been in sight.

35	...	c5?

Now he loses a pawn by force.

| 36 | ♖a4 | |

The point is that 36...a5 is quietly answered by 37 ♖a2 followed by 38 ♔c4.

36	...	♖b6
37	♖a5	♖c6
38	♔c4	♖b6
39	♖a2	

White has time to protect the second rank before consuming a pawn.

39	...	♖c6
40	♔d5	♖c8
41	♖xa6+	

Black has made the time control, but the ending is lost.

41	...	♔g5
42	♖a4	

The most accurate. 42 ♖c6 ♖h8 43 h4+ ♔g4 44 ♔xc5 ♔xg3 45 ♖f6 probably wins too, but there is no reason to give the opponent a passed pawn. Black's c-pawn remains weak.

42	...	f5
43	♖f4	

The sealed move.

43	...	♔f6
44	h4	♖e8 (D)

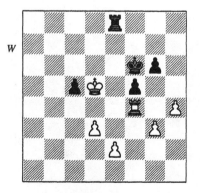

45 ♖f2

During the two-hour adjournment, I looked at the energetic 45 e4 but could find no convincing win. The main variation is as follows: 45...♖d8+ 46 ♔c4 ♔e5 (not 46...♖d4+ 47 ♔c3 ♔e5 48 exf5 with simplification to a won ending) 47 exf5 (if 47 h5 now 47...♖d4+ would follow because the pawn ending after 48 ♔c3 fxe4 49 ♖xe4+ is a draw) 47...gxf5 48 h5 (to post the rook behind the passed pawn immediately; 48 ♖f3 ♖c8 49 ♖e3+ ♔d6 is not a clear win) 48...♖g8 49 h6 ♖xg3 50 ♖h4 ♖g8 51 h7 ♖h8 52 ♔xc5 f4 53 d4+ ♔f5 54 d5 f3 and now, I thought at first, play would continue 55 d6 f2 56 ♖h1 ♔g4 57 d7 ♖xh7 58 ♖xh7 (or 58 d8♕ ♖xh1 draw) 58...f1♕ 59 ♖g7+ ♔h5! 60 d8♕ ♕c1+ 61 ♔d6 ♕h6+ with a draw.

A fantastic line, but very shaky. To begin at the end, 57 ♖f1 (instead of 57 d7) is a win – White waits for 57...♔g3 before continuing with 58 d7. White can calmly give up the rook because the advanced passed pawns and the out-of-play black king will decide the issue.

Black, in turn, can avoid all harm with 56...♔e6 (instead of 56...♔g4), and at best White will keep his now harmless d-pawn. All this means that White must be more circumspect about advancing his d-pawn. Instead of 55 d6, more accurate is 55 ♖h1 (D).

Now Black has only one answer, 55...♔e5, and it is just sufficient to

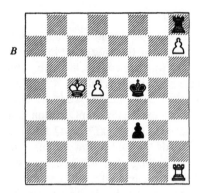

draw. For instance, 56 d6 ♖c8+ and now:

1) 57 ♔b5 ♔xd6 58 h8♕ ♖xh8 59 ♖xh8 ♔d5! and the white king is held off, which guarantees the draw: 60 ♖f8 ♔e4 61 ♔c4 ♔e3 62 ♖e8+ ♔d2, etc.

2) 57 ♔b4 is the most venomous. Black has two ways to go wrong:

2a) 57...♔xd6 58 h8♕ ♖xh8 59 ♖xh8 ♔d5 60 ♔c3 and wins.

2b) 57...f2 58 d7 ♖h8 59 ♔c5 and wins after either 59...♔e6 60 ♔c6 or 59...♖xh7 60 d8♕ ♖xh1 61 ♕d5+.

2c) 57...♖b8+ is the saving check. After 58 ♔c3, f2 is good: 59 d7 ♔e6 60 h8♕ ♖xh8 61 ♖xh8 f1♕ 62 d8♕ ♕c1+ and White cannot evade Black's checks; e.g., 63 ♔b4 ♕b2+ 64 ♔c5 ♕c3+ 65 ♔b6 ♕b2+ 66 ♔a6 ♕a1+ 67 ♔b7 ♕g7+! 68 ♔c8 ♕c3+, etc.

A more difficult complex of variations, all in all, than I had suspected at first. But my intuition had not let me down: White should not play 45 e4. I had only one short hour of adjournment time left to find something better. Finally I found the text-move,

which looks passive at first but is based on a solid foundation: White keeps intact the pawn formation d3-e2 which served him so well in the middlegame and prepares to play the rook behind the h-pawn. Black has no satisfactory way to stop White from freeing the h-pawn with 46 g4.

45   ...   ♖c8

45...♖e5+ is pointless on account of 46 ♔d6. During the adjournment I had particularly kept in mind that Black might give up his weak c-pawn to cut off the white king and get active play for his king and rook. But after the continuation 45...♖d8+ 46 ♔xc5 ♔e5 47 ♖f4! ♖c8+ 48 ♔b4 ♖c2 49 e4 ♖g2 50 d4+ ♔e6 51 exf5+ gxf5 52 ♖f3 the win is not difficult. Black therefore tries to refine the idea by first waiting for g3-g4 so that the square f4 will no longer be accessible to White's rook.

46	g4	♖d8+
47	♔xc5	♔e5
48	gxf5	gxf5 *(D)*

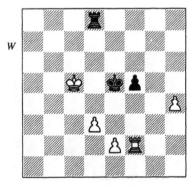

The win is very simple now; White already has a passed pawn.

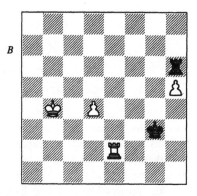

49	h5	Rc8+
50	♔b4	Rh8
51	Rh2	Rh6

If 51...♔f4 then 52 h6 is the simplest.

52 e3

Hindering the penetration of the black king.

52	...	f4
53	exf4+	♔xf4
54	d4	♔g3
55	Re2 *(D)*	

Black should have resigned here. Unashamed, he plays on for some time.

55	...	Rxh5
56	Re8	♔f4
57	♔c4	Rh1
58	d5	♔f5
59	d6	Rd1
60	♔c5	♔f6
61	♔c6	Rc1+
62	♔d7	Ra1
63	Rf8+	♔g7
64	Rf2	1-0

Game Twenty-four
Karpov – Hort
Waddinxveen 1979
English Opening

After the double-round-robin ten-player tournament in Montreal and just before the Spartakiade, Karpov was prepared to play in a small tournament of four players at Waddinxveen, held in honour of Euwe. Considering the generally peace-loving disposition at that time of the three other competitors, Hort, Kavalek, and Sosonko, it seemed he would not have too much competition for first place. This was confirmed by the final standings, although in some games the World Champion was teetering on the edge of a precipice.

When the last round started, Karpov had a lead of one and a half points over Hort, his opponent in that round. A draw thus seemed a perfectly reasonable expectation. Karpov had White, however, and with the white pieces he is never very generous with short draws. Besides, the last three games they had played against each other were drawn, which added a certain challenge.

This was Karpov's best game of the tournament. With subtle opening play he gained a great advantage, and then he deliberately played for a tactical twist which, it is true, reduced his advantage, but in a manner whereby he obtained his favourite type of position: a tight, safe pawn formation around his king, his opponent saddled with two somewhat weak pawns.

When Hort exchanged queens and adopted a passive stance, he appeared to be already lost. A fabulous technique was required to show this, however, and Karpov once again proved that he has it. He thus ended up winning the tournament two points ahead of Kavalek, who won his last game. The contrast could have been even more striking: he would have been two and a half points ahead if Sosonko had accepted Kavalek's offer of a draw in the last round.

	1	c4	♘f6
	2	♘f3	e6
	3	♘c3	c5
	4	g3	b6
	5	♗g2	♗b7
	6	0-0	

This makes the following reply possible. White usually plays 6 d4 immediately, to establish a type of position in which White has a spatial advantage and Black has a so-called hedgehog formation – that is, pawns on a6 and b6, no c-pawn, pawns on d6 and e6, and the kingside pawns on their original squares, though a pawn on g6 or h6 is sometimes acceptable.

This type of formation usually provides little excitement. A recent example is Stean-Andersson, Amsterdam 1979: 6 d4 cxd4 7 ♕xd4 ♘c6 8 ♕f4 ♗b4 9 ♗d2 0-0 10 0-0 ♗e7 11 ♖fd1 a6 12 e4 d6 13 ♕e3 ♖a7 14 ♕e2 ♕b8 15 ♗e3 ♗a8 16 ♘d2 ♖c8 17 ♖ab1 ♘d7 18 b4 ♖b7 19 f4 ♘a7 20 ♖e1 ♖bc7 21 ♕d3 h6 22 ♘e2 ♘f6 ½-½.

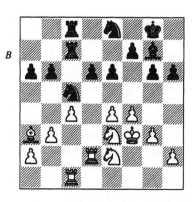

Black's eighth move has an interesting idea behind it, which is also known from the Catalan and certain variations of the Queen's Indian Defence: it provokes ♗c1-d2 to prevent White from fianchettoing his queen's bishop, which is its most harmonious development. Possibly Karpov postponed d2-d4 to avoid this.

6 ...   d5

A novelty on the sixth move! 6...♘c6 7 e4 ♕b8, as in Smejkal-Larsen, Biel 1976, is also interesting. Black had a reasonable position after 8 d4 cxd4 9 ♘xd4 ♘xd4 10 ♕xd4 ♗d6!. The most usual, however, is 6...♗e7, aiming for the 'hedgehog' mentioned earlier. In a game against Gheorghiu, Moscow 1977, Karpov showed that he knows how to handle this prickly system: 7 d4 cxd4 8 ♕xd4 d6 9 b3 0-0 10 ♖d1 ♘bd7 11 ♗b2 a6 12 ♕e3!? ♕b8 13 ♘d4 ♗xg2 14 ♔xg2 ♕b7+ 15 ♕f3 ♕xf3+ 16 ♘xf3 ♖fc8 17 ♘d4 ♖ab8 18 ♖ac1 h6 19 e4 ♘e8 20 f4 ♗f6 21 ♔f3 ♖b7 22 ♗a3 ♖bc7 23 ♘ce2 ♘c5 24 ♖d2 g6 25 ♘c2 ♗g7 26 ♘e3 and now *(D)*:

Black lost his patience and decided on 26...f5?. He was then rolled up on the kingside with remarkable speed: 27 exf5 gxf5 28 h3 h5 29 ♖g1 ♖f7 30 g4! hxg4 31 hxg4 fxg4 32 ♖xg4 ♔f8 33 ♘g3 a5 34 ♖g6 ♔e7 35 f5! ♖f6 36 ♖xf6 ♘xf6 37 ♖e2! ♖f8 38 ♗xc5 bxc5 39 fxe6 ♔xe6 40 ♘ef5+ and Black resigned. (The exclamation marks attached to White's moves are by Karpov himself.)

Hort probably had no wish to undergo such treatment. In general, he prefers to leave the well-worn theoretical paths as soon as possible.

7 cxd5   ♘xd5
8 d4   ♘xc3

The alternative is 8...♗e7 After 9 ♘xd5 Black must recapture with the bishop because 9...♕xd5 10 e4 ♕d7 11 d5 exd5 12 ♘e5! ♕e6 13 exd5 ♕xe5 14 ♖e1 ♕d4 15 ♕xd4 cxd4 16 d6 leads to great advantage for White. The above variation was given by Van Wijgerden. After 9...♗xd5 10 dxc5 ♗xc5 it seems it will not be easy for White to convert his small lead in development into a lasting advantage. Van Wijgerden gives 11 b4, but Black has nothing to fear after 11...♗e7 12 ♗b2 0-0. But 11 ♘g5 is strong. Black must now play 11...♗xg2 12 ♕xd8+ ♔xd8 13 ♔xg2 to avoid getting a weak isolated pawn on d5. After 13...♔e7 14 ♖d1 White has a small but tangible advantage.

The text leads to a position that has been seen often in recent tournament practice but without the fianchetto of Black's queen's bishop. One cannot tell from this game whether or not that is an advantage because Hort goes wrong fairly quickly.

9 bxc3   ♘d7

A normal developing move, although preparing to castle on the kingside would seem more obvious. Hort seems to have an unfortunate plan in mind.

10 ♖e1   cxd4
11 cxd4   ♗b4

This was his idea, but White will not simply allow the exchange of bishops. The more modest 11...♗e7 is correct.

12 ♗g5! (D)

A venomous zwischenzug which Hort had probably underestimated.

12 ...   f6

A serious concession. A weakness on e6 is just about the most unpleasant weakness Black can have in this type of position. However, now 12...♗e7 is only worse because of 13 ♗xe7 ♕xe7 14 ♖c1 and there is no reasonable way to prevent the rook from penetrating to c7; e.g., 14...♘f6 15 ♕a4+ ♕d7 16 ♕xd7+ ♘xd7 17 ♖c7 or 14...♕d6 15

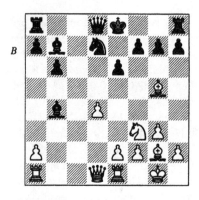

♕c2. And moving the queen away cannot be considered, since there are no suitable squares; e.g., 12...♕b8 13 ♕a4! ♗xe1 14 ♘e5 and White wins.

13 ♗d2   ♗xd2
14 ♕xd2   ♖c8

14...0-0 is no better, as 15 ♘g5 disrupts Black's pawn structure while White keeps his strong bishop: if 15...♗xg2 16 ♘xe6 wins the exchange.

15 ♕d3 (D)

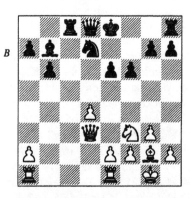

Van Wijgerden called this the best move of the game, but that was only because he underestimated White's advantage. Even stronger is 15 ♕e3!, to begin the siege of the weak e-pawn immediately. After the forced reply 15...♕e7, White continues with 16 ♖ec1. Castling is now forced, to prevent White's immediate penetration via the c-file. After 16...0-0 17 ♗h3 ♗d5 18 ♘e1 Black's position is critical, and as soon as White's knight gets to d3 Black will have to weaken himself further with g7-g5. The white bishop can later return quietly to g2. Black will not be able to get any decent counterplay because his knight stands badly on d7.

Karpov seems to have deliberately chosen the text-move over 15 ♕e3. He has seen a tactical twist, known from the Queen's Indian Defence, by which he will maintain at least a slight advantage. So he avoids the tension-filled position and instead heads straight for the more technical one.

15 ... ♕e7

Hort is right to postpone castling. After 15...0-0 16 ♘g5 fxg5 17 ♗xb7 he would have a splintered pawn structure and an unhappy knight against a strong bishop.

16 ♖ac1 0-0

Necessary now, since he must be ready to counter the penetration by White's heavy pieces along the c-file.

17 ♘g5 (D)

One of the points of his 15th move.

17 ... fxg5
15 ♗xb7 ♘c5

By means of this countertwist Black gets rid of his weak knight and

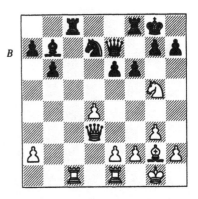

also forces his opponent to exchange a centre pawn for a wing pawn.

19 dxc5 ♕xb7
20 ♕e3

An ideal square for the queen. Alternatives offer nothing; e.g., 20 cxb6 ♖xc1 21 ♖xc1 ♕xb6 attacking f2, or 20 ♕b3 ♕e4 and now it is the black queen that is ideally placed.

20 ... ♖xc5

A slight inaccuracy which has no immediate serious consequences. The alternative 20...bxc5 leaves White with less of a choice, as 21 ♕xe6+ ♕f7 22 ♕xf7+ ♔xf7 followed by 23...♔e6 leads to a roughly equal ending and 21 ♖xc5 ♖xc5 22 ♕xc5 ♕e4 (still the ideal square for the black queen) leaves White with only a marginal edge.

21 ♖xc5 bxc5
22 ♖c1! (D)

Much stronger than the obvious 22 ♕xc5. White prevents the centralisation of the black queen.

22 ... ♕d5

Another possibility is 22...♖f5 to aim for a rook ending. After 23 ♕xe6+

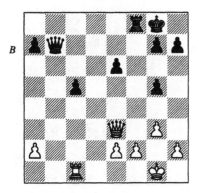

♛f7 White can't avoid the endgame, since his f-pawn is hanging. But the rook ending after 24 ♛c8+ ♛f8 25 ♛xf8+ ♚xf8 26 e4 ♜e5 27 ♜c4 is no forced draw; e.g.:

1) 27...g4 28 h3 h5 29 hxg4 hxg4 30 ♚f1 ♚f7 31 ♚e2 ♚f6 32 ♚e3 ♚g5 33 ♜a4 ♜e7 34 ♜a5 ♜c7 35 ♚d3 and Black gradually runs out of good moves.

2) 27...♚e7 28 f4 exf4 29 gxf4 ♜h5 30 ♚g2 (much stronger than Böhm's 30 e5, which Black meets by 30...♜h4 31 ♚g2 g5) 30...♚d6 31 ♜a4 ♚c6 32 ♜xa7 and now Van Wijgerden's continuation 32...c4 33 ♜xg7 c3 34 ♚f3 looks hopeless for Black; e.g., 34...c2 35 ♜g1 ♚c5 36 ♜c1 ♜xh2 37 a4 and the white passed pawns decide. Much tougher, however, is 32...g6 to prevent White from getting two connected passed pawns. Black would then have reasonable drawing chances.

All in all, Hort had little reason to go in for this. The text-move is more solid since White's remaining pawns will all be on the kingside.

23 ♜xc5   ♛xa2
24 ♜xg5

This is the position the World Champion was aiming for. His advantage is not great, but it is quite enduring.

24 ...   ♛b1+?

Preparing to exchange queens. However, the rook ending looks untenable. 24...♜f5 is correct. The point is that after the exchange of rooks a draw would be unavoidable: 25 ♜xf5 ♛b1+ 26 ♚g2 ♛xf5 27 ♛xa7 ♛e4+ and recovers the pawn on e2. This means that 25 ♜g4 would be the only winning try, but Black would not stand much worse after 25...a5. His passed pawn would ensure counterplay.

25 ♚g2   ♛b6
26 ♜e5

White has absolutely no objection to a rook endgame.

26 ...   ♛xe3
27 ♜xe3 (D)

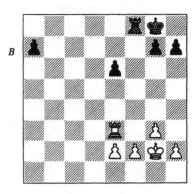

The most critical position of the game. Hort now defends his weak pawn on a7 with his rook on the second rank, but, as the game shows, this method fails to build a tight defensive line. Most commentators recommend 27...♔f7 28 ♖a3 h5 as the best defence. Böhm writes that the resulting four-against-three endgame does not look lost, and Van Wijgerden claims that sooner or later White must play g3-g4 with a probable draw.

I will subject this ending to a closer examination, continuing after 29 ♖xa7+ ♔f6 30 ♖a5. Black has two plausible replies.

1) 30...g6 is the most solid: Black tries firmly to hold his ground.

I will now show the several methods White has at his disposal so that we can form a good idea of this ending in its totality. I will label the methods *X, Y,* and *Z.*

Method X

White aims for the pawn structure e3-f4-g4, as given by Van Wijgerden and later achieved in the game. He easily reaches the following position:

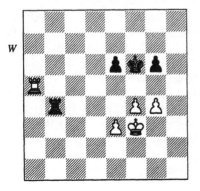

How does White make progress? He gains nothing tangible with 1 g5+ ♔f7 2 ♖a7+ ♔f8, nor with 1 ♖a7 g5. The only try is to bring the king nearer. After, say, 1 ♔e2 ♖b3 2 ♔d2 ♔f7 3 ♖c5 ♖a3 4 g5 ♔e7 5 ♖c7+ ♔f8 6 ♖c3 ♖a4 with the threat of forcing a draw immediately with 7...e5 8 fxe5 ♖g4, White makes no progress.

This method therefore seems to have little chance of success. White's king fails to penetrate.

Method Y

White aims for this position:

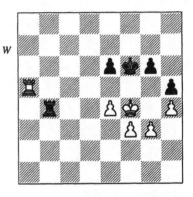

This is a far more effective set-up. White has clearly revealed the darker side of ...h7-h5: in many cases White's king can penetrate via g5. The black rook cannot be driven off the fourth rank, but White continues with 1 g4. The white king penetrates decisively after 1...hxg4 2 fxg4 ♖c4 3 g5+ ♔f7 4 ♖a7+ ♔f8 5 ♔e5.

But is White able to reach this diagram starting from the position after

30...g6? A brief variation shows that he comes out one tempo short: 31 ♔f3 ♖b8 32 ♔f4 ♖b2 33 ♖e5 and now not 33...g5+ 34 ♖xg5 ♖xe2 35 ♖xh5 ♖xf2+ 36 ♔g4 and White wins, but 33...♖b4+! 34 e4 ♖b2 with a draw. White lacks the extra move h2-h4.

Method Z
White's king tries to penetrate via h4, and he plays 31 f4 ♖b8 32 e4! ♖b2+ 33 ♔h3 *(D)*.

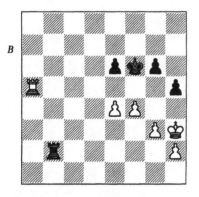

The threat is now 34 e5+ ♔f7 35 ♖a7+ ♔f8 36 ♔h4, or 34...♔f5 35 ♖a8 followed by 36 ♖f8+ and 37 ♖f6. Black has two ways of meeting this:

Z1) 33...e5. A very interesting try indeed. White can capture the pawn in two ways or can give check to cut off the black king. After 34 ♖a6+ exactly the same position would occur as in the game Timman-Meulders, Amsterdam 1978. Meulders retreated his king to the most natural and correct square, f7. If instead 34...♔g7 (I will use the move numbering of the present game

for the sake of convenience; Timman-Meulders was actually at move 43 here), Black loses in a studylike manner: 35 f5! gxf5 36 exf5 ♖f2 37 ♖g6+ ♔h7 *(D)* (or 37...♔f7 38 ♖g5 e4 39 ♖xh5 e3 40 ♖h4 and wins).

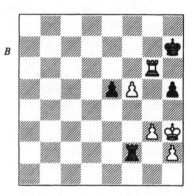

38 ♔h4!! ♖xh2+ (or 38...♖xf5 39 ♖g5 ♖f2 40 h3 and wins) 39 ♔g5 ♖h3 40 ♔f6 e4 41 ♖g7+ ♔h8 (or 41...♔h6 42 ♔f7 with the intention 43 ♔g8 and 44 ♖g6 mate) 42 g4! with mate soon after 42...hxg4 43 ♔g6. More resistance is offered by 42...♖a3, but White wins with 43 ♖e7 – but not 43 ♔g6? ♖g3! with a draw.

The game continuation was instructive: 34...♔f7 (instead of 34...♔g7) 35 fxe5 ♖e2? 36 ♖a7+ ♔f8 37 ♔h4 ♖xe4+ 38 ♔g5 ♖xe5+ 39 ♔xg6 ♖e2 40 ♖f7+ ♔e8 41 h3! ♖g2 42 ♖f3 h4 43 g4 ♖g3 44 ♖f4! ♖xh3 45 g5 ♔e7 46 ♔g7 ♔e6 47 g6 ♔e5 48 ♖f1 ♖g3 49 ♔f7 and Black resigned. He could have drawn with 35...g5!; e.g., 36 ♖h6 g4+ 37 ♔h4 ♖xh2+ 38 ♔g5 ♖g2 39 e6+ ♔e7 40 ♔f4 ♖f2+ 41 ♔e5 ♖a2 42

🜚h7+ 🜚e8 and White can make no progress.

This implies that 34 🜚a6+ is not sufficient to win and that White must try 34 🜚xe5, which is a very normal move anyway (against Meulders I did not have this possibility because my rook was on a4 instead of a5). Black now replies 34...🜚e2 and it is problematical how White can cash in his two healthy extra pawns because his king and rook are both tied down. Pointless is 35 g4 hxg4+ 36 🜚g3 🜚g7 (the most accurate, although 36...🜚f7 is adequate too) and White has no winning chances at all. Therefore he must try 35 🜚e8 🜚f7 36 🜚a8 🜚xe4 37 🜚h4 *(D)* and the king threatens to penetrate into Black's position via g5 (and possibly h6). The poor position of Black's rook makes his defensive task hopeless.

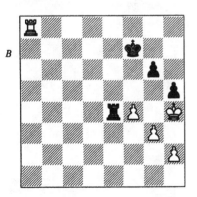

Z1a) 37...🜚f6 38 🜚a6+ 🜚f5 39 h3! and the threatened 40 g4+ cannot be adequately met; for example, 39...🜚e1 40 g4+ hxg4 41 hxg4+ 🜚xf4 42 🜚f6+

followed by 43 🜚xg6 and wins, or 39...g5+ 40 🜚xh5 gxf4 41 g4+ 🜚e5 42 🜚g5! followed by 43 🜚f6 and the white passed pawns decide.

Z1b) 37...🜚e2 38 🜚g5 (but certainly not 38 h3 🜚h2! and draws) 38...🜚xh2 39 🜚a7+ 🜚e8 40 🜚xg6 🜚g2 41 🜚h7 🜚xg3+ 42 🜚f6 🜚g4 43 f5 h4 44 🜚h8+ 🜚d7 45 🜚f7 and the game would be drawn only if Black's king could support the h-pawn in time – but there is no chance of that.

Z2) 33...🜚f2 *(D)*.

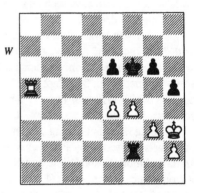

A very refined defence. The point is that the white rook is tied down after 34 e5+ 🜚f5 35 🜚a8 g5 36 🜚f8+ 🜚e4. White can win a second pawn with check after 36 fxg5 (instead of 36 🜚f8+) 36...🜚xg5 37 🜚g8+ 🜚h6 38 🜚e8, but it is insufficient for victory after 38...🜚e2 39 🜚xe6+ 🜚g5. The white king stands too poorly; e.g., 40 🜚e8 🜚h6 41 e6 🜚g6 42 e7 🜚g7.

On 33...🜚f2 White quietly replies 34 🜚b5 *(D)*. Remarkably, Black is in zugzwang.

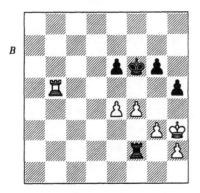

Of course he can enter variation Z, with 34...e5, but we have seen that it is not enough to draw. The other try is 34...h4, but then White wins smoothly with 35 ♔xh4 ♖xh2+ 36 ♔g4 and the white king's penetration via g5 is not to be stopped; e.g., 36...♖g2 37 e5+ ♔f7 38 ♖b7+ ♔f8 and now 39 ♖b3 followed by 40 ♔g5 is the simplest.

2) 30...e5!. This fighting continuation was suggested by Polugaevsky. Initially I thought that White now had a won game after 31 f4 exf4 32 gxf4 g6 33 e4 *(D)*, based on variations after 33...♖b8 34 ♖a7!.

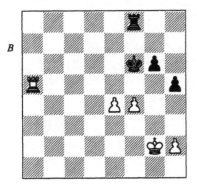

Remarkably enough, in this type of endgame it can be better for the king of the defending side to be cut off on the eighth rank than on the sixth. Therefore Black has to withdraw his king with 33...♔g7 or 33...♔f7. After 34 ♔g3 ♖b8 35 e5 ♖b4 there is no win, because 36 ♖a7+ is parried by 36...♔g8. This last variation is actually fairly simple, despite the fact that it was a long time before I realised this.

Conclusion: The black plan of immediately giving up the a-pawn and taking up a position with a pawn on h5 is sufficient to draw.

27	...	♖e8
28	♖a3	♖e7
29	♖a5	

Under these circumstances it does no harm to prevent h7-h5.

29	...	♔f7
30	h4	h6
31	g4	♔f6
32	f4 *(D)*	

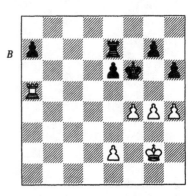

Now that Black cannot exchange pawns, White can build up a mighty pawn front without worrying that his king will be unable to penetrate.

32	...	♖b7
33	♔f3	♖c7
34	♖a6	

Provoking ...g7-g6. After 34...♔f7, 35 f5 already comes into consideration. White's passed e-pawn would be extremely strong, and White's king could penetrate via h5 after the exchange on f5.

| 34 | ... | g6 |
| 35 | ♖a5 | |

Preventing 35...h5 for sure.

| 35 | ... | ♖d7 |
| 36 | e3 | |

Another quiet preparatory move.

| 36 | ... | ♖b7 |
| 37 | h5 *(D)* | |

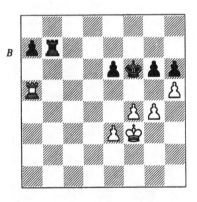

The time is ripe for this strategic advance. Note the importance of having provoked ...g7-g6. White threatens to capture on g6, after which it would be simple to obtain two connected passed pawns. Black's reply is therefore forced.

| 37 | ... | g5 |
| 38 | ♖a6 | |

He will again work with the threat f4-f5. The alternative is 38 fxg5+ to get a protected passed pawn. But Black's position might be difficult to overcome.

| 38 | ... | gxf4 |

For the first and last time in the game, Black could have tried to derive some profit from the presence of his insignificant passed a-pawn, namely by playing 38...♖b3.

The idea is now to exchange on f4 and to force White to recapture with the king. White then has two plans:

1) 39 f5. I gave this thrust in my original notes, supposing that the pawn ending after 39...♖b6 40 ♖xb6 axb6 41 e4 would be won on account of White's protected passed pawn. Not until thirteen years later did I realise that Black can hold the pawn ending. For instance: 41...♔e5 42 ♔e3 exf5 43 exf5 ♔d5 44 ♔d3 b5 45 ♔c3 ♔c5 46 ♔b3 ♔d5 47 ♔b4 ♔c6 48 f6 ♔d6 49 ♔xb5 ♔e6 50 ♔c5 ♔xf6 51 ♔d6.

If Black were to allow his king to be driven back to g7 he would lose. With 51...♔f7, however, he stands his ground, both after 52 ♔e5 ♔e7 and after 52 ♔d7 ♔f6, when after 53 ♔e8 the black king moves out to e5, whereupon both sides will queen at the same time.

2) 39 fxg5+ hxg5 40 ♖xa7. The correct plan. White's winning plan consists in the rook manoeuvre ♖a7-h7-h6-g6. Black can do little to

counter this, as is evident from the variation 40...♖b4 41 ♖h7 e5 42 ♖h6+ ♔f7 43 ♖g6 e4+ 44 ♔e2 ♖b5 45 ♔d1 ♖c5 46 ♔d2 when Black is in zugzwang: he has to allow the white king onto the c-file. The win then proceeds systematically; e.g. 46...♖d5+ 47 ♔c2 ♖d3 48 ♖xg5 ♖xe3 49 h6, followed by 50 ♖g7+ and 51 g5.

| 40 | ♔g2 | ♖b7 |
| 41 | ♔g3 | ♔f7 |

This is tougher than 41...♖b3+ 42 ♔h4 ♖b4 43 ♖xa7 ♖xf4 44 ♖h7 with an easy win.

42 ♖a4

Always systematic. He protects the fourth rank for his king before breaking through with g4-g5. The immediate 42 g5 is not so simple: 42...hxg5 43 hxg5 ♖b3+ 44 ♔f4 ♖b4+ 45 ♔e5 ♖b5+ and Black keeps on checking.

42	...	♔g7
43	g5	♖c7
44	♖a5	

The sealed move. Now that Black's king no longer protects the e-pawn, White need not worry about the variation given on White's 42nd move.

| 44 | ... | ♔g8 |
| 45 | ♖b5 | *(D)* |

Note that the World Champion is in no hurry to create a protected passed pawn with g5-g6. Under no circumstances can Black take on g5.

| 45 | ... | ♔f7 |
| 46 | ♔g4 | a6 |

At last this pawn can take a step forward.

47 ♖b8

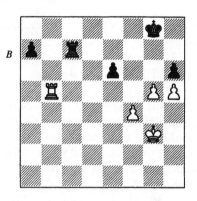

This penetration carries the unanswerable threat 48 ♖h8 (47...♔g7 48 ♖e8 ♔f7 49 ♖h8).

| 47 | ... | ♖c1 |

Hort, in desperation, surrenders the seventh rank. 47...hxg5 is equally hopeless but a little more difficult for White. Van Wijgerden gives two nice variations after 48 fxg5 ♖c4+ 49 ♔f3 ♖c3+ 50 ♔e4 ♖c4+ 51 ♔e3 *(D)*:

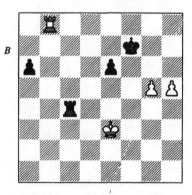

1) 51...♖g4 (51...♖c3+ 52 ♔d4 only helps White) 52 g6+ ♔g7 53 ♖b7+ ♔g8 54 ♔f3 ♖g5 55 ♖h7 e5 (otherwise 56 ♔f4) 56 ♔e4 a5 57 ♔d5

a4 58 ♔e6 and the white king is in time to seal the mating net around the black king.

2) 51...♖h4 52 g6+ ♔g7 53 ♖b7+ ♔g8 54 ♖h7 a5 55 ♔f3 a4 56 ♔g3 ♖h1 57 ♔g4 a3 58 ♖a7 ♖a1 59 ♔g5 and the white king is again in time. Mate in two is threatened.

48 g6+

The simplest, now that Black has given up the seventh rank.

48	...	♔g7
49	♖b7+	♔f8
50	♖b6	♖g1+
51	♔f3	♖f1+

52	♔e4	♖e1+
53	♔d4	♔e7
54	♖xa6	♔f6
55	♖a7	

Cuts off the black king.

55	...	e5+

Final desperation.

56	fxe5+	♖xe5
57	♖a6+	1-0

White didn't fall into it: the ending would be drawn after 57 ♖f7+ ♔e6 58 ♖e7+?? ♔xe7 59 ♔xe5 ♔f8. Black resigned after the text-move due to 57...♖e6 58 g7 or 57...♔f5 58 g7 ♖e8 59 ♖xh6 and queening is not far off.

Index of Players

Numbers refer to pages.
A bold number indicates that the first named played was White.

Index of Openings